TRACING

YOUR

ALABAMA

PAST

TRACING

YOUR

ALABAMA

PAST

Robert Scott Davis

University Press of Mississippi / *Jackson*

www.upress.state.ms.us

Copyright © 2003 by Robert Scott Davis

Manufactured in the United States of America
11 10 09 08 07 06 05 04 03   4 3 2 1
∞

Library of Congress Cataloging-in-Publication Data

Davis, Robert Scott, 1954–
    Tracing your Alabama past / Robert Scott Davis.
        p.   cm.
    ISBN 1-57806-491-0 (cloth : alk. paper)—ISBN 1-57806-492-9
(pbk. : alk. paper)
    1. Alabama—Genealogy—Handbooks, manuals, etc.   2.
Alabama—Genealogy—Bibliography.   I. Title.

F325 .D39   2003
929′.1′0720761—dc21   2002005475

British Library Cataloging-in-Publication Data available

For Royal Laney and Carolina Nigg

CONTENTS

MAPS AND CHARTS

ACKNOWLEDGMENTS

Many people contributed to making this work possible. My brother Gus composed the many maps. The staffs of Southern History of the Birmingham Public Library and the Alabama Department of Archives and History provided valuable suggestions and corrections, as did Elizabeth Willauer, Kenneth H. Thomas Jr., Ted O. Brooke, Lloyd Bockstruck, and Carolina Nigg. Responsibility for the results, however, rests with me. Dr. Edwin C. Bridges, director of the Alabama Department of Archives and History, urged me to write this book years before I even came to Alabama. The University Press of Mississippi made the same request a few years ago, after I had been hired as director of the Family and Regional History Program at Wallace State College, Hanceville, Alabama.

My being here came about through the efforts of Dr. James C. Bailey, president of Wallace State, upon the recommendation of Dr. Bridges. Dr. Bailey established and continues to generously support a truly unique program to help students and the general public appreciate the heritage of north central Alabama. May what began with him and his community college come to be common everywhere.

Helping to build this program has been a wonderful learning experience for me, made all the better by the camaraderie of the staff, Betty, Cherie, Dean, Darlene, Iman, and Martha, as well as my many students and visitors. My research and learning has also benefited tremendously from my association with Bill Simpson and the Cullman Public Library and the North Central Alabama Genealogical Society.

TRACING
YOUR
ALABAMA
PAST

1. HISTORICAL BACKGROUND

In many ways, Alabama best represents all of the southern United States. Even in geography and climate, the state contains significant elements of the mineralogy and topography of the entire region. The extreme north of modern Alabama consists of a large portion of the Tennessee River Valley, where the cities of Decatur, Florence, and Huntsville grew up. Southeastern Alabama adjoins the Chattahoochee River, as does neighboring southwestern Georgia. Northeastern Alabama exists as a mirror image of the adjoining areas of Georgia, while western Alabama resembles eastern Mississippi. Alabama's gulf coast belongs to the same region as Florida's panhandle. Through the center of the state, the Alabama, Coosa, Warrior, and many other rivers—a huge network—combine and, at Mobile, join the Gulf of Mexico, as do other classic rivers and ancient sea ports of the South.

Alabama's pleasant climate, geology, rivers, caves, fossils, plants, and wildlife are also legends. More unique plants and animals exist in Alabama's environment than almost anywhere else. The state even receives an especially large share of the natural outer space objects that come to Earth, the famous "stars" that fell on Alabama.

Beginning in prehistoric times, the area that became Alabama represented the coming together of the diverse peoples of the South. Human beings have lived in today's Alabama for almost as long as people have lived in the Western Hemisphere, as shown in the remains found in Russell Cave and elsewhere. By the time of the arrival of Hernando de Soto's Spanish army in the 1540s, Alabama had significant populations of the Chickasaws (northwest; final removal 1836), Choctaws (southwest and central west; final removal 1834), Cherokees (northeast; final removal 1838), and Creeks (south and central two-thirds of today's Alabama; final removal 1836). Some remnants of these tribes, particularly the Porch Creeks of Atmore, still reside in Alabama.

As early as 1513, the Spanish explored at least the coast of today's Alabama. In 1699, French explorers covered the same area and, in 1702, established the first permanent white settlement, Mobile, as the capital of Louisiana. They moved the settlement to the present site of the city of Mobile in 1712. The French also established Fort Toulouse in Alabama in 1717. The colonial capital moved out of Alabama forever in 1720. The coastal area became part of British West Florida from 1763 until 1780, when it was captured by the Spanish. The state of Georgia made various claims to the land of today's Alabama north of the thirty-first latitude, although Georgia made no settlements and exercised no local authority in the area. Anglo-American and African American families did settle in what became Alabama as citizens of the European nations that claimed the region.

In 1802, Georgia gave up all claims to the land that today is Alabama to the United States government. American troops seized Mobile from Spain on April 15, 1813. The federal government generally recognized the land claims made under the previous national governments. The first offices for granting land opened at St. Stephens, near Mobile, in 1806 and at Huntsville in 1811, making the future state of Alabama a federal land state for purposes of granting unclaimed lands. The area had been vaguely included in the unorganized federal territories south of the Ohio River until made part of the Mississippi Territory in 1798. From colonial times through 1836, violent conflict often occurred between white settlers and the Creek Indians, giving rise to the expression "God willing and the Creeks don't rise [up]." The most famous of these clashes were the Creeks' success at Fort Mims (August 30, 1813) and the victory of a combined United States and American Indian force over the Creeks at Horseshoe Bend (March 27, 1814).

Today's Alabama began as the Alabama Territory in 1817, with St. Stephens as the capital. (The name Alabama comes from a Choctaw word that means "clearers of the thicket.") On December 14, 1819, President James Monroe signed the final resolution to create the State of Alabama. Huntsville served as the temporary state capital until the government officially moved to Cahawba in 1819. Tuscaloosa became the state capital in 1825, before the seat of government moved permanently to Montgomery in 1847. The state opened its first penitentiary at Wetumpka in 1841 and a mental institution at Tuscaloosa in 1852. The state university first accepted students in 1831.

Statehood brought increased settlement from Georgia, South Carolina, Tennessee, and other southern states. Aside from purchasers of federal lands and squatters, many families moved to Alabama to obtain military bounty land for federal service prior to 1855. Warrants for military land were no longer issued after 1858, and land for such grants was no longer located after 1863. Much of the state has navigable rivers and mineral wealth that also encouraged development. The coming of the railroads and steamboats in the 1820s to 1860s opened more lands to settlement and development.

The Confederate States of America began in Montgomery in 1861, and the resulting Civil War for four years brought Alabama both increased industrial activity and severe wartime shortages. Although the state contributed tens of thousands of soldiers to the war effort, Alabama civilians saw very little of the fighting and destruction until the last months of the war. Alabamians, black and white, contributed men to both armies. For much of the war, federal forces occupied the Tennessee River Valley in the north of the state.

The post-Civil War Reconstruction era (1865–1874) provided special opportunities for the many newcomers of various nationalities coming to Alabama. The federal Homestead Act of 1862 gave land to non-Confederates willing to develop farms and homes here. Generous federal acts for granting lands to encourage railroad development, combined with northern capital and expertise, opened vast areas of an already traditionally diverse southern state to new mining, manufacturing, and agriculture. Today's city of Birmingham, begun at a former Confederate iron works in 1871, grew from these seeds. Alabama's reconstruction legislature expanded access to local government through the creation of several new counties.

The most cosmopolitan areas in Alabama, Birmingham and Mobile, did not have the state's only ethnic diversity. French supporters of the deposed emperor Napoleon I and their servants, for example, founded Demopolis much earlier, and some of their descendants still live in Marengo (named for Napoleon's great victory), Hale, and Greene Counties. Cullman County had a large German population brought to Alabama by Johann Cullmann to take advantage of lands made available by the Homestead Act and the new railroads. People of many other backgrounds also came. Families of Scandinavian descent from the Midwest settled at Thorsby, while persons with Highland Scot ancestry founded Scotland and Inverness, Alabama. Northerners with dreams of founding an intellectual utopia created the town of Fairhope.

Federal programs during the Great Depression of the 1930s, followed by the World War II and Cold War military buildups, provided federal funds for interstate highways, river improvements, dams, military bases, and much more that helped fuel modern development in the state. The state's struggles with civil rights ultimately brought legal and social equality to the entire nation, while also producing a number of extensive works on local and social history. Alabama's central location and wide variety of topography encouraged a growing industry in tourism and retirement. This same geography and history inspired and created an exceptional number of artists, musicians, politicians, writers, and scientists of national and international reputation.

Early American high hopes for Alabama's potential inspired an unusually high number of special local sources, such as Sanborn fire insurance maps for new towns. Some of these dreams became the realities of Anniston, Birmingham, Cullman, Florence, and Mobile while other towns such as St. Stephens and Cahawba passed into history. Their stories inspired a great general interest in the state, even from its early years. The Alabama Historical Society began in 1850, and the following year the first history of the state appeared in print, Albert James Pickett's *History of Alabama, and Incidentally of Georgia and Mississippi*.

In records, Alabama has also been blessed among the southern states. Extensive archives of all of the nations that governed Alabama survive, as do a wide variety of local government records. As a territory and a state, Alabama borrowed the best ideas on records keeping from older states and added some of its own. Alabama created the first modern state archives, and what has remained one of the best in the United States, in 1901. The archives have the executive records of all of Alabama's governors' administrations, from 1817 to almost the present day, and many other types of records of exceptional research value found nowhere else. Today, among the many good ideas in records keeping to come out of Alabama has been the creation of local archives operated by county governments in conjunction with local historical and genealogical societies. Some of these archives are funded by special records fees.

For historical background on Alabama, some general works include the following:

Badger, R. Reid, and Lawrence A. Clayton, eds. *Alabama and the Borderlands from Prehistory to Statehood.* Tuscaloosa: University of Alabama Press, 1985.

Flynt, J. Wayne. *Poor but Proud: Alabama's Poor Whites.* Tuscaloosa: University of Alabama Press, 1989.

Moore, Albert B. *History of Alabama.* Nashville, Tenn.: Benson Printing, 1951.

Rogers, William, et al. *Alabama: The History of a Deep South State.* Tuscaloosa: University of Alabama Press, 1994.

Trover, Ellen Lloyd. *Chronology and Documentary Handbook of the State of Alabama.* New York: Oceana Publications, 1972.

Alabama politics have been covered in general histories far better than many other general areas through such works as Walter L. Fleming, *Civil War and Reconstruction in Alabama* (New York: Macmillan, 1905); and Samuel L. Webb, *Two-Party Politics in the One-Party South: Alabama's Hill Country, 1874–1920* (Tuscaloosa: University of Alabama, 1997).

2. INTERNET, BOOKS, BIBLIOGRAPHIES, PERIODICALS, NEWSPAPERS, AND MANUSCRIPTS

RESEARCH IN GENERAL

The web site of the Alabama Department of Archives and History includes extensive current, historical, and genealogical information useful for research, including many important Alabama Internet and postal addresses. The Internet address is http://www.archives.state.al.us.

Information on individual Alabama counties should also be sought in Marcia K. Smith, *Alabama County Data and Resources*, 2nd ed. (Titus, Ala.: The Author, 1999). For Alabama in general, several compilations were published many years ago by Thomas M. Owen, including *History of Alabama and Dictionary of Biography* (1921) and *The Story of Alabama* (1949). Researchers might also consult *Memorial Record of Alabama*, 2 vols. (Madison, Wis.: Brant & Fuller, 1893) and *The Encyclopedia of Alabama* (St. Clair Shores, Mich.: Somerset Publishers, 1999).

Many books have been published on methods and materials for historical research in the United States. Among the more popular of such works there are Emily Anne Croom, *The Genealogist's Companion and Sourcebook* (Cincinnati: Betterway Books, 1998); Ronald Gross, *The Independent Scholar's Handbook* (Berkeley: Ten Speed Press, 1974); and the current edition of Jacques Barzun and Henry F. Graff, *The Modern Researcher;* also see Stacy A. Anderson, "Indexes and Databases at State Libraries, Archives, and Bureaus of Vital Records," *Heritage Quest* (July–August 2001): 68–71. Similar works on specific types of research, such as federal records, will be discussed elsewhere. So many works come out on such topics as research on the Internet that any attempt at a bibliography must immediately become outdated.

SPECIAL NOTE ON THE INTERNET

The Internet has become an indispensable tool for any serious historical research. Throughout this work, web sites will be referred to for additional information. Sites include indexes, texts, and access to interlibrary loans of materials. Discussion groups and web sites such as Genweb and Genforum also allow for the exchange of questions, ideas, information, and help by e-mail.

However, the Internet also has numerous shortcomings, not all of which will ever be worked out. New sites appear and old ones disappear so rapidly as to make any discussion out of date, even as posted on the Internet. Addresses change; information posted on individual sites appears and disappears; and different answers appear to the same question at different times, when asked in the same major database web sites. Information is posted without documentation. When articles and books are digitized onto the web, sometimes pages are not copied without any warning that the work is incomplete. Even telephone directories on the Internet can sometimes be years out of date.

The latest editions of the following works, and others, can help in at least introducing the Internet's vast resources:

Crowe, Elizabeth Powell. *Genealogy Online: Researching Your Roots.* Summit, Pa.: McGraw-Hill, 2000.

Kemp, Thomas Jay. *The Genealogists Virtual Library Full Text Books on the World Wide Web.* Wilmington, Del.: Scholarly Resources, 2001.

————. *Virtual Roots: A Guide to Genealogy and Local History on the World Wide Web*. Wilmington, Del.: Scholarly Resources, 2000.

McClure, Rhoda. *The Complete Idiot's Guide to Online: Genealogy*. Indianapolis, Ind.: MacMillan, 2000.

Renick, Barbara, and Richard S. Wilson. *The Internet for Genealogists: A Beginners Guide*. LaHabra, Calif.: Compuology, 1999.

Trinkle, Dennis A., and Scott A. Merriman. *The History Highway 2000: A Guide to Internet Users*. Armonk, N.Y.: M. E. Sharpe, 2000.

Wilson, Richard S. *Publishing Your Family History on the Internet*. LaHabra, Calif.: Compuology, 2000.

Some generalizations can be made. Almost all libraries, archives, and historic sites now have web sites on the Internet, although usefulness and content vary as much as do these individual organizations. Search engines such as Google and mega search engines like Dogpile usually will take you where you need to go on the Internet. Most libraries have some form of free on-line book catalog, and ALICAT (Alabama Library Information CATalog, described elsewhere), while it lasts, includes most of the books in most of Alabama's public libraries.

The best web site for Alabama research is that of the Alabama Department of Archives and History (http://www.archives.state.al.us). This site, as explained in more detail elsewhere, includes addresses (postal and web) to societies, libraries, and state agencies; bibliographies; descriptions of manuscript collections, newspapers, and government records at the Alabama Archives; and much more of value to researchers. Special additions to this ever-changing web site are being planned.

Genealogy has become the second most popular and the most profitable use of the Internet. Sources for family history research also serve to help in any biographical and historical research. CyndisList, FamilySearch, Rootsweb, Ancestry.com, Genealogy.com, Heritage Quest, GenForum, GenWeb, and many more web sites provide personal information on individuals but also (with the exception of FamilySearch) some access to information on subjects by keyword, that is, by typing in any text words as if given names. Large scholarly publishing companies, listed elsewhere but also frequently changing names, are preparing to tap into this market by creating massive new databases; but, as with their mammoth publications, these will only be affordable by large, usually academic, libraries.

Similarly, many nongenealogical and nonlibrary web sites also have value for historical research in all forms. Valuable Civil War research sites have become particularly numerous. Many of these other sites will be mentioned elsewhere in this publication.

BOOKS, THESES, DISSERTATIONS, AND BIBLIOGRAPHIES

All of Alabama's public libraries and many colleges and universities share information on their respective holdings through the ALICAT (Alabama Library Information CATalog) computer system. It can be accessed at any of the member libraries and on the Internet at http://Alabama.brodart.com/search/ax/browse.html.

Aside from the book catalogs available at the specific libraries, many Alabama libraries, including the Birmingham and Huntsville public libraries, have their catalogs accessible through the Internet. Alabama books and source materials can also be identified through national computer databases, on the Internet, such as the catalog of the Library of Congress.

Several bibliographies of Alabama books exist in print. Specifically for Alabama, the researcher should consult

Barefield, Marilyn Davis. *Researching in Alabama,* Rev. ed. Birmingham: Birmingham Public Library, 1998.

Brannen, Ralph N. *Alabama Bibliography: Books, Articles, Theses, Dissertations.* Oxford, Ala.: The Author, 1996).

Brown, Lynda W., et al. *Alabama History: An Annotated Bibliography.* Westport, Conn.: Greenwood Press, 1998.

Collier, Marcia K. Smith. *Alabama County Data and Resources,* 2nd ed. Titus, Ala.: The Author, 1999.

Ellison, Rhoda C. *Check List of Alabama Imprints, 1807–1870.* University, Ala.: University of Alabama Press, 1946.

Ward, Robert David. *Bibliography of County Histories of Alabama.* Birmingham: Birmingham Public Library, 1991.

Alabama also has or has representation in specialty bibliographies such as

Adams, Katherine J., and Lewis L. Gould. *Inside the Natchez Trace Collection: New Sources for Southern History*. Baton Rouge: Louisiana State University Press, 1999.

Derfer, Lisa A. *Pamphlets in American History*. Sanford, N.C.: Microfilming Corporation of America, 1982.

Hoole, William Stanley. *Alabama Bibliography: A Short-Title Catalogue of the Publications of Peter Alexander Brannon, Former Director of the Alabama Department of Archives and History*. Tuscaloosa: Confederate Publications, 1984.

Hummel, Ray O. *Southeastern Broadsides before 1877: A Bibliography*. Richmond: Virginia State Library, 1971. Alabama is on pages 31–67.

Ross, Charlotte Tankersley, ed. *Bibliography of Southern Appalachia*. Knoxville: University of Tennessee Press, 1976.

Wright, J. *Criminal Activity in the Deep South, 1700–1930: An Annotated Bibliography*. New York: Greenwood Press, 1989.

Many special topical studies prove especially useful for directing researchers to source materials. These works include, among others,

Blevins, Brooks. *Cattle in the Cotton Fields: A History of Cattle Raising in Alabama*. Tuscaloosa: University of Alabama Press, 1997.

Brantley, William H. *Banking in Alabama, 1816–1860*. 2 vols. Birmingham: Birmingham Printing Company, 1961.

Brown, Edwin L., and Colin J. Davis, eds. *It Is Union and Liberty: Alabama Coal Miners, 1898–1998*. Tuscaloosa: University of Alabama Press, 1998.

Carter, E. A., and V. G. Seaquist. *Extreme Weather History and Climate Atlas for Alabama*. Huntsville, Ala.: Strode, 1984.

Cline, Wayne. *Alabama Railroads*. Tuscaloosa: University of Alabama Press, 1997. For other sources see Holly T. Hansen, *The Directory of North American Railroads, Associations, Societies, Archives, Libraries, Museums, and Their Collections* (Wilmington, Del.: Scholarly Resources, 1999).

Dean, Blanche E., et al. *Wildflowers of Alabama*. Tuscaloosa: University of Alabama Press, 1995.

Evans, Carol Muse. *The Complete Guide to Alabama Weather*. Birmingham: Seacoast Publishing, 1999.

Gibbons, Whit., et al. *Poisonous Plants and Venomous Animals of Alabama*. Tuscaloosa: University of Alabama Press, 1997.

Greer, Jennifer. *Alabama Gardener's Guide*. Franklin, Tenn.: Cool Springs Press, 1997.

Jackson, Harvey H., III. *Rivers of History: Life on the Coosa, Tallapoosa, Cahaba, and Alabama*. Tuscaloosa: University of Alabama Press, 1995. For other information on steamboats, see Peter Maust, " 'Congress Could Do Nothing Better': Promoting Steamboat Safety in Antebellum America," *Prologue: The Quarterly of the National Archives* 32 (2000): 100–13.

Lawson, Thomas, Jr. *Logging Railroads of Alabama*. Birmingham: Craftsman Printing, 1996.

Miller, Hobson. *Myths, Mysteries, and Legends of Alabama*. Birmingham: Seacoast Publishing. 1995.

Mueller, Edward A. *Perilous Journeys: A History of Steamboating on the Chattahoochee, Apalachicola, and Flint Rivers*. Eufaula: Historic Chattahoochee Commission, 1990.

Neville, Bert. *Directory of River Packets in the Mobile-Alabama-Warrior-Tombigbee Trades, 1818–1932*. Selma, Ala.: The Author, 1962.

Rivers of Alabama. Huntsville: Strode Press 1968.

Sharpe, Patricia S. *Alabama Trails*. Tuscaloosa: University of Alabama Press, 1996.

Thurmond, John T., and Douglas E. Jones. *Fossil Vertebrates of Alabama*. University, Ala.: University of Alabama Press, 1981.

Willoughby, Lynn. *Fair to Middlin': The Antebellum Cotton Trade of the Apalachicola/Chattahoochee River Valley*. Tuscaloosa: University of Alabama Press, 1993.

———. *Flowing through Time: a History of the Lower Chattahoochee River*. Tuscaloosa: University of Alabama Press, 1995.

Other resources exist for natural history studies in Alabama, such as Thomas A. Imhof's *Alabama Birds* (Tuscaloosa: University of Alabama

Press, 1976). *Wild Alabama* is a journal of natural history exploration published by Wild Alabama, P.O. Box 117, Moulton, AL 35650-0117. The library of the Geological Survey of Alabama and the State Oil and Gas Board of Alabama has an extensive collection of printed and other resource materials on mining, soil, oil, gas, and even plants. Located on the campus of the University of Alabama in Tuscaloosa, this institution can be contacted through its web site. The Alabama Geological Society publishes a number of valuable works on the state's natural history, including Jim Lacefield's *Lost Worlds in Alabama Rocks: A Guide to the State's Ancient Life and Landscapes* (2000). The Alabama Department of Archives and History has records of mine inspections, 1906–1909, among other state publications and materials relating to geology, forestry, and natural resources. Extensive information on Alabama rivers and other waterways can be found in the files of the United States Army, Corps of Engineers, Mobile District, Technical Library, P.O. Box 2288, 109 St. Joseph Street, Room 5023, Mobile, AL 36628.

The Alabama Department of Archives and History has a bibliography of theses and dissertations on Alabama on its web site. For the whole country, see the current editions of such sources as *Dissertations in History* and *Doctoral Dissertations in History*, found in the reference areas of all major research libraries. The Alabama Archives, in addition to an extensive Alabama-oriented library, also has a well-organized almanac collection (LPR 133) and pamphlet collections (LPR 117–19).

PERIODICALS

Most genealogical periodicals and some issues of historical periodicals are included in *PERiodical Source Index*, or PERSI (1987–), a nationwide annual subject index from 1847 to the present prepared by the staff of the Allen County-Fort Wayne Public Library. References to articles not on counties or specific families are listed under "US" in the geographic section of the index. The most recent edition is on computer CD-ROM disk and is also accessible on the Internet through Ancestry.com. Electronic access also allows for special keyword searches. The current edition of *Genealogical Research in the Tutwiler Collection of Southern History and Literature* identifies all Alabama and most southern periodicals included in PERSI.

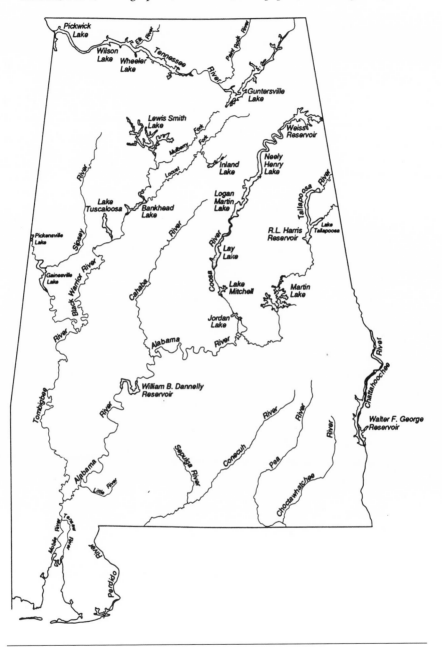

Alabama: Major Rivers and Lakes

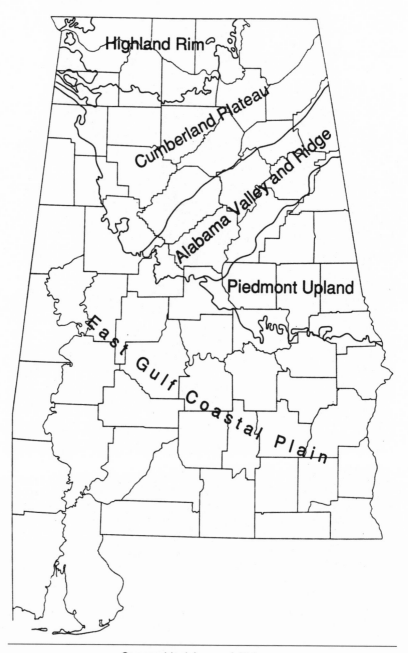

Geographical Areas of Alabama

For specific information on Alabama genealogical periodicals see chapter 14 in this volume, "City, County, and Community Sources."

Texts of many periodicals of value in historical research can be found through such web sites as the Alabama Virtual Library, accessible through all Alabama libraries of any size. A bibliography of periodical and newspaper articles (as well as some books) that can be accessed for free by anyone on the Internet is on the web site RSAP: Resources to Research Periodicals.

Many genealogical newspaper columns are listed in Anita Cheek Milner's *Newspaper Genealogical Column Directory*, 6th ed. (Bowie, Md.: Heritage Books, 1996). Many web sites on the Internet list genealogical columns, especially those of major newspapers. Especially useful is the web site of the International Society of Family History Writers and Editors, formerly the Council of Genealogy Columnists. Local public libraries often collect genealogical columns that cover their respective areas.

Lists of articles in Alabama's four historical journals are available at the web site of the Alabama Department of Archives and History. These publications include *Alabama Historical Quarterly* (1930–1982), published by the Alabama Department of Archives and History but no longer in publication; *Alabama Review* (1948 to present), published by the Alabama Historical Association and the University of Alabama Press; *Alabama Heritage* (1986 to present), published by the University of Alabama; and *Gulf Coast Historical Review* (1985 to present), published by the History Department of the University of South Alabama. The Alabama Center for Traditional Culture, 410 N. Hull Street, Montgomery, AL 36104, also publishes historical articles in *Tributaries: Journal of the Alabama Folklife Association*.

For the various national bibliographies/indexes to historical research articles, see Emily Anne Croom, *The Genealogist's Companion and Sourcebook* (Cincinnati: Betterway Books, 1998), 115–23. Historical articles on Alabama appear in many regional and national journals such as *Journal of Southern History*, which has an annual bibliography of major historical publications on the South. Alabama is also covered in such national bibliographies as *C.R.I.S.: The Combined Retrospective Index Set to Journals in History, 1838–1974; Historical Abstracts, America: History and Life*; the current edition of *The American Historical Association's Guide to Historical Lit-*

erature; and the *Humanities Index.* The latter replaced the *Social Sciences and Humanities Index* and *International Index to Periodicals.*

NEWSPAPERS

The Alabama Department of Archives and History has the most extensive collections of Alabama newspapers, originals and copies on microfilm, anywhere. The newspaper microfilm can be borrowed on interlibrary loan. A list of the newspapers on microfilm appears in its web site, arranged by county; also see Rhoda C. Ellison, *History and Bibliography of Alabama Newspapers in the Nineteenth Century* (University, Ala.: University of Alabama Press, 1954); and William Joseph Plott, *A Checklist of Alabama Newspapers Published since 1900* (University, Ala.: n.p., 1982). Information on what currently exists at local libraries is found in chapter 14 of this volume, "City, County, and Community Sources." Some national bibliographies of newspaper holdings include Clarence S. Brigham, *History and Bibliography of American Newspapers, 1690–1820* (Worcester: American Antiquarian Society, 1947); Winifred Gregory, *American Newspapers, 1821–1936: A Union List of Files Available in the United States and Canada* (New York: Wilson Company, 1937); and *Newspapers in Microfilm: United States, 1948–1972* (Washington, D.C.: Library of Congress, 1973).

Alabama governors began sending condolences, which no longer exist, to families of persons recently dead in the late 1940s. The newspaper funeral notices used for that purpose are filed in the family folders of the Alabama Department of Archives and History. Similar funeral notices, and also the anniversary notices, from 1950 to 1978, were filed separately, in alphabetical order, at the Alabama Archives and were microfilmed. All of this microfilm is widely available at libraries in Alabama and on loan through LDS (Latter-Day Saint) family history centers. For some 1985 to 1987 Alabama obituaries from the *Times-Daily* newspaper of Florence, Alabama, see George Edwin Lyon, *Northwest Alabama Obituaries,* 3 vols. (Cullman: Gregath, 1985–1988). Many Alabama public libraries maintain funeral notice and obituary files of local deaths; see chapter 14 of this volume, "City, County, and Community Sources," and Betty M. Jarboe, *Obituaries: A Guide to Sources* (Boston: G. K. Hall, 1982).

Many Alabama genealogical periodicals have published information from early newspapers for the counties that these journals cover, respectively. Some newspaper abstracts for some counties have also been published as separate books, such as Betty Taylor's abstracts from Guntersville (Marshall County) newspapers. Several books gather at least some personal information from newspapers that covered the entire state: Pauline Jones Gandrud and Kathleen Paul Jones, *Marriage, Death, and Legal Notices from Early Alabama Newspapers, 1819–1893* (Greenville, S.C.: Southern Historical Press, 1981); Helen S. Foley, *Marriage and Death Notices from Alabama Newspapers and Family Records, 1819–1890* (Greenville, S.C.: Southern Historical Press, 1981); and Michael Kelsey, Nancy Graff Floyd, and Ginny Guinn Parsons, *Miscellaneous Alabama Newspaper Abstracts,* 2 vols. [covering 1821–1877] (Bowie, Md.: Heritage Books, 1995–1996). Michael Kelsey, Nancy Graff Floyd, and Ginny Guinn Parsons have also published *The Southern Argus: Obituaries, Death Notices, and Implied Deaths, June 1869 through 1874* (Bowie, Md.: Heritage Books, 1995) and *Marriage and Death Notices from the South Western Baptist Newspaper* (Bowie, Md.: Heritage Books, 1995).

Some newspapers outside of Alabama include information on Alabamians. For example, the newspapers abstracted in Elizabeth Evans Kilbourne's *Columbus, Georgia, Newspaper Clippings (Columbus Enquirer),* 6 vols. to date [covering 1832–1849, so far] (Savannah: The Author, 1997–), and *Terrell County, Georgia Newspaper Clippings,* 5 vols. to date [covering 1866–1889, so far] (Savannah: The Author, 1996–), include references to numerous Alabamians.

PRIVATE MANUSCRIPTS AND ARCHIVES

Alabama's archives and records repositories are described in *Archives and Manuscripts in Alabama: A Repository Guide* (Montgomery: Society of Alabama Archivists, 1997) and in the current edition of the national *Directory of Archives and Manuscript Repositories.* Addresses and other information on many of the state's manuscript and government records repositories can also be found at the web site of the Alabama Department of Archives and History and in Marcia K. Smith Collier's *Alabama County*

Data and Resources, 2nd ed. (Titus, Ala.: The Author, 1999). The web site "Repositories of Primary Sources: Eastern United States" lists for Alabama: Air Force Historical Research Agency; Alabama Department of Archives and History; Alabama State University; Auburn University (Montgomery); Auburn University Archives; Auburn University Special Collections; Birmingham Museum of Art; Birmingham Public Library; Horseshoe Bend National Battlefield Park; Mobile Public Library; Redstone Scientific Information Center; Russell Cave National Monument; Samford University; Tuskegee Institute National Historic Site; University of Alabama at Birmingham; University of Alabama at Huntsville; University of Alabama (Tuscaloosa); University of South Alabama; and University of West Alabama. Most of these institutions also have web sites on the Internet.

Among the published guides to manuscript holdings of Alabama libraries and archives there are *A Guide to the Collections of the Department of Archives and Manuscripts, Linn-Henley Research Library, Birmingham Public Library* (Birmingham: Birmingham Public Library, 1986); *An Alphabetical Index to Historical Manuscript Collections with Subject, Geographic, and Chronological Indexes, Wm. Stanley Hoole Special Collections Library, the University of Alabama* (n.p., 1988); and John S. Lupold, *Chattahoochee Valley Sources and Resources: An Annotated Bibliography,* 2 vols. (Eufaula, Ala.: Historic Chattahoochee Commission, 1993). Volume one of the latter includes Barbour, Chambers, Dale, Henry, Houston, Lee, and Russell Counties. Another source of information on Alabama manuscripts is Lucille Griffith's *Alabama: A Documentary History to 1900,* Rev. ed. (Tuscaloosa: University of Alabama Press, 1972).

Manuscript holdings for Alabama have descriptions in such national resources as the Research Library Information Network (RLIN), currently accessible through the Internet, and Online Computer Library Center (OCLC). The latter is accessed through subscribing university libraries and some archives, including the Birmingham Public Library (the Jefferson County Library Cooperative). OCLC is also included in the Alabama Virtual Library, accessible in each of Alabama's libraries. RLIN includes private manuscript collections in the Alabama Department of Archives and History and in the National Union Catalog of Manuscript Collections. For more information on these resources see Mary McCampbell Bell, Clifford

Dwyer, and William Abbot Henderson, "Finding Manuscript Collections: NUCMC, NIDS, and RLIN," *National Genealogical Society Quarterly* 77 (1989): 208–18; and *What the OCLC Online Union Catalog Means to Me: A Collection of Essays* (Dublin, Ohio: OCLC, 1997). The Information Exchange Database, Manuscripts Society, Special Collections, University Libraries, University of Arkansas, Fayetteville, AK 72701, maintains data on many historical manuscripts in private possession.

The Church of Jesus Christ of Latter-Day Saints (LDS) maintains thousands of family history centers around the world. Currently, twenty-eight of these operations are in Alabama, usually located in its churches and open to the general public during selected hours each week. Through these centers, researchers have access to some three million microfilm reels of copies of records from around the world, including most Alabama county records before 1920. For addresses and hours of family history centers visit the Internet web site Familysearch.com. For descriptions of the materials microfilmed by the LDS Church see Johni Cerny and Wendy Elliott, *The Library: A Guide to the LDS Family History Library* (Salt Lake City: Ancestry, 1988).

The Library of Congress, 101 Independence Avenue SE, Washington, DC 20540-4660, still has the reputation as the world's greatest research center. For a basic overview of its resources for research, see James C. Neagles, *The Library of Congress: A Guide to Genealogical and Historical Research* (Salt Lake City: Ancestry, 1990).

Near the above, the Daughters of the American Revolution Library, 1776 D Street, Washington, DC 20006-5392, provides highly accessible and unique resources for Alabama and American research. Chapters of the DAR across the nation contribute to this organization's extensive historical and genealogical library with indexed typescripts of private and local government records. Members of the DAR have to provide genealogical and personal data back to ancestors of the American Revolution. This information, often thoroughly documented, is almost always available to the general public. For information on the DAR Library see Eric Grundset and Steven B. Rhodes, *American Genealogical Research at the Daughters of the American Revolution Library* (Washington, D.C.: DAR, 1997), and the library's regularly updated, published bibliography of family histories. Lists of the patriot ancestors documented by the members of the DAR are found in Daughter's of the American Revolution, *Patriot Index,* 3 vols.(Washington, D.C.: DAR, 1990–1994); *Index of the Rolls of Honor (Ancestor Index),* 2 vols. (Washington, D.C.: DAR, 1988); *Genealogy Guide Master Index of Genealogy in the Daughters of the American Revolution Magazine* (Washington, D.C.: DAR, 1994); and in Ethel Beck Marty, Carolyn Luttrell, and Alice Geron, *Membership Roll and Register of Ancestors: Alabama Society, Daughters of the American Revolution,* 5 vols. (Washington, D.C.: DAR, 1949–).

Several other archives and libraries outside of Alabama have extensive Alabama manuscript holdings and even published catalogs of these holdings. The most important of these are the Southern Historical Collection of the Wilson Library of the University of North Carolina at Chapel Hill and the Manuscripts Department of the William R. Perkins Library of Duke University. The manuscript holdings of both libraries can be accessed through the Internet. For East Tennessee families that settled in north Alabama, researchers should plan a visit to the McClung Historical Collection, East Tennessee Historical Center, 500 West Church Avenue, Knoxville, Tennessee. The Alabama sources in the National Archives and Records Administration will be discussed throughout this book but especially in chapter 13, "Other Special Federal Sources."

MISCELLANEOUS NATIONAL SOURCES

Many broad national works include significant source material on Alabama. Several of the major publishers of reference works and microfilm compilations for libraries have sources for specific groups that include Alabamians, notably University Publications of America, Gale Publishing, Research Publications/Primary Source; K. G. Saur; and Scholarly Resources. Many of their published indexes and other resources are being copied onto databases on the Internet. Some national guides and bibliographies in print of special value for Alabama research include

Arksey, Laura, Nancy Pries, and Marcia Reed. *American Diaries: An Annotated Bibliography of Published American Diaries and Journals.* 2 vols., 1492–1980. Detroit, Mich.: Gale Research, 1983. This work has a geographic index.

Bentley, Elizabeth Petty. *The Genealogist Address Book.* Baltimore, Md.: Genealogical Publishing Company.

————. *County Courthouse* [address] *Book.* Baltimore, Md.: Genealogical Publishing Company.

————. *Directory of Family Associations.* Baltimore, Md.: Genealogical Publishing Company.

Bremer, Ronald A. *Compendium of Historical Sources: The How and Where of American Genealogy.* Bountiful, Utah: American Genealogical Publishing Company, 1997.

Eichholz, Alice. *Ancestry's Red Book: American State, County, and Town Sources.* Rev. ed. Salt Lake City: Ancestry, 1992. The best guide to the general sources available for each state.

Filby, P. William. *A Bibliography of American County History.* Baltimore: Genealogical Publishing Company, 1985.

————. *Directory of American Libraries with Genealogy or Local History Collections.* Wilmington: Scholarly Resources, 1988.

Kirkham, E. Kay. *An Index to Some of the Family Records of the Southern States.* Logan, Utah: Everton Publishers, 1979.

Meyerink, Kory. *Printed Sources: A Guide to Published Genealogical Records.* Salt Lake City: Ancestry, 1997.

Schreiner-Yantis, Netti, and Marian Hoffman. *Genealogical and Local History Books in Print.* 5th ed. Baltimore: Genealogical Publishing Company, 1996.

Smith, Jessie Carnie. *Ethnic Genealogy: A Research Guide.* Westport, Conn.: Greenwood Press, 1983.

Szucs, Loretto Dennis, and Sandra Hargreaves Luebking. *The Source: A Guidebook to American Genealogy,* Rev. ed. Salt Lake City, Utah: Ancestry, 1997.

Wasserman, Paul, and Alice E. Kennington. *Ethnic Information Sources of the United States.* Detroit, Mich.: Gale Research, 1983.

3. MAPS AND PLACES

LOCATIONS IN ALABAMA

Many sources exist for finding locations in Alabama, such as the indexes to federal topographical maps discussed below. For historical locations see W. Craig Remington and Thomas J. Kallsen, *Historical Atlas of Alabama*, 2 volumes to date (Tuscaloosa: Department of Geography, 1997–). Volume 1 covers historical locations and volume 2 maps cemeteries while identifying the most prominent families buried therein. A third volume, locating place names on Alabama rivers, is being prepared for publication. Other works include

Bahn, Filbert S. *American Place Names of Long Ago: A Republication of Cram's Unrivaled Atlas of the World, as Based on the Census of 1890*. Baltimore: Genealogical Publishing Company, 1998.
The Encyclopedia of Alabama. St. Clair Shores, Mich.: Somerset Publishers, 1999.
Foscue, Virginia O. *Place Names in Alabama*. Tuscaloosa: University of Alabama Press, 1989.
Harris, W. Stuart. *Dead Towns of Alabama*. University: University of Alabama Press, 1977.
Parker, J. Carlyle. *City, County, Town, and Township Index to the 1850 Federal Census Schedules*. Detroit: Gale, 1976.
Read, William A. *Indian Place Names in Alabama*. Rev. ed. Tuscaloosa: University of Alabama Press, 1984.

Works Projects Administration, *Alabama: A Guide to the Deep South*. New
York: Richard D. Smith, 1941.

A nationwide index to the current federal topographical maps has been
published as *Omni Gazetteer of the United States of America* (Detroit: Om-
nigraphics, 1991). Volume 4 includes Alabama. The index to these maps
can also be accessed through the Internet at the web site of the United
States Geological Survey (USGS) and also through Topozone.com. This
index allows instant direct access to the actual maps of these locations. Federal topographical maps, showing buildings, elevations, creeks, roads, cemeteries, etc., past and present, and related federal aerial photographs can
also be obtained for a fee from National Cartographic Information Center,
U.S. Geological Survey, 507 National Center, Reston, VA 22092. Alabama's
first topographical maps date to the 1890s, although many areas of Alabama were not so mapped until recent times. Many libraries and some
stores across Alabama have federal topographical maps. The map collections of the Department of Geography of the University of Alabama and
the Southern History Collection of the Birmingham Public Library have
many of the historical topographical maps. A set of nonfederal Alabama
topographical maps, with an index, has been published as *Alabama Atlas
and Gazetteer: Topo Maps of the Entire State* (Yarmouth, Maine: DeLorme,
1998).

Federal aerial photographs for use in topographical maps begin in the
late 1930s. For background information on them see Charles E. Taylor and
Richard E. Spurr, *Aerial Photographs in the National Archives* (Washington,
D.C.: National Archives, 1973). Copies of federal aerial photographs can
also be ordered from National Cartographic Information Center, U.S.
Geological Survey, 507 National Center, Reston, VA 22092. The Map Li-
brary of the Department of Geography of the University of Alabama at
Tuscaloosa has a large collection of these photographs for Alabama.

SANBORN MAPS FOR CITIES AND TOWNS

Sanborn fire insurance maps show individual building floor plans,
streets, and other important information for over one hundred Alabama

towns and cities. Proportions on these maps are usually distorted, however. The earliest of these maps for Alabama exist from the late 1880s. For historical background and research uses for such maps, see Diane L. Oswald, *Fire Insurance Maps: Their History and Application* (College Station, Tex.: Lacewing Press, 1997). General lists of Sanborn maps include Walter W. Ristow, *Fire Insurance Maps in the Library of Congress* (Washington, D.C.: Library of Congress, 1981), and the less complete R. Philip Hoehn, William S. Peterson-Hunt, and Evelyn I. Woodruff, *Union List of Sanborn Fire Insurance Maps Held by Institutions in the United States and Canada*, 2 vols. (Santa Cruz, Calif.: University of California, 1976).

The following Alabama cities and towns have Sanborn maps for the years indicated. A complete or almost complete set of these maps for Alabama is found at the Alabama Department of Archives and History; the W. Stanley Hoole Library of the University of Alabama at Tuscaloosa; and the Library of Congress. Microfilm of the Alabama maps is found at the Gorgas Library of the University of Alabama at Tuscaloosa and in the Department of Manuscripts and Archives (Birmingham Archives), the Linn Henley Research Library of the Birmingham Public Library. Many Alabama county public libraries have at least copies of their local Sanborn maps. Sanborn maps for the rest of the United States can be found in the Map Library of the Department of Geography, University of Alabama at Tuscaloosa; and the Map Division, Library of Congress. Sanborn maps can be purchased on microfilm and soon will be found on the Internet.

Sanborn Fire Insurance Maps of Alabama

Abbeville 1907–1943	Bay Minette 1927–1949
Alabama City 1926	Bessemer 1888–1959
Albertville 1927–1951	Birmingham 1885–1969
Alexander City 1894–1954	Boaz 1929–1944
Aliceville 1933	Brewton 1893–1949
Andalusia 1905–1947	Bridgeport 1892–1944
Anniston 1885–1967	Brundidge 1916–1943
Ashland 1928	Calera 1889–1938
Athens 1884–1948	Camden 1894–1938
Atmore 1927–1947	Camp Hill 1928–1948
Attalla 1892–1956	Carbon Hill 1926–1946
Auburn 1897–1949	Citronelle 1908–1926
Avondale 1914	Clanton 1917–1952

Clayton 1895–1924
Columbia 1885–1916
Columbiana 1909–1935
Cordova 1930
Cullman 1888–1959
Dadeville 1889–1934
Decatur 1884–1969
Demopolis 1884–1959
Dothan 1893–1958
Elba 1903–1943
Enterprise 1905–1951
Eufaula 1959
Evergreen 1884–1947
Fairhope 1932–1949
Fayette 1928–1949
Florala 1907–1941
Florence 1884–1963
Foley 1945
Fort Payne 1891–1955
Gadsden 1885–1969
Gainesville 1884–1925
Geneva 1893–1932
Georgiana 1916–1947
Goodwater 1894–1949
Greensboro 1884–1943
Greenville 1884–1958
Guntersville 1930–1954
Gurley 1898–1927
Haleyville 1930–1950
Hartford 1906–1951
Hartselle 1917–1951
Headland 1916–1945
Heflin 1930–1940
Huntsville 1884–1966
Hurtsboro 1916–1934
Jackson 1930–1949
Jacksonville 1885–1948
Jasper 1894–1959
Lafayette 1885–1955
Langdale 1932
Lanett 1930
Leeds 1930

Linden 1933
Livingston 1894–1934
Luverne 1893–1927
Marion 1894–1949
Mobile 1885–1991
Monroeville 1930
Montevallo 1933
Montgomery 1884–1972
Oneonta 1930–1951
Opelika 1885–1962
Opp 1930–1951
Oxford 1885–1950
Ozark 1893–1943
Pell City 1930
Phenix City 1922–1960
Piedmont 1894–1948
Prattville 1911–1950
Pritchard 1933
Red Bay 1949
Roanoke 1894–1955
Robertsdale 1947
Rogerville 1928
Russellville 1894–1960
Samson 1910–1934
Scottsboro 1917–1951
Selma 1884–1963
Sheffield 1889–1963
Shelby 1905–1923
Springville 1885–1909
Stevenson 1895–1946
Sylacauga 1894–1964
Talladega 1885–1966
Tallassee 1913–1949
Tallassee, East 1913
Thomaston 1925
Thomasville 1939
Troy 1885–1963
Tuscaloosa 1884–1967
Tuscumbia 1884–1956
Tuskegee 1895–1954
Union Springs 1885–1954
Uniontown 1884–1950

West Blocton 1939   Winfield 1942
Wetumpka 1885–1955   York 1924–1945

The National Archives has local maps of many but not all Alabama post offices and has microfilmed these as M1126 Post Office Department Reports of Site Locations, 1837–1950, rolls 1–15. This microfilm is arranged by county and then in rough alphabetical order by post office. A set of this microfilm is in the Family and Regional History Program of Wallace State College, Hanceville, and the Gorgas Library, University of Alabama, Tuscaloosa.

MODERN MAPS

The Map Library of the Department of Geography of the University of Alabama at Tuscaloosa has modern (1980s to present) county and city maps of Alabama as well as aerial photographs from c. 1950s to c. 1970s. This library also has modern and some past federal topographical maps.

Modern county road maps can be ordered from Map Sales, Alabama Department of Transportation, 1409 Coliseum Blvd. RM. R-109, Montgomery, AL 36130-3050. These maps include the township, range, and section numbers used in federal land grants and in Alabama deeds.

HISTORICAL MAPS

Historical maps can be found at a number of locations. Samford University has an extensive map collection, see *Maps: The Samford University Annotated List* (Birmingham: Samford, 1977). The William Stanley Hoole Library of the University of Alabama at Tuscaloosa and the Southern History Collection of the Birmingham Public Library have many detailed historical statewide and local maps of Alabama. Researchers need an appointment to use the original maps in the Birmingham Public Library's map collection, although photocopies of most of the maps are readily available there for researchers. For specific maps the researcher should see Birmingham Public Library, *A List of Nineteenth-Century Maps of the State of Alabama* (Birmingham: Birmingham Public Library, 1973); and Birmingham Public Library, *A List of the 16th, 17th, and 18th Century Material in the Rucker Agee Map Collection, Birmingham Public Library* (Birmingham: Birmingham Public Library, 1978).

The above libraries and the Geological Survey of Alabama Library at the University of Alabama at Tuscaloosa have copies of maps and have detailed county soil survey maps. Dating from c. 1900 to the 1950s, these maps show elevations, roads, and even some individual buildings.

The Alabama Department of Archives and History has many historical maps of Alabama. The department also has county property-owner maps for Autauga, Barbour, Bullock, Butler, Coffee, Covington, Crenshaw, Dale, Dallas, Elmore, Geneva, Henry, Houston, Lee, Lowndes, Macon, Montgomery, and Pike Counties. The Works Projects Administration prepared these maps in the 1930s. The Alabama Archives also has an extensive collection of Alabama soil-survey pamphlets and accompanying maps, 1902–1979, in collection LPR 89.

Several sources for information on county boundary changes in Alabama exist in print. However, no such work can be exact, for laws on Alabama's county and state boundaries were frequently vague and very much subject to interpretation. For changes on a county by county basis, see Peggy Tuck Sinko, *Alabama: Atlas of Historical County Boundaries* (New York: Simon & Schuster, 1996); and W. Craig Remington, *The Atlas of Alabama Counties* (Tuscaloosa: Department of Geography, University of Alabama, 2000).

Several sources exist for use in determining boundaries used in federal censuses. For county boundaries in each of the federal censuses, see William Thorndale and William Dollarhide, *Map Guide to the U.S. Federal Censuses, 1790–1920* (Baltimore: Genealogical Publishing Company, 1987). National Archives microfilm of records of boundaries used in taking the federal census includes T1210 for 1900 and T1224 for 1830–1890 and 1910–1950); also see Bruce Carpenter, "Using Soundex Alternatives: Enumeration Districts, 1880–1920," *Prologue: The Quarterly of the National Archives and Records Administration* 25 (1993): 90–93.

The following miscellaneous sources of use in exploring Alabama's historic boundaries and locations are found in the Tutwiler Collection of Southern History and Literature, Birmingham Public Library:

Abernathy, Thomas Perkins. *The Formative Period in Alabama, 1815–1828*. University: University of Alabama Press, 1965.

Brannon, Peter. "Peter Brannon's Alabama Travel Logs: A Series of Historic Stories of Trips through Alabama" (1928–1931), from *Alabama Highways Magazine*. Southern History of the Birmingham Public Library has an index to this work.

Harrell, Clifford. "Boundaries of Alabama." M.A. thesis, Alabama Polytechnic Institute, 1939.

Safford, Berney. *Hand-Book of Alabama*. 2nd ed. Birmingham: Roberts & Son, 1892. This work includes lists of voter precincts by county.

4. BIOGRAPHICAL SOURCES

The family vertical files of the Alabama Department of Archives and History provide the best single source for biographical, genealogical, and other personal information on Alabamians of the past. Arranged alphabetically, all but the most recent additions to this material have been microfilmed. The film is widely available at many libraries in Alabama and can be borrowed through the family history centers of the Church of Jesus Christ of Latter-Day Saints (LDS family history centers) around the world. The Alabama Archives has filing cabinets, in the microfilm reading room, of additional family and biographical material donated since the microfilm edition of the family files. Many Alabama public libraries also have at least local-oriented vertical files of biographical and genealogical information on individuals.

The Alabama Department of Archives and History (see chapter 5 in this volume, "Statewide and Out-of-State Libraries and Archives") also has various card catalogs and other sources of at least public service information on Alabamians. Its card catalogs include Miscellaneous Name and Subject File; Civil Commissions and Appointments; Bonds of State and County Officials [by county]; Alabama Legislators; Family Exchange Card File; Spanish Grants; and Index to [Federal] Land Books. On microfilm the Alabama Archives has registers of commissions and appointments, c. 1819–c. 1935; funeral and anniversary notices from Alabama newspapers,

1950–1979, in alphabetical order; a special index to select counties in the 1870 census of Alabama; and the Alabama military records card catalog indexes for wars from the American Revolution to World War I; and more.

Other special biographical sources are discussed elsewhere. For birth, death, and divorce records for Alabamians, see chapter 15 in this volume, "Vital Records: Births, Deaths, Divorces, and Marriages." For personal data from census records see chapter 12 in this volume, "Census Records."

Alabama also has special published compilations of family histories and biographical data. These works include

Elliott, Carl. *Annals of Northwest Alabama.* 5 vols. Northport, Ala.: Hermitage Press, 1965–1987.

England, Flora Dainwood. *Alabama Source Book.* Marion, Ala.: Coffee Printing Company, 1964. This work includes Dallas, Marengo, Perry, and Wilcox Counties.

Helms, Lavina Jordan. *Church Records of Southeast Alabama.* Enterprise, Ala.: The Author, 1995.

Horn, Robert C., and Mariemma Fuller. *Epitaphs in East-Central Alabama Cemeteries.* 4 vols. Dadeville, Ala.: Genealogical Society of East Alabama, 1985.

Ivison, Hazle R. Collins. *Alabama Tombstone Inscriptions.* Mobile: The Author, 1987.

Jacobson, Judy. *Alabama and Mississippi Connections: Historical and Biographical Sketches of Families on Both Sides of the Tombigbee River.* Baltimore: Clearfield, 1999.

Moffett, Dorothy Ivison, and William R. Armistead. *Beneath Southern Sod.* N.p., 1964.

Pettit, Madge. *Pioneers and Residents of West Central Alabama prior to the Civil War.* Bowie, Md.: Heritage Books, 1988.

Saunders, James E. *Early Settlers of Alabama.* New Orleans: The Author, 1899.

Stewart, Mrs. Frank Ross. *Northeast Alabama Scrapbook, 1883–1935.* 2 vols. Centre, Ala.: Stewart University Press, 1983.

Strickland, Jean, and Patricia N. Edwards. *The Locator File.* Moss Point, Miss.: Ben Strickland, 1999. This work covers southwest Alabama of 1850 and earlier.

Special Collections, W. Stanley Hoole Library, University of Alabama at Tuscaloosa, has the genealogical information found in the correspondence of Alabama researchers Pauline Gandrud and Kathleen Paul Jones. Their miscellaneous notes from Alabama county records and newspapers have been published.

Publications of detailed biographical and genealogical information became popular at the turn of the century and often included individuals of only local (if any real) prominence. The best single index for such material for Alabama is "Alabama Biographical Sketches," an unpublished typescript in the Southern History Collection, Birmingham Public Library. Prepared by the Works Project Administration in the 1930s, this index does not include the biographical material found in the expanded reprint of Clement Evans, ed., *Confederate Military History.* 16 vols. (Wilmington, N.C.: Broadfoot Company, 1987). Another biographical index to Alabama is *Alabama Biographical Directory* (St. Clair Shores, Mich.: Somerset Publishers, 1999).

Many national biographical sources exist that include Alabamians, such as, among others, the CD-ROM computer disk edition of *Biography and Genealogy Master Index,* 17 vols. to date (Detroit, Mich.: Gale Publishing, 1986–); the *World Biographical Index,* updated and published annually by K. G. Saur North America (an index with sources given can be accessed at the Saur web site); *Personal Name Index to "The New York Times Index"* [1851–], 25 vols. to date (Succasunna, N.J.: Roxbury Data Interface, 1976 and 1989), available in Social Science of the main branch of Birmingham Public Library; volume seven of *C.R.I.S.: The Combined Retrospective Index Set to Journals in History, 1838–1974,* 11 vols. (Washington, D.C.: Carrollton Press, 1977); and the "U.S. Biography Index" (an index to biographical information in books without indexes) and other card catalogs of the Local History and Genealogy Room of the Library of Congress, Jefferson Annex, Washington, D.C.

Many nationwide federal sources for such information can be found in *Genealogical and Biographical Research: A Select Catalog of National Archives Microfilm Publications* (Washington, D.C.: National Archives, 1983). The latter work includes information on National Archives microfilm of letters of recommendation made to United States presidents for federal employment, arranged by presidential administration, 1797–1877. For biographical data on some of the leaders on the southern frontier see Dan L. Thrapp, *Encyclopedia of Frontier Biography,* 3 vols. (Signal Mountain, Tenn.: Mountain Press, 1995).

Several other compilations of biographies of politicians and prominent bureaucrats also exist, including

Biographical Directory of the American Congress, 1774–1996. Alexandria, Va.: Congressional Quarterly Company, 1997.

Lanman, Charles. *Biographical Annals of the Civil Government of the United States* (Washington, D.C.: James Anglin, 1876). From the latter, the article "Some Prominent Alabamians of the Early Republic," *Alabama Family History and Genealogy News* 19, no. 4 (1998): 24, was compiled.

Miller, Cynthia Pease. *A Guide to Research Collections of Former Members of the United States House of Representatives, 1789–1987.* Washington, D.C.: Government Printing Office, 1988.

Paul, Karen Dawley. *Guide to Research Collections of Former United States Senators, 1789–1995.* Washington. D.C.: Government Printing Office, 1995.

Quatannens, Jo Anne McCormick. *Senators of the United States: A Historical Biography.* Washington, D.C.; Government Printing Office, 1995.

Ritter, Charles F., and Jon L. Wakelyn. *American Legislative Leaders, 1850–1910.* Westport, Conn.: Greenwood, 1989.

Stewart, John Craig. *The Governors of Alabama.* Gretna, La.: Pelican Publishing, 1975.

Watson, Elbert L. *Alabama United States Senators.* Huntsville, Ala.: Strode Publishers, 1982.

BUSINESSMEN AND PROFESSIONALS

Special sources also exist on craftsmen and businessmen, such as John S. Craig, *Craig's Daguerreian Registry* (Torrington, Conn.: The Author, 1996), a biographical reference on early photographers. Aside from books of biographical sketches and indexes to biographical materials on specific professions, there is also the microfiche of the bibliography of personal and professional records of some fifty thousand southern artisans to

1820 compiled by the Museum of Early Southern Decorative Arts of Winston-Salem, North Carolina.

In addition to the city directories, there have also been directories of Alabama businessmen/businesses and gazetteers providing information on Alabama towns, cities, counties, businesses, professionals, and sometimes even planters. The directories are arranged alphabetically by town and by type of business. Alabama is included in *The Southern Business Directory and General Commercial Advertiser* (Charleston: Walker & James, 1854). A few south Alabama counties had business directories in the 1850s to 1861. Statewide directories of businesses in Alabama began as early as 1881 with *The Alabama State Gazetteer and Business Directory* (Lynchburg, Va.: Southern Directory and Publishing Company, 1881). No library has a complete collection of these directories, although some are found in the Library of Congress and the Birmingham Public Library. For modern information on businesses, consult such sources as *International Directory of Company Histories,* 16 vols. to date (Detroit, Mich.: St. James Press, 1984–). A special source for Alabama is *Summary of Statutes of Alabama Affecting Railroad Corporations* (n.p., 1908).

Over the years, many directories and reference works have appeared on companies that did mining in Alabama, including, among others,

Armes, Ethel. *The Story of Coal and Iron in Alabama.* Birmingham: Birmingham Chamber of Commerce, 1910.

Bennett, James R. *Tannehill and the Growth of the Alabama Iron Industry.* McCalla, Ala.: Alabama Historic Iron Works Commission, 1999.

DeJarnette, Donald W. *Directory of Underground Coal Mines in Alabama.* Tuscaloosa: Geological Survey of Alabama, 1986.

Directory of Commercial Minerals in Georgia and Alabama along the Central of Georgia Railway. Buffalo, N.Y.: Matthews-Northrup Works, 1923.

Lewis, W. David. *Sloss Furnaces and the Rise of the Birmingham District.* Tuscaloosa: University of Alabama Press, 1994.

Also helpful for Alabama mining research are the various editions of *Alabama Mining and Manufacturing Directory, Directory of Alabama Manufacturers and Manufactures,* and *Alabama Directory of Mining and Manu-*

facturing. For other sources see Theodore J. Hull, "Electronic Records Relevant to Research on Mining," *Prologue: The Quarterly of the National Archives and Records Administration* 31 (1999): 101–9.

As early as 1841, Lewis Tappen's Mercantile Agency offered for sale credit ratings of individual business efforts. His company evolved into R. G. Dun and Co., which began publishing credit ratings as the *Mercantile Agency's Reference Book* in 1859. As Dun and Bradstreet, the company still publishes credit ratings today. Because these and similar yearly compilations by their competitors were only leased to individual customers and were collected for destruction at the end of each year, few of these compilations survive. The Library of Congress (on microfilm); the Baker Library of Harvard Business School; and the New York Public Library likely have the most complete collections of these works. For historical background on these records, see James D. Norris, *R. G. Dun & Co., 1841–1900* (Westport, Conn.: Greenwood Press, 1978).

The R. G. Dun Collection of manuscript credit reports for Alabama and the rest of the country, starting in 1848 and continuing to the early 1880s, is in the Baker Library, Harvard University, Boston, MA 02163, and can be searched for a fee. For more information see the Baker Library's web site. When writing to the Baker Library to ask for information from the R. G. Dun Collection, include the name of the business or businessmen, the state, the county, and the town (if known). These records are not open to genealogists.

MEDICAL PROFESSIONALS

In addition to such sources as those cited above, many reference materials exist for information on medical professionals. Almost every county probate court in Alabama, respectively, has a local register of medical professionals, usually beginning by the 1870s. The Alabama Department of Archives and History has the medical examinations files of the Alabama Board of Medical Examiners, 1881–1962. The Family and Regional History Program at Wallace State College has a copy of the index. A printed source is Patsy R. Page, *Directory of Alabama Physicians, 1886* (Alachua, Fla.: Page Publications, 1995). Historical publications, such as those located through past volumes of *Bibliography of the History of Medicine*, sometimes also provide biographical information. For background on the practice of medicine in Alabama, see Howard L. Holley, *A History of Medicine in Alabama* (Birmingham: University of Alabama at Birmingham School of Medicine, 1982). For nursing sources, see Interagency Council on Library Resources for Nursing, *Guide to Archival Sources in Nursing* (West Long Branch, N.J.: The Author, 1960).

For nationwide indexes to biographical information on physicians, including for Alabama, see the sources listed below. The National Genealogical Society also has the American Medical Association Deceased Physicians' File and related sources; for information consult the National Genealogical Society web site.

Atkinson, William B. *The Physicians and Surgeons of the United States*. Philadelphia: Charles Robson, 1878.

Hafner, Arthur W. *Directory of Deceased American Physicians, 1804–1929*. 2 vols. Chicago: American Medical Association, 1989.

Holloway, Lisabeth M. *Medical Obituaries: American Physicians' Biographical Notices . . . before 1907*. New York: Garland Publishing, 1981.

Kaufman, Martin. *Dictionary of American Medical Biography*. Westport, Conn.: Greenwood, 1984.

Williams, Stephen W. *American Medical Biography*. Greenfield, Mass.: L. Merriam, 1845.

ATTORNEYS

Several sources also include at least some information on lawyers. The Alabama Department of Archives and History has biographical files of deceased members of the Alabama Bar Association, 1922 to the present, and some photographs for the period 1879–1915. Past volumes of the annual proceedings of the Alabama Bar Association sometimes contain memorials of deceased members. For lists of Alabama attorneys, see Walter B. Jones, "Alabama Lawyers, 1818–1948," *Alabama Lawyer* 9 (1948): 123–93; and *The Alabama Bar Directory* (1985–), published by the Desk Book Committee of the Alabama State Bar.

The only attempt at a complete list of lawyers for the whole United

States ever published is *Martindale's American Law Directory* (New York: Martindale, 1868). The Hubbell (now Martindale and Hubbell) Company has published lists of attorneys since 1871, but these lists are selective. Available at many law libraries, the later Martindale lists for 1874 to 1878 and 1888 and forward often do include at least some professional information. The Family and Regional History Program, Wallace State College, Hanceville, has microfiche of the Hubbell and Martindale lists, 1868–1900. Phi Delta Phi, the national fraternity of lawyers, began in 1865 and keeps biographical data on members, past and present.

FEDERAL EMPLOYEES

For career information on federal employees and office seekers, see Claire Prelchtel-Kluskens, "Documenting the Career of Federal Employees," *Prologue: The Quarterly of the National Archives and Records Administration* 26 (1994): 180–83; and *Genealogical and Biographical Research: A Select Catalog of National Archives Microfilm Publications* (Washington, D.C.: National Archives, 1983). Published lists of federal employees from 1816 to 1825 frequently give state or country of birth for individuals; see "Some Alabama Federal Employees with Place of Birth," *AlaBenton Genealogical Quarterly* 10 (1993): 40–46. Many of these books to 1959 are in the microfilm reading room of the Alabama Department of Archives and History. Records of Appointments of Postmasters, 1789 to 1832, appears in National Archives microfilm M1131; and for Alabama for 1832–1971, in reels 1–3 of National Archives microfilm M841. For career information on federal military officers, several sources exist, including Edward W. Callahan, *List of the Officers of the Navy of the United States and of the Marine Corps from 1775 to 1900* (New York: L. R. Hamersly & Co., 1901); Francis B. Hietman, *Historical Register of Officers of the Continental Army . . . April 1775 to December 1783* (Washington, D.C.: Rare Book Shop, 1914); and Francis B. Hietman, *Historical Register and Directory of the United States Army . . . September 29, 1789, to March 2, 1903* (Washington, D.C.: Government Printing Office, 1903).

MASONIC AND OTHER GROUPS

No statewide compilation of Masonic biographical information has been created, although some of it has survived in miscellaneous sources.

The Grand Lodge of Alabama, which began in 1821, may be reached at P.O. Box 6195, Montgomery, AL 36106. For information on Masonic research, see Jill Rueble Hughes, "Researching Masonic Records," *Heritage Quest,* no. 42 (1992): 15–18; and John S. Yates, *Researching Masonic Records* (Wichita Falls, Kans.: The Author, 1995). Alabama's lodges of the International Order of the Odd Fellows have an Internet web site. For other organizations, see the current edition of Elizabeth Petty Bentley, *The Genealogist Address Book* (Baltimore, Md.: Genealogical Publishing Company); and Alan Axelrod, *The International Encyclopedia of Secret Societies and Fraternal Orders* (New York: Facts on File, 1997).

ALABAMA WRITERS

Alabamians frequently appear in national and southern compilations of information on writers. The Alabama Writers Forum, Alabama State Council on the Arts, 201 Monroe Street, Montgomery, AL 36130-1800, publishes *Alabama Literary Resources Directory*, a guide to current authors and writers groups in the state, and *First Draft: The Journal of the Alabama Writers' Forum* (1993–).

WOMEN'S SOURCES

Statistical studies on labor, medicine, and politics centered on Alabama women have been published over the years, some even as periodicals. To find other sources, see *Sources for Research in Women's History: A Preliminary Survey of Holdings in Alabama Institutions* (Montgomery: Alabama Department of Archives and History, 1985). Aside from individual biographies, local histories, and regional studies, books on Alabama women as a specific subject or as a collection of biographies exist. Some of these works include

Bernhard, Virginia, ed. *Hidden Histories of Women in the New South.* Columbia: University of Missouri Press, 1994.

Boucher, Ann. *Alabama Women: Roles and Rebels.* Troy, Ala.: Troy State University Press, 1978.

Robbins, Mary La Fayette. *Alabama Women in Literature.* Selma, Ala.: Selma Printing Company, 1895.

Sterkx, H. E. *Partners in Rebellion: Alabama Women in the Civil War.* Rutherford: Farleigh Dickinson University Press, 1970.

————. *Some Notable Alabama Women during the Civil War.* University, Ala.: Alabama Civil War Centennial Commission, 1962.

Thomas, Mary M. *The New Woman in Alabama: Social Reforms and Suffrage, 1890–1920.* Tuscaloosa: University of Alabama Press, 1992.

————, ed., *Stepping out of the Shadows: Alabama Women, 1819–1990.* Tuscaloosa: University of Alabama Press, 1994.

Toffell, Miriam Abigail. *A Collection of Biographies of Women Who Made a Difference in Alabama.* Birmingham, Ala.: The League of Women Voters, 1995.

Yelverton, Mildred G. *They Also Served: Twenty-Five Remarkable Alabama Women.* Dothan, Ala.: Ampersand Publishing, 1993.

Special national sources for women also exist and prove helpful in Alabama research; see, for example, the special women's research issue of *Heritage Quest* (May–June 2001), and

Blanton, DeAnne. "Women Soldiers of the Civil War." *Prologue: The Quarterly of the National Archives and Records Administration* 25 (1993): 27–34.

Carmack, Sharon D. *A Genealogist's Guide to Discovering Your Female Ancestor.* Cincinnati: Beltway Books, 1998.

Conway, Jill K. *The Female Experience in Eighteenth- and Nineteenth-Century America: A Guide to the History of American Women.* Princeton: Princeton University Press, 1985.

Hinding, Andrea. *Women's History Sources: A Guide to Archives and Manuscript Collections.* New York: Bowker, 1979.

Jones, Edward T. *Notable American Women, 1607–1950.* 3 vols. Cambridge, Mass.: Harvard, 1971.

Schaefer, Christina K. *The Hidden Half of the Family: A Sourcebook for Women's Genealogy.* Baltimore: Genealogical Publishing Company, 1999.

Seeley, Charlotte Palmer. *American Women and the U. S. Armed Forces: A Guide to the Records of Military Agencies in the National Archives Relating to American Women.* Washington, D.C.: National Archives, 1992.

INFORMATION ON PERSONS LIVING TODAY

Several works describe how to use modern sources, such as the Internet, for research on people in any state. These works include, among many others, Richard S. Johnson, *Find Anyone Fast by Phone, Fax, Mail, and Computer* (Burlington, N.C.: MIE Publishing, 1995); Joseph J. Culligan, *You, Too, Can Find Anybody* (North Miami, Fla.: Hallmark Press, 1993); Ted L. Gunderson, *How to Locate Anyone Anywhere without Leaving Home* (New York: E. P. Dutton, 1989); and Loretto Dennis Szucs and Sandra Hargreaves Luebking, *The Source: A Guidebook to American Genealogy*. Rev. ed. (Salt Lake City, Utah: Ancestry, 1997). Specifically for the Internet, see, among many other works available, Thomas Jay Kemp, *Virtual Roots: A Guide to Genealogy and Local History on the World Wide Web* (Wilmington, Del.: Scholarly Resources, 1996); and Barbara Renick and Richard S. Wilson, *The Internet for Genealogists: A Beginners Guide* (La Habra, Calif.: Compuology, 1997).

Several of the sources described in such works are widely and commercially available, such as the Social Security death index (also found at all LDS family history centers) and the national telephone directories. These sources and others are also accessible through the Internet. Some examples of such web sites include Ancestry.com, Familysearch.com, and GenealogyLibrary.com. The already extensive Alabama and genealogy resources available on the Internet grow by the hour.

5. STATEWIDE AND OUT-OF-STATE LIBRARIES AND ARCHIVES

Alabama has dozens of libraries, archives, and other repositories for historical and genealogical research, most of which have web sites on the Internet. Repositories of more than local interest appear below. For special local sources, also see chapter 14 in this volume, "City, County, and Community Sources"; and Daniel R. Cusick, ed., *Alabama Foundation Directory* (Birmingham: Birmingham Public Library, 1996). For other institutions, see the current editions of *Ancestry's Red Book*; *Directory of Archives and Manuscript Repositories*; *American Library Directory*; and *Directory of Historical Organizations in the United States and Canada*. Books and some microfilms in Alabama's public libraries and some colleges are cataloged in the Alabama Library Information CATalog (ALICAT), which can be accessed at any Alabama public library and over the Internet.

THE ALABAMA DEPARTMENT OF ARCHIVES AND HISTORY

The Alabama Department of Archives and History, 624 Washington Ave., P.O. Box 300100, Montgomery, AL 36130-0100, is the oldest modern state department of archives in the United States, having begun in 1901. Its extensive collections of private papers and complete collections of official papers of governors are cataloged on computer on the Research Library Information Network (RLIN), currently accessible through the Internet. The web site for the Alabama Archives is http://www.archives.state.al.us. The Alabama Archives also has microfilm of federal records, such as censuses, that relate to Alabama and microfilm of the most important early county records for all Alabama counties except for Houston, Mobile, and Morgan Counties. This microfilm is supplemented with some original county records donated from across the state.

The following lists of the public finding aids of the Alabama Archives give a good general idea of the department's holdings. Card catalogs include Books; Miscellaneous Name and Subject File; Civil Commissions and Appointments; Bonds of State and County Officials [by county]; Alabama Legislators; Family Exchange Card File; Spanish Grants; Index to [Federal] Land Books; Towns/Cities Incorporated; Private Manuscripts; Manuscript Collections [by category]; and the Allen Rankin File [a subject index to Rankin's newspaper articles on Alabama]. Binders include Books and Serials in RLIN; Pamphlets; Alabama Pamphlet Collection; J. L. M. Pamphlet Catalog; CSA Muster Rolls; CSA Regimental History Files; CSA Unit Index; Newspaper—Finding Aids; Private Records—Finding Aids; State Records—Finding Aids; Local Records—Finding Aids; Various Legislative Indexes; and Maps. Many of the holdings of the Alabama Department of Archives and History will be discussed in detail elsewhere.

The Alabama Department of Archives and History is the repository for the official state government records. Most state agencies had administrative materials, subject files, publications, and public relations files that are now at the archives and inventoried under the name of each agency. Inventoried under the "Archives and History, Department of," the researcher will find numerous subject files, including Works Projects Administration record surveys (see *The WPA Historical Records Survey: A Guide to the Unpublished Inventories, Indexes, and Transcripts* [Chicago: Society of American Archivists, 1980]), county files, the Scottsboro Boys case records (ALAV92-A28, SG 12 528), place names, governors, and military records resources. The latter is especially extensive for the Civil War.

Other special state records at the Alabama Archives have inventories under the names of their respective departments. Each such inventory includes a department history. For example, airport inspection files, 1934 to present, can be found under "Aeronautics, Department of"; miscellaneous local photographs can be found under "Federal Civil Works Administration," "Development Office," and "Education, Superintendent of." Under the last heading can also be found validations of out-of-state teaching certificates, 1920–1921. Under "Corrections, Board of," the researcher can find blueprints of county jails, made c. 1911–c. 1934, and county jail and alms house inspection reports, c. 1907–c. 1934. (Additional information can frequently be found in local county grand jury proceedings in the respective individual Alabama counties.) Various inspection reports, 1901–1933, survive in the records of "Fire Marshal." Applications for pardons, 1846–1921, can be found under "Pardons and Paroles, Board of," while gin permits, 1932–1940, and cotton warehouse reports, 1930–1936, are found under "Agriculture and Industries, Department of." Miscellaneous county tax insolvent lists, 1820–1866, and certificates for land sold for taxes, c. 1866–c. 1939, have been inventoried under "Auditor, State"; but other records of certificates of land sold for taxes, 1868–1924, should be sought under "Tax Commissioner." The "Auditor, State" records also include railroad returns, 1860–1907, and records of the Bank of the State of Alabama, 1831–1857.

The Alabama Department of Archives and History also has the subject files of the state's Historical Commission. The Alabama Historical Commission, 468 South Perry Street, Montgomery, AL 36130-0900, maintains information on historic preservation and archaeology within the state. Access to this agency's files is made by appointment. For information on the commission, see the current editions of its publications *A Plan for Action* and *A Guide for Services and Resources.* Aside from the available books on architecture in specific localities, several works have been done for the whole state by Robert Gamble, including *Historic Architecture in Alabama: a Primer of Styles and Types, 1810–1930* (Tuscaloosa: University of Alabama Press, 1990).

Some national sources on historic preservation also include Alabama, such as the files of the Historic American Buildings Survey and the Historic

American Engineering Record on the Internet. A related source is National Trust for Historic Preservation Library, *Index to Historic Preservation Periodicals*, 2 vols. (Boston: G. K. Hall, 1988, 1992).

Not all of Alabama's state records still exist. The earliest prison records do not survive, for example, although the Alabama Department of Archives and History has on microfilm "Records of Deaths of State Convicts in Alabama, 1884–1952," as well as state convict records for 1885 to 1952 and county convict records for 1931 to 1954. This same record group has applications for employment at the state prison, 1921–1939. For sources on the early history of Alabama's state prison, see Mary Ann Neeley, "Painful Circumstances: Glimpses of the Alabama Penitentiary, 1846–1852," *Alabama Review* 44 (1991): 3–16.

Several digests of federal court and state supreme court cases exist for Alabama. The most complete of these for courts in Alabama is *Alabama Digest*. For a composite index, by plaintiff, to all American legal cases printed in all state supreme court cases, including Alabama, from 1656 to 1906, see the *1906 Decennial Edition of the American Digest* (St. Paul Minn.: West Publishing Company, 1912). The Alabama Department of Archives and History has the records of the state's supreme and appeals courts through 1980 (1989, for criminal appeals). The researcher must know the court term and, for appeals court cases, the case number for 1978 and later. For information on locating federal and state court cases, see Stephen Elias and Susan Levinkind, *Legal Research: How to Find and Understand the Law* (Berkeley, Calif.: Nolo Press, 1997); and Ellen Greenberg, *The Supreme Court Explained* (New York: W. W. Norton, 1997). Surviving Alabama federal court case files not still held by the individual courts are archived in the National Archives Southeast Region (currently at, but soon to move from, 1557 St. Joseph Avenue, East Point, GA 30344).

OTHER STATEWIDE AND REGIONAL LIBRARIES AND ARCHIVES IN AND FOR ALABAMA

In addition to the major libraries listed below, other collection repositories appear in *Archives and Manuscripts in Alabama: A Repository Guide* (n.p.: Society of Alabama Archives, 1997) and in the Alabama Department of Archives and History's web site. These other libraries include the Air Force Historical Research Agency; Alabama A & M University Archives and Special Collections; Alabama Center for Traditional Culture; Alabama Power Corporate Archives; Alabama Space and Rocket Center Archives; Auburn University Archives; Auburn University at Montgomery Archives and Special Collections; Oakwood College Archives and Museum (relating to African American Seventh-Day Adventists); Tuskegee University Booker T. Washington Collection (includes African American history); University of Alabama at Birmingham Archives (relating to health science); USS *Alabama* Battleship Memorial Park Archives; and Woman's Missionary Union Hunt Library and Archives.

The Tutwiler Collection of Southern History and Literature is at the Birmingham Public Library, 2100 Park Place, Birmingham, AL 35203 (currently open Mon.–Tues.: 9–8; Wed.–Sat.: 9–6; Sun.: 2–6). This library has one of the most extensive book and periodical collections in the world for southern research and also for the American Civil War in the South. In addition to a large collection of federal census microfilm, the library's massive holdings include a complete set of the Revolutionary War pension claims, the DAR lineage books, the *Compendium of American Genealogy*, the Lyman C. Draper Collection, and historical map collections. The originals in the latter are open only by appointment, but photocopies of the most commonly used maps are readily available to researchers. The holdings of this institution include some unique copies of Works Projects Administration transcripts of Alabama historical records and some of the typescripts of local Alabama records prepared by the state's chapters of the Daughters of the American Revolution. For an outline of the research materials in the Tutwiler Collection and the Department of Archives and Manuscripts, see the current edition of *Genealogical Research in the Tutwiler Collection of Southern History and Literature* and the library's bibliographies for such topics as African American and Native American research.

The Birmingham Public Library also has other resources of value to researchers. It is a federal government documents repository. The library also has the Department of Archives and Manuscripts, containing Birmingham-oriented archives of government records and private manuscripts, open Mondays through Fridays. Archives and Manuscripts also has broader collections, including the materials of the Southern Women's Archives and the Alabama Historical Commission's Oral History Project. The latter took in Baldwin, Barbour, Bullock, Chambers, Clarke, Clay, Colbert, Conecuh, Covington, Dallas, Fayette, Greene, Jefferson, Lamar, Lauderdale, Lee, Macon, Madison, Marion, Shelby, Tuscaloosa, Walker, and Winston Counties. The Social Science Division of the library has the indexes and microfilm of the back issues of the *New York Times* for 1851 to 1989.

The printed holdings of the Birmingham Public Library and the Jefferson County Library Co-operative are cataloged on the Internet through the Jefferson County Cooperative Library System's web site. The Southern History Collection of the Birmingham Public Library is next door to the Jefferson County courthouse.

The Family and Regional History Program, Wallace State College, P.O. Box 2000, Hanceville, AL 35077-2000, offers courses and also field trips for genealogical research. The genealogical collection, concentrating on Alabama, the southeastern United States, the American Revolution, the Civil War, and southern Native American research, is completely open to the general public. Many of its microfilms are available nowhere else in Alabama or the South. Regular hours are 8 to 8, Monday through Thursday, and 8 to 4 on Friday. During the summer, library hours, Monday through Thursday, are 8 to 6. The library also acts as a LDS Family History Center for borrowing for the public from the some 3 million microfilm reels of worldwide records held by the Genealogical Society of Utah.

Special Collections, Harwell G. Davis Library, Samford University Library, 800 Lakeshore Drive, Birmingham, AL 35229, has a good general genealogical library, including some materials not at the Birmingham Public Library (above). Its current hours are Monday, 8 to 8, and Tuesday through Friday, 8 to 4:30. This library is also the archives for the Alabama Baptist Convention and has extensive Baptist research files. Its holdings include indexes to *The Alabama Baptist;* the McCubbins Collection of records of Rowan County, North Carolina; the Patton, Leslie and Company Papers of old East Florida; and research flies of Alabama genealogist Maud

McLure Kelly. The library is also a federal documents repository. Its extensive newspaper microfilm collection includes several Alabama newspapers and the Georgia Baptist Convention's *Christian Index*. The library's microfilms of Alabama church records of all denominations was created from original records loaned by individual churches.

The Heritage Room, Huntsville Public Library, 915 Monroe Street, P.O. Box 443, Huntsville, AL 35804, is located near the Von Braun Civic Center; this library's current hours are Monday through Wednesday, 9 to 9; Thursday through Saturday, 9 to 5; and Sunday, 2 to 5. Its genealogical collection includes books on midwestern and other states not found elsewhere in the South. The unusually large census collection includes all of the surviving federal censuses through 1850 and most of the census for 1860 and 1870. The library also has the Lyman C. Draper (southern frontier) Collection; DAR lineage books; the seventeenth- and eighteenth-century South Carolina land memorials; the *Virginia Gazette*, 1736–1780; Dahlonega (Georgia) newspapers, 1875–1878; a number of National Archives microfilms of American Indian records; and the McCubbins Collection (Old Rowan and Iredell Counties in North Carolina). The Huntsville library is also home to the Madison County Archives of historical government records. The library's book catalog can be accessed through the Huntsville-Madison County Public Library web site: http://www.hpl.lib.al.us.

The William Stanley Hoole Special Collections Library, University of Alabama Libraries, Box 870266, Tuscaloosa, AL 35487-0266, has extensive private manuscript collections, including some family papers and the extensive Alabama genealogical research files of Pauline Gandrud and Kathleen Paul Jones. The library is open 8 to 4:30, Monday through Friday, and 8 to 8:45 on Thursdays. For more information, see the web site: http://www.lib.ua.edu/hoole/gen.htm.

A number of other libraries have special collections of interest to Alabama researchers or researchers of Alabama, including

> The Alabama Room, Anniston Public Library, 108 East Tenth Street, P.O. Box 308, Anniston, AL 36202, has collections with a special emphasis on

Calhoun County, Alabama; Creek and Cherokee Indians; the Revolutionary War pension claims; and miscellaneous county records microfilm for
Georgia, North Carolina, South Carolina, and Virginia. It has the Leo-
nardo Andrea Collection of South Carolina genealogical research. The library also sells a number of books of abstracts of Calhoun County records.

The Houston Cole Library, Jacksonville State University, N. Pelbarn Road,
Jacksonville, AL 36265, is a federal government records depository, although its federal records publications are integrated into its general collection. This library has on microfilm several collections of colonial
records, including those for South Carolina as well as some of the Lyman
C. Draper Collection; records of the Freedman's Bureau in Alabama; an
index to African American Federal soldiers; compiled service records for
U.S. soldiers, 1784–1811; a collection of English county histories; and federal census records for Florida, Mississippi, North Carolina, South Carolina, and Virginia, through 1910, and Kentucky, through 1900 (no
soundex).

The Gadsden Public Library, 254 College Street, Gadsden, AL 35999, has a
genealogical collection that includes a complete set of the Revolutionary
War pension claims and such federal census records as North and South
Carolina through 1910; the Ohio and Oklahoma soundexes for 1900; Mississippi censuses and soundexes through 1910 and the 1920 census; the
Kentucky soundexes for 1900 and 1910; the Louisiana 1900 census and 1910
soundex; Florida and Virginia census records through 1910 (no soundexes);
and Texas censuses through 1920 and soundexes, 1880–1910.

The Chattanooga-Hamilton County Public Library, 1001 Broad Street, Chattanooga, TN 37402, is a good resource for the areas of the four states near
Chattanooga. The library is renowned for its local biographical information and family folders collections.

The Ralph P. Draughon Library, Auburn University Library, Auburn University, AL 36849, has a genealogy research collection open by appointment and private manuscript collections that include some family papers.

6. SPECIAL AFRICAN AMERICAN RESEARCH MATERIALS

GENERAL

For African American research in general, several works exist. These sources include, among others, Charles L. Blockson, *Black Genealogy* (Baltimore: Black Classic Press, 1991); Jessie Carney Smith, *Ethnic Genealogy* (Westport, Conn.: Greenwood, 1983); and J. L. Dillard, *Black Names* (New York: Moulton, 1976).

Sources for specific research in Alabama African Americans exist beyond broad regional studies, local sources, and individual biographies, including many web sites on the Internet. Among the works in print there are

Bailey, Richard. *Neither Carpetbaggers nor Scalawags: Black Officeholders during the Reconstruction of Alabama, 1867–1878.* Montgomery: R. Bailey, 1991.

Bond, Horace M. *Negro Education in Alabama: A Study in Cotton and Steel.* New York: Athenaeum, 1969.

Boothe, Charles O. *The Cyclopedia of the Colored Baptists of Alabama: Their Leaders and Their Work.* Birmingham: Alabama Publishing, 1895.

Curtin, Mary E. "Legacies of Struggle: Black Prisoners in the Making of Postbellum Alabama, 1865–1895." Ph.D. diss., Duke University, 1992.

Driskell, Glenda J. "Traditional Black Music and Musicians in Rural Alabama." Ph.D. diss., University of Alabama, 1985.

Edwards, Otis B. "An Economic History of the Negro in Agriculture in Dallas, Macon, and Madison Counties, Alabama, 1910–1950." Ph.D. diss., University of Nebraska, 1955.

Hine, Darlene Clark. *Black Women in America: An Historical Encyclopedia.* Brooklyn, N.Y.: Carson, 1993.

Kolchin, Peter. *First Freedom: the Responses of Alabama's Blacks to Emancipation and Reconstruction.* Westport, Conn.: Greenwood Press, 1972.

Letwin, Daniel. *The Challenge of Interracial Unionism: Alabama Coal Miners, 1878–1921.* Chapel Hill: University of North Carolina Press, 1998.

Lowery, Charles D., and John F. Marszalek. *Encyclopedia of African American Civil Rights.* Westport, Conn.: Greenwood Press, 1992.

Methodism for Two Centuries . . . Black United Methodist Churches, the North Alabama Conference. N.p., n.d.

Mobe, Thomas Truxtun. *Black Soldiers, Black Sailors, Black Ink: Research Guide to African-Americans in the U.S. Military History, 1526–1900.* Chesapeake Bay, Md.: Moebs Publishing, 1994. For other sources, see Trevor K. Plante, "Researching African Americans in the U.S. Army, 1866–1890: Buffalo Soldiers and Black Infantrymen," *Prologue: Quarterly of the National Archives* 33 (2001): 56–61.

Mooreman, Joseph H. *Leaders of the Colored Race in Alabama.* Mobile: News Publishing, 1928.

Reid, Stephen N. *History of Colored Baptists in Alabama.* N.p., n.d.

Who's Who in Colored America: A Biographical Dictionary of Notable Living Persons of Negro Descent in America. 4 vols. New York: Who's Who, 1927–1937.

Young, Henry J. *Major Black Religious Leaders, 1755–1940.* Nashville: Abingdon, 1977.

Alabama African American heritage organizations include the Black Heritage Council of the Alabama Historical Commission, 468 South Perry Street, Montgomery, AL 36130–0900. Among miscellaneous sources for

African Americans, researchers will find city directories, such as those listed in chapter 14 in this volume, "City, County, and Community Sources," especially useful in urban areas and more helpful in some ways than federal census records.

Several other general reference works also include some specific information on Alabama. These sources include

Christopher, Maurine. *America's Black Congressmen* (New York: Thomas Y. Crowell, 1971)

Foner, Eric. *Freedom's Lawmakers: A Directory of Black Office Holders during Reconstruction* (New York: Oxford, 1993)

Littlefield, Daniel F., Jr. *Africans and Creeks: From the Colonial Period to the Civil War* (Westport, Conn.: Greenwood Press, 1990).

Savage, Beth L. *African American Historic Places* (Washington, D.C.: National Park Service, 1994)

Schweninger, Loren. *Black Property Owners in the South, 1790–1915* (Urbana: University of Chicago Press, 1990)

Many individual libraries and archives, including the National Archives Southeast Region, have free brochures on their African American history sources; also see the Alabama Department of Archives and History's booklet: *Microfilm Records: Black History* (n.d.). Southern History of the Birmingham Public Library has a bibliography: "African American Genealogy." Some general sources include

Abajian, James de T. *Blacks in Selected Newspapers, Censuses, and Other Sources.* 3 vols., plus supplement. Boston: G. K. Hall, 1977–1985. Also see "African-American Newspapers: The Nineteenth Century," a computer source available from Scholarly Resources.

Alabama Center for Higher Education. *Union List of Black Americana: Afro-American Holdings of the Libraries of the Colleges of the Alabama Center for Higher Education.* Birmingham: The Author, 1974.

Greene, Robert Ewell. *Black Defenders of America, 1775–1973.* Chicago: Johnson Publishing Company, 1973.

Gubert, Betty Kaplan. *Early Black Bibliographies, 1863–1918.* New York: Garland, 1982.

La Brie, Henry G. *The Black Newspaper in America: A Guide*. Kennebunk-port, Maine: Mercer House Press, 1973.

Newman, Richard. *Black Access: A Bibliography of Afro-American Bibliogra-phies*. Westport, Conn.: Greenwood, 1984.

Schatz, Walter. *Directory of Afro-American Sources*. New York: Bowker, 1975.

Woodson, Carter G. *A Century of Negro Migration*. Washington, D.C.: As-sociation for the Study of Negro Life and History, 1918.

The National Archives and Records Administration has published sev-eral sources for African American research. Those works by Debra L. New-man include *List of Free Black Heads of Households in the First Federal Census, 1790* (Alabama is not included as there is no 1790 census of Ala-bama); *List of Black Servicemen from the War Department Collection of Rev-olutionary War Records; Black History; Selected Documents Pertaining to Black Workers among the Records of the Department of Labor and Its Compo-nent Bureaus, 1902–1969*. Also see the special African American issue of *Pro-logue: The Quarterly of the National Archives and Records Administration* 29, no. 2 (1997). Another source is Barbara D. Walker, *Index to the Journal of the Afro-American Historical and Genealogical Society Quarterly* (Bowie, Md.: Heritage Books, 1992). For some other sources, see chapter 17 in this volume, "Special Reconstruction Era Resources."

Debra L. Newman's *Black History: A Guide to Civilian Records in the National Archives* (Washington, D.C.: National Archives and Records Ad-ministration, 1984) includes descriptions of federal records that document acts of violence and actions of groups such as the Ku Klux Klan against African Americans. Another source is *Report of the Joint Select Committee Appointed to Inquire into the Condition of Affairs in the Late Insurrectionary States*, 13 vols. (Washington, D.C.: Government Printing Office, 1872), Se-rial number 1484–1496. Alabama is included in volumes 8 through 10. Other printed works on this topic include William D. Bell, "The Recon-struction Ku Klux Klan . . . Analysis of the Alabama Klan Episode, 1866–1874" (Masters thesis, Louisiana State University, 1973); Glenn Alan Feldman, "The Ku Klux Klan in Alabama, 1915–1954" (Ph.D. diss., Auburn

University, 1996); and Glenn Alan Feldman, *Politics, Society, and the Klan in Alabama, 1915–1949* (Tuscaloosa: University of Alabama Press, 1999).

SPECIAL SLAVE HISTORY RESOURCES

Especially for research of individual slaves, several guides exist. These works include David H. Streets, *Slave Genealogy: A Research Guide with Case Studies* (Bowie, Md.: Heritage Books, 1986); Mary L. Jackson Fears, *Slave Ancestral Research: It's Something Else* (Bowie, Md.: Heritage Books, 1995); and Allen D. Austin, *African Moslems in Antebellum America: A Sourcebook* (New York: Garland Publishing, 1984).

Several other works provide useful background information on slave life in Alabama and elsewhere, such as Kenneth Stampp, *The Peculiar Institution: Slavery in the Ante-Bellum South* (New York: Vintage Books, 1956); Ella Forbes, *African-American Women during the Civil War* (New York: Garland Publishing, 1998); and Herbert G. Gutman, *The Black Family in Slavery and Freedom, 1750–1925* (New York: Pantheon Books, 1976). The Alabama Department of Archives and History has an extensive pamphlet collection relating to slavery (LPR 109).

Individual slaves often appear in records only as statistics or by given names only, as in such county records as estate proceedings, bills of sale (often found in deed books), etc. Slaves in federal census records, 1790–1860, appear only as statistics, even in the separate mortality and slave population schedules of the censuses of 1850 and 1860; see chapter 12 in this volume, "Census Records."

Without some special information to help identify the owners or even the individual slaves on the larger plantations, tracing a slave family is extremely difficult. The National Archives and other repositories have fragmentary documents that identify owners of slaves and former owners of freedmen, often scattered among unrelated records, and without useful indexes. See, for example, the previously cited guides to records at the National Archives. Identities of former owners of several freedmen (some from Bullock and Montgomery Counties in Alabama) appear in records of failed attempts to win pensions for former slaves: see "Some Former Slaves and Their Masters," *Heritage Quest*, no. 69 (May–June 1997): 85–87. A few other federal sources that help to identify former owners of slaves, but almost never Alabama slaves, are cited in Kenneth W. Munden and Henry Putney Beers, *The Union: A Guide to Federal Archives Relating to the Civil War* (Washington, D.C.: National Archives and Records Administration, 1986). Information on thousands of African Americans as slaves can be found in the surviving records of the Freedman's Savings and Trust Company; see chapter 17 in this volume, "Special Reconstruction Era Resources."

Interviews made with former slaves by the Works Projects Administration are found in George P. Rawick, ed., *The American Slave: A Composite Biography* (Westport, Conn.: Greenwood Publishing, 1972). The Alabama slave reminiscences are in volume 6 of the original series and in volume 1 of the two supplements (1972–1977). An index to persons interviewed and a geographical index to all of these volumes is Donald M. Jacobs's *Index to the American Slave* (Westport, Conn.: Greenwood Press, 1981). The Library of Congress has placed these interviews on the Internet at its web site.

7. CHURCH AND RELIGIOUS GROUPS

Researchers should be aware that most Alabamians were and are Baptists and Methodists, religions that almost never keep registers of births, deaths, or marriages. Church minutes, however, can sometimes prove residence, provide names of members who could be relatives, and imply migration (as well as sometimes give explicit reasons for the migration). The largest collection of Alabama church records on microfilm is in Special Collections, Harwell G. Davis Library, Samford University Library, 800 Lakeshore Drive, Birmingham, AL 35229. This library microfilms Alabama historical church records of all denominations.

For national repositories of church records see the latest edition of Elizabeth Bentley's *The Genealogist's Address Book* (Baltimore: Genealogical Publishing Company). Other such sources include Henry Smith Stroupe, *The Religious Press in the South Atlantic States, 1802–1865: An Annotated Bibliography with Historical Introduction and Notes* (Durham, N.C.: Duke University Press, 1956); Charles H. Lippy, *Bibliography of Religion in the South* (Macon: Mercer University Press, 1985); Fran Carter-Walker, *Searching American Church Records* (Bountiful, Utah: American Genealogical Lending Library, 1993); and John T. Humphrey, *Understanding and Using Baptismal Records* (Washington, D.C.: Humphrey Publications, 1996). For guides on how to write a church history see Wallace Guy Smeltzer, *How to*

Write and Publish the History of a United Methodist Church (Lake Junaluska, N.C.: Methodist Church, 1969).

Resources for Alabama Baptists in general are extensive. Special Collections, Harwell G. Davis Library, Samford University Library, 800 Lakeshore Drive, Birmingham, AL 35229, is the archives for the Alabama Baptist Convention. The library's holdings include indexes to *The Alabama Baptist* and microfilm of the Georgia Baptist Convention's *Christian Index*. For background on Alabama Baptists, see J. Wayne Flynt, *Alabama Baptists: Southern Baptists in the Heart of Dixie* (Tuscaloosa: University of Alabama Press, 1998); Benjamin Franklin Riley, *History of the Baptists of Alabama* (Birmingham: Roberts and Son, 1895); F. Wilbur Helmbold, *Brief Sketches of Some Alabama Baptist Associations* (Birmingham: Samford University, 1970); and Ray M. Atchison and Arthur L. Walker, *Historical Studies of Alabama Baptist Churches and Associations: A Check List* (Birmingham: Howard College Library, 1958).

Studies of groups within the Alabama Baptist organization also exist. These works include Cynthia Adams Wise, *The Alabama Baptist Children's Home: The First 100 Years* (Montgomery: Brown, 1991); and Catherine B. Allen, *A Century to Celebrate: History of Woman's Missionary Union* (Birmingham: Woman's Missionary Union, 1987). Another source is the back issues of the periodical *The Alabama Baptist Historian* (1964–), published by the Alabama Baptist Historical Society and Wilbur Hembolt, "Baptist Periodicals of Alabama," *Alabama Baptist Historian* 2 (2) (1996). Regional and national works of value in Primitive Baptist research include Reden H. Pittman, *Biographical History of Primitive or Old School Baptist Ministers of the United States* (1909; reprint, Stone Mountain, Ga.: Primitive Baptist Publications, 1984); David Montgomery and Mark Green, eds., *Biographical History of Primitive or Old School Baptist Ministers of the United States Volume II* (Lampasas, Tx.: Primitive Baptist Heritage Corporation, 2001); and Jerry A. Newsome, *A Modest History of Primitive Baptists in the United States* (n.p., n.d.).

For historical and some biographical material on Alabama Methodists, see Anson West, *A History of Methodism in Alabama* (1893; reprint, Spartanburg, S.C.: Reprint Company, 1983); Marion Elias Lazenby, *History of Methodism in Alabama and West Florida* (North Alabama Conference and

Alabama-West Florida Conference, 1960); and Nancy E. Sims, *A Selective Bibliography of the Methodist Church in Alabama* (Birmingham: The Author, 1978). Selective studies include Franklin Shackelford Moseley, *160 Years of Methodism in South Alabama and Northwest Florida* (Hannibal, Mo.: American Yearbook Company, 1968); James E. Elliott, "A History of Methodism in Western Alabama, 1818–1870" (Masters thesis, University of Alabama at Tuscaloosa, 1947); W. T. Andrews, *Memorial Sketches of the Lives and Labors of the Deceased Ministers of the North Alabama Conference, Methodist Episcopal Church, South (1870–1912)* (Nashville, Tenn.: Publishing House of the M. E. Church, South, 1912); and Ruth Sykes Ford, *A History of the Woman's Society of Christian Service of the North Alabama Conference of the Methodist Church* (Huntsville: The Society, 1963). For Alabama's African American Methodists, see W. H. Mixon, *History of the African Methodist Episcopal Church in Alabama with Biographical Sketches* (Nashville, Tenn.: A.M.E. Church Sunday School Union, 1902), and *Methodism for Two Centuries Proclaiming Grace and Freedom: Black United Methodist Churches, the North Alabama Conference* (n.p., n.d.).

Regional works on the Methodists have a great deal of material on Alabamians. These sources include Brent Holcomb, *Marriage and Death Notices from the Southern Christian Advocate*, 2 vols. (Greenville, S.C.: Southern Historical Press, 1979–1980), covering 1835–1867; Brent Holcomb, *Marriage Notices from the Southern Christian Advocate, 1867–1878* (Columbia, S.C.: The Author, 1994); and Brent Holcomb, *Death and Obituary Notices from the Southern Christian Advocate, 1867–1878* (Columbia: The Author, 1993). Some Alabama Methodist ministers are also found in Harold Lawrence's *Methodist Preachers in Georgia, 1783–1900* (Milledgeville, Ga.: Boyd Publishing, 1984) and *Methodist Preachers in Georgia, 1783–1900: A Supplement* (Milledgeville, Ga.: Boyd Publishing, 1995).

Similarly, Presbyterian sources for Alabama include works for more than just one state, such as Fred J. Hood, *Reformed America: The Middle and Southern States, 1783–1837* (University, Ala.: University of Alabama Press, 1980); E. C. Scott, *Ministerial Directory of the Presbyterian Church, U.S., 1861–1941* (Austin, Tex.: Von Boechman Co., 1942); Brent Holcomb, *Marriage and Death Notices from the Charleston Observer, 1827–1845* (Greenville, S.C.: A Press, 1980); and Lowery Ware, *Associate Reformed*

Presbyterian Death and Marriage Notices . . . 1843–1863 (Columbia, S.C.: SCMAR, 1993). Works for research specifically on Alabama Presbyterians include James Williams Marshall, *The Presbyterian Church in Alabama* (Montgomery: Presbyterian Historical Society of Alabama, 1977); *Minutes of the Alabama Synod of the Cumberland Presbyterian Church, 1855–1887* (Birmingham: Works Projects Administration, 1937); and Aleathea Thompson Cobbs, *Presbyterian Women of the Synod of Alabama* (Mobile: Woman's Auxiliary of the Synod of Alabama, 1936).

Records of the oldest Roman Catholic Church in Alabama have been indexed in *Index to the Records of Old Mobile Cathedral of the Immaculate Conception . . . 1704–1891* (Pascagoula, Miss.: Jackson County Genealogical Society, 1992). For historical background on this faith, see Austin Carroll, *A Catholic History of Alabama and the Floridas,* 2 vols. (New York: P. J. Kenedy, 1908).

Aside from works on local churches, sources on other religions in Alabama also exist. These materials include, for the Lutherans, Brent Holcomb, *Marriage and Death Notices from the Lutheran Observer, 1831–1861, and the Southern Lutheran, 1861–1865* (Greenville, S.C.: Southern Historical Press, l979); and, for the Disciples of Christ, George H. Watson and Mildred B. Watson, *History of the Christian Churches in the Alabama Area* (St. Louis: Bethany Press, 1965).

Research is currently being done on the history of Alabama's Jews. Some materials for Alabama exist in the Museum of the Southern Jewish Experience, P.O. Box 16528, Jackson, MS 39236–6528.

8. PREHISTORIC AND NATIVE AMERICAN SOURCES

For prehistoric Native American research in Alabama, see John A. Walthall, *Prehistoric Indians of the Southeast: Archaeology of Alabama and the Middle South* (Tuscaloosa: University of Alabama Press, 1990); David L. DeJarnette, ed., *Handbook of Alabama Archaeology* (Huntsville: Alabama Archaeological Society, 1964); Ned J. Jenkins and Richard A. Krause, *The Tombigbee Watershed in Southeastern Prehistory* (Tuscaloosa: University of Alabama Press, 1986); William Snyder Webb and Charles G. Wilder, *An Archaeological Survey of Guntersville Basin on the Tennessee River in Northern Alabama* (Lexington: University of Kentucky Press, 1951); Prieur Jay Higginbotham, *The Mobile Indians* (Mobile: Sir Rey's, 1966); and W. Philip Krebs, *Ten Thousand Years of Alabama Prehistory* (Tuscaloosa: Alabama State Museum of Natural History, 1986). Prehistoric Alabama also has a journal: *Journal of Alabama Archaeology* (37 vols. to date, 1955–), published by the Alabama Archaeological Society.

Native Americans after European contact are discussed in several works. Specifically for Alabama, researchers should consult *Indians of Alabama* (Hamburg, Mich.: North America Book Distribution, 1999); William A. Read, *Indian Place Names in Alabama* (1937; reprint, Tuscaloosa: University of Alabama Press, 1984); John Franklin Phillips, *The American Indian in*

Alabama and the Southeast (Nashville, Tenn.: Parthenon Press, 1986); Marie West Cromer, *Modern Indians of Alabama* (Birmingham: Southern University Press, 1984); and J. Anthony Paredes, ed., *Indians of the Southeastern United States in the Late Twentieth Century* (Tuscaloosa; University of Alabama Press, 1992). For land cessions by the tribes of Alabama, see Charles C. Royce, *Indian Land Cessions in the United States* (Washington, D.C.: Government Printing Office, 1900).

The Alabama Department of Archives and History maintains at its web site a Native American page that includes current addresses of private and public organizations relating to Native Americans. The state agency is the Indian Affairs Commission, 669 S. Lawrence Street, Montgomery, AL 36130.

Researchers attempting to document family lore of Native American heritage should be warned that many such tales have no documentation. Persons of Native American ancestry frequently appear in records as being white, black, or mulatto (the only official racial designations used on the federal censuses until the 1870 census). Typically, when a "grandmother" is remembered in family lore as a "Cherokee Princess," any real Native American ancestors almost invariably prove to be several generations further back in the family tree than remembered and not Cherokee but members of some now lost tribe of coastal North Carolina or Virginia. Other families remember African American and Caucasian ancestors with physical features common to Native Americans as Indians. For some of the more easily documented relationships of "red, white, and black," see Angela Y. Walton-Raji, *Black Indian Genealogy Research: African American Ancestors among the Five Civilized Tribes* (Bowie, Md.: Heritage Books, 1993).

However, the records that do exist for southeastern American Indians can be a rich source of personal information not found elsewhere. Some references to Alabama Indian improvements are occasionally found in county tract books and other records at individual courthouses. Some federal land grants mention previous Native American residents; see chapter 11 in this volume, "Federal Land Records."

Numerous guides, source material, and other printed works have become available in recent years to aid in this area. Many libraries and archives have brochures and bibliographies of their respective Indian resources, such as *American Indian Records in the Alabama Room* [Annis-ton-Calhoun County Public Library] (n.p., n.d.). The National Archives Southeastern Region (currently at, but soon to move from, 1557 St. Joseph Avenue, East Point, GA 30344) has a free brochure on its extensive collection of National Archives microfilms of southeastern American Indian tribes. The *South Eastern Native American Exchange*, P.O. Box 161424, Mobile, AL 36616 (1993–), is a periodical devoted to Native American research in the Old South but especially for Alabama. For other sources for Native American research on all tribes that lived in Alabama, see Laurie Beth Duffy, *Who's Looking for Whom in Native American Ancestry* (Bowie, Md.: Heritage Books, 1997); Ronald Chepesiuk and Arnold M. Shankman, *American Indian Archival Material: A Guide to Holdings in the Southeast* (Westport, Conn.: Greenwood, 1982); Ronald Kanen, *A Bibliography of the Creeks and Other Native Americans of the Southeast* (Wakulla Springs, Fla.: Muskogee Press, 1983); and George E. Lankford, *Native American Legends* (Little Rock, Ark.: August House, 1987).

Records of the earliest white involvements with the American Indians survive largely in materials found in the British archives and libraries. Much of this material has not been microfilmed, indexed, or published. The materials that are in print include William L. Lewis and James A. Lewis, *A Guide to Cherokee Documents in Foreign Archives* (Metuchen, N.J.: Scarecrow Press, 1983); the volumes on American Indian affairs in *The Colonial Records of South Carolina* series; and Theresa M. Hicks, *South Carolina Indians, Indian Traders, and Other Ethnic Connections* (Columbia: Peppercorn Publications, 1997). Many white men living among the Indians are mentioned in Benjamin Hawkins, *Letters, Journals, and Writings of Benjamin Hawkins, 1798–1816*, ed. C. L. Grant (Savannah: Beehive Press, 1980).

Most Native American records are federal. The best guide to those sources is Edward E. Hill, *Guide to Records in the National Archives of the United States Relating to American Indians* (Washington, D.C.: National Archives, 1981). Other guides, catalogs, and bibliographies for these records include *American Indians: A Select Catalog of National Archives Microfilm Publications* (Washington, D.C.: National Archives, 1995); and Steven L. Johnson, *Guide to American Indian Documents in the Congressional Serial Set: 1817–1899* (New York: Clearwater Publications, 1977). For broader bibliographies and guides, see Arlene B. Hirschfelder, Mary Gloyne Byler, and Michael A. Dorris, *Guide to Research on North American Indians* (Chicago: American Library Association, 1983); E. Kay Kirkham, *Our Native Americans and Their Records of Genealogical Value,* 2 vols. (Logan, Utah: Everton, 1984); and Jessie Carney Smith, *Ethnic Genealogy* (Westport, Conn.: Greenwood Press, 1983). Many encyclopedic compilations on Native American subjects also exist.

SPECIAL CHEROKEE SOURCES

Specifically for Cherokee Indian research, see Tony Mack McClure, *Cherokee Proud: A Guide for Tracing and Honoring Your Cherokee Ancestors* (Somerville, Tenn.: Chunannee Books, 1996). For historical background, the researcher could start with Duane H. King, *The Cherokee Indian Nation: A Troubled History* (Knoxville: University of Tennessee Press, 1979). Many of the early records of the Cherokees are abstracted in William L. Lewis and James A. Lewis, *A Guide to Cherokee Documents in Foreign Archives* (Metuchen, N.J.: Scarecrow Press, 1983); and Paul Kutsche, *A Guide to Cherokee Documents in the Northeastern United States* (Metuchen, N.J.: Scarecrow Press, 1986). Lists of white men living among the Cherokees, 1796–1797, appear on pages 328–29 of Dorothy Williams Potter's *Passports of Southeastern Pioneers, 1770–1823* (Baltimore: Genealogical Publishing Company, 1982). Sharron Standifer Ashton has published an 1835 Cherokee voting list in *Indians and Intruders,* vol. 2 (Norman, Okla.: Ashton Books, 1997). Bob Blankenship has published the names from the various censuses (rolls or enrollments) of the Cherokees in *Cherokee Roots,* 2 vols. (Cherokee, N.C.: The Author, 1992). Other works valuable for identifying individuals include Emmet Starr, *History of the Cherokee Indians* (Muskogee, Okla.: Oklahoma Yesterday, 1984), for genealogies of many of the prominent Cherokee families; Jack D. Baker and David Keith Hampton, *Old Cherokee Families: Notes of Dr. Emmet Starr,* 3 vols. (Oklahoma City: Baker Publishing, 1988); and George Morrison Bell Sr., *Genealogy of "Old and New Cherokee Indian Families"* (Bartlesville, Okla.: The Author, 1972). The Georgia Department of Archives and History has a series of indexed typescripts of early records called "Cherokee Indian Letters." The typescripts

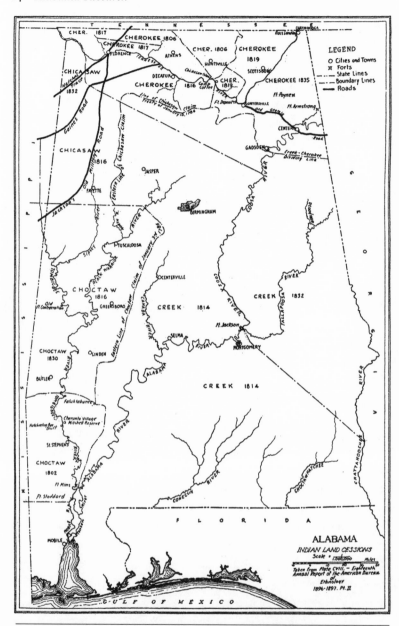

Indian Land Sessions in Alabama

are also available on microfilm through LDS family history centers and at Wallace State College, Hanceville, Alabama. Many early issues of the *Georgia Genealogical Society Quarterly* contained extensive information on pre-removal Cherokee and Creek Indian families. These issues are included in the *Georgia Genealogical Society Quarterly*'s twenty-year every name index. Many books on Georgia Cherokee communities have been published.

A number of records survive relating to Cherokee Indian claims from the War of 1812 through the 1840s; for example, see the "Cherokee 'Trail of Tears' Claims," *Georgia Genealogical Magazine* 36 (1996): 293–99. Many Cherokee claims are included in National Archives microcopy M574 Special Files, 1807–1904, Bureau of Indian Affairs, a copy of which is at the National Archives Southeast Region (currently at, but soon to move from, 1557 St. Joseph Avenue, East Point, GA 30344). Cherokee Indian property evaluations made just prior to the removal of 1838 are found in entries 217 to 251 of Record Group 75, Bureau of Indian Affairs, National Archives, 700 Pennsylvania Ave. NW, Washington, DC 20408-0001.

Genealogically rich claims filed in 1909 from more than forty thousand families, most of them in the southeastern United States, claiming Cherokee descent are included in National Archives microcopy M1104 Eastern Cherokee Applications of the United States Court of Claims, 1906–1909. Known as the "Guion Miller" claims, they have two indexes published by Bob Blankenship in one volume as *Guion Miller Roll 'Plus'* (Cherokee, N.C.: Cherokee Roots, n.d.) and a set of indexes by Jeff Bowen, *Cherokee Descendants*, 4 vols. (Signal Mountain, Tenn.: Mountain Press, 1994–1997). Indexed abstracts of these claims are being published by Jerry Wright Jordan, *Cherokee by Blood*, 9 vols. to date (Bowie, Md.: Heritage Books, 1987–). Another source of information from these records is Billy Dubois Edgington and Carrol Anne Buswell, *Vital Information from the Guion Miller Roll* (Mill Creek, Wash.: Indian Scout Publications, 1999).

SPECIAL CHICKASAW SOURCES

For Chickasaw families that lived in Alabama, see K. M. Armstrong and Bob Curry, *Chickasaw Rolls: Annuity Rolls of 1857–1860 and the "1855" Chickasaw Roll of 1856* (Bowie, Md.: Heritage Books, 1995). A list of traders among the Chickasaws for 1766 appears in Sharron Standifer Ashton, *Indians and Intruders* (Norman, Okla.: Ashton Publishing, 1996). Historical articles on the Chickasaws appear in *The Journal of Chickasaw History*, published by the Chickasaw Historical Society. The Family and Regional History program at Wallace State College, Hanceville, Alabama, has Chickasaw muster rolls, 1837–1839, and an 1847 census roll.

SPECIAL CHOCTAW SOURCES

For a guide to Alabama's Choctaw research, see Jacqueline Anderson Matte, *They Say the Wind Is Red: The Alabama Choctaw* (Red Level, Ala.: Greenberry, 1999). Many members of this tribe in Alabama before removal appear in Ben Strickland and Jean Strickland, *Records of the Choctaw Trading Post: St. Stephens, Mississippi Territory,* 2 vols. (Moss Point, Miss.: The Authors, 1984–1990); Betty C. Wiltshire, *Register of Choctaw Emigrants to the West, 1831 and 1832* (Carrollton, Miss.: Pioneer Publishing, 1993); and *Henry Sale Halbert's Complete Roll of All Choctaw Claimants and Their Heirs Existing under the Treaties of the United States and the Choctaw Nation* (St. Louis: Robert D. Patterson Stationary Company, 1889). The Alabama Department of Archives and History, in its collection of pre-statehood official records, has a payroll for the Choctaw Indian regiment for 1814.

SPECIAL CREEK SOURCES

For Creek Indian research, see the last section of Billie Ford Snider, *Full Name Indexes Eastern Creek Indians* (Pensacola: Antique Compiling, 1993). The National Archives Southeast Region (currently at, but soon to move from, 1557 St. Joseph Avenue, East Point, GA 30344) has an extensive collection of National Archives microfilms of southeastern American Indian tribes, including the claims made by Creek orphans for damages from the Creek Removal of 1836. National Archives Southeast Region has a handout on Native American research. Many of these microfilms are also available in the Family and Regional History Program, Wallace State College, Hanceville, Alabama.

Some travel accounts and memoirs of chiefly Alabama Creek families exist. The most famous of these works include George Stiggins, *Creek Indian History*, ed. Virginia Pounds (Birmingham, Ala.: Birmingham Public Library Press, 1989); Johann Christian Burckard, *Partners in the Lord's Work: The Diary of Two Moravian Missionaries in the Creek Indian Country, 1807–1813* (Atlanta: Georgia State College, 1969); and Thomas S. Woodward, *Woodward's Reminiscences of the Creek, or Muscogee Indians* (Montgomery, Ala.: Babrett & Wimbisu, 1859). Alvie L. Davidson has published a detailed index to *Woodward's Reminiscences*. Similar sources can found in Jeffrey C. Benton, comp., *The Very Worst Road: Travelers' Accounts of Crossing Alabama's Old Creek Indian Territory, 1820–1847* (Eufaula, Ala.: Historic Chattahoochee Commission, 1998); and Henry D. Sutherland Jr. and Jerry Elijah Brown, *The Federal Road through Georgia, the Creek Nation, and Alabama* (Tuscaloosa: University of Alabama, 1989). Some white men and their children living among the Creeks also appear in *Index to the Records of Old Mobile Cathedral of the Immaculate Conception, 1704–1891* (Pascagoula, Miss.: Jackson County Genealogical Society, 1994).

A number of other sources exist for research on individual Creeks. For modern Creek Indian claims and a general guide to Creek research sources, see Billie Ford Snider, *Full Name Indexes: Creek Indians East of the Mississippi* (The Author, 1993). The Georgia Department of Archives and History has a series of indexed typescripts of early Creek Indian records called "Creek Indian Letters." The typescripts are also available on microfilm through LDS family history centers and at Wallace State College, Hanceville, Alabama. Many early issues of the *Georgia Genealogical Society Quarterly* contain extensive information on Alabama's pre-removal Creek Indian families, including publication of National Archives microcopy T275, the Parsons and Abbott census or roll of the Creeks in 1832 (vol. 8, nos. 2 and 3), which has also been published by James L. Douthat as *1832 Creek Census* (Signal Mountain, Tenn.: Mountain Press, 1994). These issues are included in the *Georgia Genealogical Society Quarterly*'s twenty-year every name index. An 1831 list of white "intruders" in the Creek nation appears in Sharron S. Ashton, *Indians and Intruders*, 2 vols. (Norman, Okla.: Ashton Books, 1997). For Creek Indian property claims, see *Creek Documents* (Signal Mountain, Tenn.: Mountain Press, 1997). The Guion

Miller claims, mentioned above under "Special Cherokee Sources," also include claims representing more than one thousand Alabama Creeks.

DAWES COMMISSION RECORDS OF THE FIVE CIVILIZED TRIBES

Applications by descendants of Oklahoma Cherokee, Chickasaw, Choctaw, Creek, and Seminole families for land in 1898 through 1914 are found in the records of the Dawes Commission in the National Archives Southwest Region, P.O. Box 6216, Fort Worth, TX 76115-6216. For historical background and the use of these records, see Kent Carter, *The Dawes Commission and the Allotment of the Five Civilized Tribes, 1893–1914* (Orem, Utah: Ancestry, 1999). Many of the applicants for these lands document Alabama ancestors. Generally, only those applications that were accepted are indexed. However, the National Archives Southwest Region now has a computerized index to doubtful and rejected Cherokee applications and is preparing a more comprehensive index to all of the Dawes records. It is partially available now on the National Archives web site at http://www. nara.gov/nara/nail.html.

Currently, to search for an accepted application, look in the alphabetical indexes on reel 1 of the National Archives microfilm of the enrollment cards (M1186). These indexes provide the Dawes Roll numbers used in National Archives microcopy T529 Final Roll of the Five Civilized Tribes. The rolls on that microfilm provide the "Census Card" or "Field No." that is used to access the genealogically valuable applications for enrollment on National Archives microcopy M1301 and the cards used to cross reference the applications on microcopy M1186. The accepted Cherokee claims are indexed by surname in Bob Blankenship's *Dawes Roll 'Plus'* (Cherokee, N.C.: Cherokee Roots, n.d.); and Jo Ann Curls Page, *Index to the Cherokee Freedmen [former slaves] Enrollment Cards of the Dawes Commission, 1901– 1906* (Bowie, Md.: Heritage Books, 1996). Related sources include National Archives microcopy M1314 Index to Letters Received by the Commission to the Five Civilized Tribes.

A number of valuable reference books on the Five Civilized Tribes in Oklahoma have been published, many of which can be found in the Family and Regional History Collection of Wallace State College, in Hanceville, Alabama. These works include, among many others, James W. Tyner and Alice Timmons, *Our People and Where They Rest,* 11 vols. (The Authors, 1969), records of Cherokee cemeteries in Oklahoma; and Sharron Standifer Ashton, *Indians and Intruders,* 2 vols. to date (Norman, Okla.: Ashton Books, 1996–).

9. COLONIAL AND TERRITORIAL SOURCES

The white and black settlement of today's Alabama began in 1702 with the founding of city of Mobile, one of America's oldest cities. Mobile has been governed by France, Great Britain, Spain, the Confederacy, and the United States. For historical background on early Mobile see, among many other works,

Andrews, Johnnie. *Fort Toulouse Colonials: A Compendium of the Colonial Families of Central Alabama, 1717–1823*. Pritchard, Ala.: Bienville Historical Society, 1987.

———. *Mobile Land Grants, 1710–1795*. Pritchard, Ala.: Bienville Museum, 1973.

Cox, Isaac Joslin. *The West Florida Controversy, 1798–1813*. 1912; reprint, Gloucester: Peter Smith, 1967.

Hamilton, Peter J. *Colonial Mobile*. 1910; reprint, University: University of Alabama Press, 1976.

Higginbotham, Jay. *Old Mobile: Fort Louis de la Louisiane, 1702–1711*. Mobile: Museum of the City of Mobile, 1977.

Johnson, Cecil. *British West Florida, 1763–1783*. New Haven: Yale University Press, 1943.

Thomas, Daniel H. *Fort Toulouse: The French Outpost at the Alabamas on the Coosa*. Tuscaloosa: University of Alabama Press, 1989.

Many sources for records of early settlers of the Mobile area also exist. The Mobile Municipal Archives, 700 Pennsylvania Ave. NW, P.O. Box 1827, Mobile, AL 36633, has local records, 1715–1901, transcribed by the Works Projects Administration. Copies of these materials are also found in the Family and Regional History program, Wallace State College, Hanceville, Alabama. The Mobile County Probate Court Records Department, P.O. Box 7, Mobile, AL 36601, has also been microfilming and indexing local records for 1715 to 1850. The Local History and Genealogy Division, Mobile Public Library, 701 Government Street, Mobile, AL 36602, has transcripts of colonial British, French, and Spanish records of Alabama. Some of the original records, beginning in 1714, for the French government of what became Alabama are housed in the Louisiana State Museum Historical Center in New Orleans, Louisiana. Other resources for the area's early history are found in Special Collections and West Florida Archives, John C. Pace Library, University of West Florida, 11000 University Parkway, Pensacola, FL 32514-5750. For information on other records of colonial Mobile, see Henry Putney Beers, *French and Spanish Records of Louisiana: A Bibliographical Guide to Archive and Manuscript Sources* (Baton Rouge: University of Alabama Press, 1989); *Pre-Federal Maps in the National Archives: An Annotated List* (Washington, D.C.: National Archives and Records Administration, 1971); and Howard H. Wehmann, *A Guide to Pre-Federal Records in the National Archives* (Washington, D.C.: National Archives and Records Administration, 1989).

Many French, Spanish, and English records of what became the Mobile area of Alabama have been published. Among these works, the researcher can consult

Andrews, Johnnie, Jr. *Mobile Church Records, 1704–1813: A Partial Reconstructed List.* Pritchard, Ala.: Bienville Historical Society, 1967.

———. *Spanish Census Reports at Mobile* [1786, 1787, 1789, 1805] Mobile: Bienville Historical Society, 1973.

Arthur, Stanley Clisby. *Index to the Dispatches of the Spanish Governors of Louisiana, 1766–1792.* New Orleans: Polyanthos, 1975.

De Ville, Winston. *British Burials and Births on the Gulf Coast: Records of the Church of England in West Florida, 1768–1770.* Ville Platte, La.: The Author, 1986.

————. *English Land Grants in West Florida: A Register for the States of Alabama, Mississippi, and Parts of Florida and Louisiana, 1766–1776*. Ville Platte, La.: The Author, 1986.

Feldman, Lawrence H. Feldman. *Anglo-Americans in Spanish Archives*. Baltimore: Genealogical Publishing Company, 1991.

Forsyth, Alice D. *Louisiana Marriage Contracts . . . 1725–1758*. New Orleans: Polyanthos, 1980.

Lepre, Jerome. *Index to the Records of Old Mobile's Cathedral of the Immaculate Conception*. Pascagoula, Miss.: Jackson County Genealogical Society, 1992.

Snider, Billie Ford, and Janice B. Palmer. *Spanish Plat Book of Land Records of the District of Pensacola, Province of West Florida: British and Spanish Land Grants, 1763–1821*. Pensacola: Antique Compiling, 1994. The Alabama Department of Archives and History also has a card catalog: "Spanish Grants."

Strickland, Jean, and Patricia N. Edwards. *Index to the Archives of Spanish West Florida, 1782–1810*. Moss Point, Miss.: Ben Strickland, 1975.

————. *Records of Spanish West Florida, 1806–1811*. Moss Point, Miss.: Ben Strickland, 1999.

The federal government recognized the grants of lands made by France, Great Britain, and Spain in the Mobile area. Information on those grants is found in the claims volumes of the *American State Papers* series, indexed by Philip W. McMullin in his *Grassroots of America* (Conway, Ark.: Gendex, 1972). For more information on this history, see David Lightner, "Private Land Claims in Alabama," *Alabama Review* 20 (1967): 187–204.

Alabama became a territory in 1817 (previously, it was part of the Mississippi Territory) and a state in 1818 or 1819. Many of the records of the region are found today in the Mississippi Department of Archives and History or the National Archives and Records Administration. Much of this material is in well-indexed, published volumes, including Jacqueline Anderson Matte, *Old St. Stephens: Historical Records Survey* (St. Stephens, Ala.: St. Stephens Historic Commission, 1999), and a series by Jean Strickland that includes *Washington County, Mississippi Territory, 1803–1816 Tax Rolls* (1980) and *Residents of the Southeastern Mississippi Territory: Census,*

Tax Rolls, and Petitions, 4 vols. to date (1995–). Commissions of civil and military officials for the Alabama Territory and the first years of the State of Alabama are published in *Alabama Historical Quarterly* 6 (1944): 122–328. Federal records appear in *The Territorial Papers of the United States* (volumes 4 though 6 and 18).

10. MIGRATION SOURCES TO AND FROM ALABAMA

Military, federal land, territorial, and colonial records discussed elsewhere frequently document migration to Alabama by giving place of birth or previous residence. The most famous source for documentation of early travels to "the old southwest" is Dorothy Williams Potter's *Passports of Southeastern Pioneers, 1770–1823* (Baltimore: Genealogical Publishing Company, 1982); also see Hugh B. Johnston Jr., *They Moved Away: North Carolinians Who Went to Other States* (Wilson, N.C.: Wilson County Genealogical Society, 1997).

Federal censuses record place of birth, beginning with 1850 (the seventh census); see chapter 12 in this volume, "Census Records." Nationwide indexes to census records exist through 1850 and for 1880; and Heritage Quest has published CD-ROM computer disk indexes to the 1870 census. The index includes place of birth. Individual indexes for Alabama exist in various forms for 1830 to 1930.

The American Civil War created a number of special sources for documenting migration to and from Alabama. The state censuses of resident Confederate veterans for 1907 and 1921, available on microfilm at the Alabama Department of Archives and History and at various libraries, including LDS family history centers, give county and state of birth for almost every veteran, including those who moved to Alabama after the war. The 1907 census has also been published; see chapter 16 in this volume, "Military Records." County and state of birth also appear in most of the service records of the First Alabama Cavalry Regiment, United States Army, raised in Winston and surrounding counties; see Glenda McWhirter Todd, *First Alabama Cavalry USA* (Bowie, Md.: Heritage Books, 1999). Such information also occasionally appears in Confederate compiled service records in National Archives microfilms. Many Alabama migrations are documented in Bobbie J. McLane and Capitola Glazner, *Arkansas 1911 Census of Confederate Veterans*, 4 vols. (Hot Springs: Arkansas Ancestors, 1977–1988). Carolyn M. Rowe has published the 1867 voter returns for Walker and Winston Counties in Alabama; they provide county and date of birth of almost every man listed.

ALABAMIANS IN THE CALIFORNIA GOLD RUSH

Many records exist of Alabamians in the California gold rush. The names of persons born in or residents of Alabama in the California gold fields in the 1850s appear in the California gold miners census of 1852, available on loan at LDS family history centers and in the genealogy collection at Wallace State College in Hanceville, Alabama. California also has federal census records for 1850 and 1860. Other sources for documentation of participation in the great gold rush include

Allsworth, Mary Dean. *Gleanings from Alta, California: Marriages and Deaths Reported in the First Newspaper Published in California, 1846–1850.* Rancho Cordova, Calif.: Dean Publishing, 1980.

Carr, Peter E. *San Francisco Passenger Departure Lists.* 5 vols. to date. San Luis Obispo, Calif.: TCI Genealogical Resources, 1994–.

Dove, Lois A. *Wagon Trains, 1849–1865.* Sacramento, Calif.: L. A. Dove, 1989.

Hawkins, C. W. *Index to the Argonauts of California.* Baton Rouge, La.: Polyanthos Press, 1986.

Parker, J. Carlyle. *Gold Rush Days: Vital Statistics Copied from Early Newspapers of Stockton, California, 1850–1854.* Stockton: San Joaquin Genealogical Society, 1977.

Parker, Nathan C. *Personal Name Index to the 1856 City Directories of California*. Detroit, Mich.: Gale Research, 1980.

Rasmussen, Louis J. *California Wagon Train Lists* [1849–1852]. Colma, Calif.: San Francisco Historic Records, 1997.

―――. *San Francisco Ship Passenger Lists* [1850–1853]. 4 vols. Colma, Calif.: San Francisco Historic Record and Genealogy Bulletin, 1965–1970. For later arrivals in California, see Louis J. Rasmussen, *Railway Passenger Lists* [1870–1873] (Colma, Calif.: San Francisco Historic Records, 1966).

NATURALIZATIONS, PASSENGER LISTS, AND FOREIGN BIRTHS

Most records that indicate foreign birth for Alabama residents are federal. United States census records, for example, indicate foreign-born persons beginning with the 1830 census. The number of years naturalized is given for each foreign-born U.S. citizen beginning with the 1900 census. Contrary to published reports, the 1920 federal census almost never gives village and province of birth. For background on naturalization records, see John J. Newman, *American Naturalization Processes and Procedures, 1780–1985* (Springfield, Ind.: Indiana Historical Society, 1985); Christina K. Shaefer, *Guide to Naturalization Records of the United States* (Baltimore: Genealogical Publishing Company, 1995); and Loretto Dennis Szucs, *They Became Americans: Finding Naturalization Records and Ethnic Origins* (Salt Lake City, Utah: Ancestry, 1998). Starting in 1906, almost all jurisdictions, except for the federal courts, ceased performing naturalizations.

Some Alabama specific records document naturalizations. The Alabama Department of Archives and History has 1867–1868 voter lists that provide naturalization information on hundreds of foreign-born males. These returns have been published for Marion, Mobile, Walker, and Winston Counties by Carolyn M. Rowe; also see Clinton P. King and Meriem A. Barlow, *Naturalization Records Mobile, Alabama, 1833–1906* (Baltimore: Gateway Press, 1986). Other naturalization records have been abstracted by local Alabama genealogical societies in periodicals and books, such as Kaye Marie Couch Leigeber, *German Colonization: Cullman County, Alabama* (Cullman: Gregath Company, 1982).

For background on using passenger lists, the researcher should consult John P. Colletta, *They Came in Ships* (Salt Lake City, Utah: Ancestry, 1989). The National Archives Southeast Region (currently at, but soon to move from, 1557 St. Joseph Avenue, East Point, GA 30344) has an extensive collection of National Archives microfilm of passenger arrival lists and federal court naturalization records for the other southeastern states. The Birmingham Public Library has on microfilm indexes to passenger arrival lists for New York (1820–1846; the passenger lists themselves are on microfilm at the Georgia Department of Archives and History), New Orleans (to 1900; also the passenger lists themselves, 1820–1902), and the other Gulf and Atlantic ports (1820–1874; for the southeastern United States, 1890–1926). National Archives microfilms of passenger lists and indexes to passenger lists are described in *Immigrant and Passenger Arrivals: A Guide to National Archives Microfilm* (Washington, D.C.: National Archives Trust, 1983). National Archives microfilms can be borrowed through LDS family history centers.

Several indexes to passenger lists, chiefly for specific ethnic groups that passed through the port of New York, have been published for selected years, most of which are available at the Birmingham Public Library. These works, many of which also have computer CD-ROM versions, include the Irish (1846–1865), Germans (1850–1888), Italians (1880–1891), and Russians (1875–1891). Broader works that include Alabama also exist, including

Boyer, Carl. *Ship Passenger Lists: The South (1538–1825)*. Newhall, Calif.: The Author, 1979.

Coldham, Peter Wilson. *American Wills and Administrations in the Prerogative Court of Canterbury, 1610–1857*. Baltimore: Genealogical Publishing Company, 1989.

Filby, P. William, and Mary K. Meyer. *Passenger and Immigration Lists Index*. 14 vols. to date. Detroit: Gale Publishing Co., 1982–.

Harris, Ruth-Ann M., and Donald M. Jacobs. *The Search for Missing Friends: Irish Immigrant Advertisements Placed in the Boston Pilot*. 5 vols. to date. Boston: New England Historic Genealogical Society, 1989–1999.

Immigrant and Passenger Arrivals: A Select Catalog of National Archives Microfilm Publications. Washington, D.C.: National Archives, 1983).

PASSPORT RECORDS

Most Americans before World War I (i.e., 1914) traveled abroad without passports. For information on passport records that do exist and how to access them, see John P. Colletta, "U.S. Passport Applications: Leads to Immigration and Naturalization Records," *Heritage Quest*, no. 71 (September–October 1997): 9–15; Kathie O. Nicastro and Claire Prechtel-Kluskens, "Passport Applications," *Prologue: The Quarterly of the National Archives and Records Administration* 25 (1993): 390–95; and National Archives microcopy M1371 Registers and Indexes for Passport Applications, 1810–1906 and M1490 Passport Applications, 1906–1923.

11. FEDERAL LAND RECORDS

Alabama is a federal land state, which means that all land ownership based upon land grants comes through the United States government. (All states are federal land or "public domain" states except for the original thirteen states and Hawaii, Kentucky, Maine, Tennessee, Texas, Vermont, and West Virginia.) Several books have been published on the history of federal and/or public lands. Among the best are Benjamin H. Hibbard, *A History of Public Land Policies* (New York: Macmillen, 1924); and Vernon R. Cartstensen, ed., *The Public Lands: Studies in the History of the Public Domain* (Madison: University of Wisconsin Press, 1963). For using these records, researchers should consult the special federal lands issue of *Heritage Quest* 15, no. 3 (May–June 1999); James C. Barsi, *The Basic Researcher's Guide to Homesteads and Other Federal Land Records* (Colorado Springs: Nuthatch Grove Press, 1996); and the National Archives' booklet *Research in Land Entry Files of the General Land Office* (Washington, D.C.: National Archives Trust, 1998). An excellent discussion of federal lands in Alabama, starting in 1820, is in the introductory chapters of Wyley Donald Ward's *Original Land Sales and Grants in Covington County, Alabama* (Spartanburg, S.C.: Reprint Company, 1991). Other works on Alabama land grants include June O. Reese, *Alabama Land Sales, 1823–1832: Statewide Conveyances of "University Lands" to Private Ownership* (n.p., 1995); and Fern C.

Ainsworth, *Private Land Claims: Alabama, Arkansas, Florida* (Natchitoches, La.: The Author, 1978).

The system used by the federal government to grant lands in federal land states such as Alabama is based upon a report compiled by a committee headed by Thomas Jefferson in 1784. The resulting ordinance of 1785 determined that federal lands would be organized into squares of six miles by six miles, called townships. The townships are not numbered but are located by the intersections of numbered range (north-south or longitude) lines with numbered township (east-west or latitude) lines. Township lines are each one mile apart, as are the range lines. These township lines and range lines are still used today on deeds, Alabama county road maps, federal topographical maps, and other records as a means of locating property.

Each such square township was subdivided into smaller squares, each of one mile by one mile (640 acres), called sections. Each section within a township has a number. All property in Alabama is identified by the intersection of a township's line with a range's line, followed by the section number within the township. For example, township 34, range 19, section 12, would refer you to where township 34's line intersects with range 19's line to form section number 12. Each section is usually described in terms of quarter sections (160 acres each) and quarter-quarter sections (40 acres each), e.g., the northwestern quarter of the southeastern quarter of the section.

Obtaining federal lands often proved complicated and expensive. The ordinance of 1785 allowed only cash sales. The acts of 1796 and 1800 allowed settlers to buy lands on credit through four cash payments of eighty dollars each. The act of 1820 reverted back to only cash sales. Under the act of May 18, 1796, federal lands as small as 320 acres (half sections) could be sold. By the act of March 26, 1804, quarter sections (160 acres) could be sold, and, in 1817, under certain conditions, half-quarter sections (80 acres) were sold. By 1820, quarter-quarter sections, 40 acre tracts, were available everywhere for sale.

Lands were granted through land offices. Each land office served a specific district. District boundaries changed over the years, and researchers should consult the maps in the books below for boundaries at different periods. Alabama's last land office, Montgomery, closed in 1927, and all

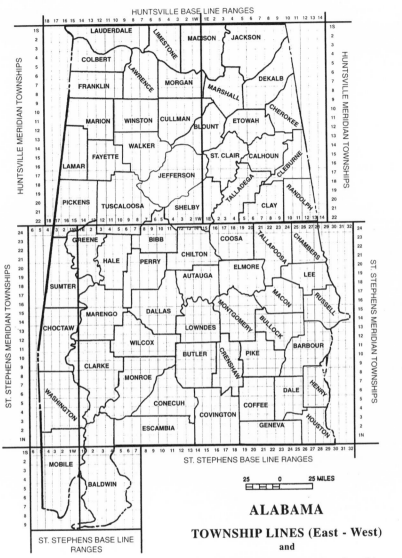

ALABAMA

TOWNSHIP LINES (East - West)
and
RANGE LINES (North - South)

SOURCE: ALABAMA STATE PLANNING AND INDUSTRIAL DEVELOPMENT BOARD
MAP DESIGN: GUS WELBORN

Alabama Township Lines and Range Lines

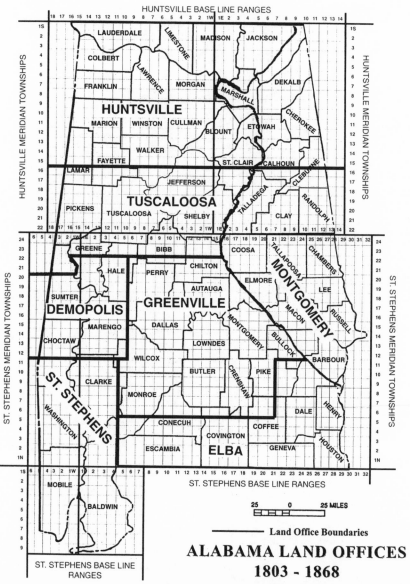

ALABAMA LAND OFFICES
1803 - 1868

See Text for Creation and Closings
of Land Offices

SOURCE: ALABAMA STATE PLANNING AND INDUSTRIAL DEVELOPMENT BOARD
MAP DESIGN: GUS WELBORN

Alabama Land Offices, 1803–1868

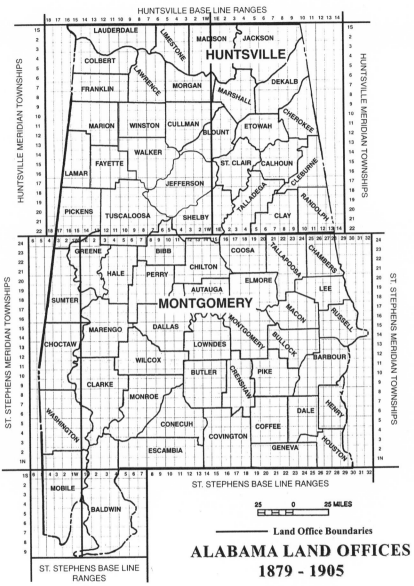

Alabama Land Offices, 1879–1905

remaining unclaimed land was then transferred to the Federal Land Bank. For maps and information on the first of these offices, see Malcom J. Rohrbough, *The Land Office Business: The Settlement and Administration of American Lands, 1789–1837* (New York: Oxford University Press, 1968). The land offices in Alabama were as follows:

> Cahaba or Conecuh Courthouse (opened August 4, 1817, in Milledgeville, Georgia, from lands formerly under St. Stephens Land Office; moved to Cahaba and opened there on October 20, 1818; moved to Greenville, June 15, 1856). Many names from land entry books and other records for this office at the Alabama Department of Archives and History appear in Marilyn Davis Hahn's *Old Cahaba Land Office Records and Military Warrants, 1817–1853*, rev. ed. (Greenville, S.C.: Southern Historical Press, 1986).
>
> Demopolis (opened by July 15, 1833, with lands formerly under the jurisdiction of the St. Stephens and Cahaba Land Offices; moved to Montgomery, March 30, 1866). Many names from land entry books and other records at the Alabama Department of Archives and History for this office appear in Marilyn Davis Hahn's *Old Demopolis Land Office Records and Military Warrants, 1818–1860, and Records of the Vine and Olive Colony* (Greenville, S.C.: Southern Historical Press, 1983). The Vine and Olive Colony refers to exiled followers of the Emperor Napoleon who settled in Marengo County, Alabama, under the federal Act of March 3, 1817.
>
> Elba (opened April 1, 1854, from lands formerly of the Sparta Land Office; moved to Montgomery, March 30, 1866). Many names from land entry books and other records for this office from the Alabama Department of Archives and History; Hoole Library of the University of Alabama; and the Scruggs Collection of the Birmingham Archives, Birmingham Public Library, appear in Marilyn Davis Hahn's *Old Sparta and Elba Land Office Records and Military Warrants, 1822–1860* (Greenville, S.C.: Southern Historical Press, 1983).
>
> Greenville (opened June 16, 1856, from lands formerly of the Cahaba Land Office; moved to Montgomery, March 30, 1866).
>
> Huntsville (opened July 27, 1810, for former Indian lands; moved from Nashville, Tennessee, to "Twickenham," i.e., Huntsville, by act of February 11, 1811; moved to Montgomery by March 1, 1905). Many names from land entry books and other records for this office at the Alabama Department of Archives and History appear in Marilyn Davis Barefield's *Old Huntsville Land Office Records and Military Warrants, 1810–1854* (Greenville, S.C.: Southern Historical Press, 1985).
>
> Mardisville (opened January 1834 from lands formerly under Montevallo

Land Office and Indian lands; moved to Lebanon, April 12, 1842; moved to Centre by August 1, 1858; moved to Huntsville, March 30, 1865; moved to Montgomery, May 26, 1866). Many names from land entry books and other records at the Alabama Department of Archives and History for this office appear in Marilyn Davis Barefield's *Old Mardisville, Lebanon, and Centre Land Office Records and Military Warrants, 1834–1860* (Birmingham, Ala.: Southern University Press, 1990).

Montevallo (opened December 20, 1833, from lands formerly under the Huntsville Land Office; moved to Mardisville by January 1834).

Montgomery (opened January 1, 1834, from former Creek Indian lands in eastern Alabama; closed 1927). Many names from land entry books and other records at the Alabama Department of Archives and History for this office appear in Marilyn Davis Barefield's *Old Montgomery Land Office Records and Military Warrants, 1834–1869* (Birmingham, Ala.: Southern University Press, 1991).

Sparta or Conecuh Court House (opened August 1, 1822, from lands formerly under Cahaba Land Office; moved to Elba, April 1, 1854). Many names from land entry books and other records at the Alabama Department of Archives and History for this office appear in Marilyn Davis Hahn's *Old Sparta and Elba Land Office Records and Military Warrants, 1822–1860* (Greenville, S.C.: Southern Historical Press, 1983).

St. Stephens (opened December 26, 1806, from former Indian territory; moved to Mobile in 1867; Mobile moved to Montgomery on March 29, 1879). Many names from land entry books and other records for this office at the Alabama Department of Archives and History appear in Marilyn Davis Hahn's *Old St. Stephen's Land Office Records and American State Papers Public Lands,* vol. 1, *1768–1888* (Greenville, S.C.: Southern Historical Press, 1983).

Tuscaloosa (opened by July 2, 1821, most of its lands had been under the Huntsville Land Office, although the southernmost two townships were from St. Stephens and Cahaba Land Offices; moved to Montgomery, March 30, 1866). Many names from land entry books and other records for this office at the Alabama Department of Archives and History appear in Marilyn Davis Barefield's *Old Tuskaloosa Land Office Records and Military Warrants, 1821–1855* (Greenville, S.C.: Southern Historical Press, 1984).

With the exception of military bounty and homestead land grants (see below), federal land records usually contain no personal data. For any grant, typically, the paperwork provides little information beyond the name of the applicant, the applicant's place of residence when applying for the grant, description of the location of the land, and date of application. Case files can, in a few instances, give information on heirs or other data; see William Dollarhide, "Federal Land Records: Send Me the Case Files!" *Heritage Quest* 15 (May–June 1999): 21–32.

These records of the individual land offices exist in many places. The Alabama Department of Archives and History has 550 receipt books that show the purchases of federal lands. The Alabama Archives also has at least partial indexes to some fifty of these volumes. The William Stanley Hoole Library of the University of Alabama at Tuscaloosa has many other records. Federal copies of the land office records are in the National Archives, 700 Pennsylvania Ave. NW, Washington, DC 20408-0001 (which has an alphabetical name index to land grantees and applicants to land grants to 1908 for Alabama, Alaska, Arizona, Florida, Louisiana, Nevada, and Utah), and in the Bureau of Land Management, Eastern States Office, 7450 Boston Boulevard, Springfield, VA 22153. The Bureau of Land Management (BLM) records frequently contain notes and cross references not found in other copies.

The Bureau of Land Management also has an index to patents issued to land grantees, excluding the persons paying in installments (on credit), 1796–1820, and homestead applications not completed. This index is widely available on CD-ROM computer disk and, with the patents themselves, through the bureau's Internet web site: http://www.glore.blm.gov. Bill Tubbs is publishing this information for Alabama and parts of Mississippi on a county by county basis, with accompanying local maps.

Each probate court in each Alabama county has a county tract book for its respective county, wherein information on land grants within the county appears, arranged by township lines, range lines, and section numbers. Some of these county tract books have been published. For example, Margaret Matthews Cowart has put into print these records for Colbert, Franklin, Jackson, Laurence, Limestone, Madison, Marshall, and Morgan Counties. A state copy of the county tract books is at the Alabama Department of Archives and History.

MILITARY BOUNTY LAND GRANTS IN ALABAMA

Conditions for receiving land for military service varied over the years; for historical background, see James W. Oberly, *Sixty Million Acres:*

American Veterans and the Public Lands before the Civil War (Kent, Ohio: Kent State University Press, 1990). For use of these records, see E. Wade Hone, "Federal Military Bounty Lands," *Heritage Quest* 15 (May–June 1999): 9–16. Originally, federal bounty land for veterans and heirs of veterans of the War of 1812 (1812–1815) could only be taken out in designated districts in Arkansas, Illinois, and Missouri. An act of 1842 allowed the claimants to receive their land in any federal land state, including Alabama. Until 1852, veterans or heirs of veterans could not sell their bounty land claims, but they could accept government land script in lieu of a grant and, starting in 1830, could sell that script to anyone. Acts of 1850 and 1855 offered bounty lands to veterans and heirs of veterans of all conflicts from 1790 on, and the act of 1855 granted bounty lands on service of as little as fourteen days. In 1856, bounty lands were offered based upon Revolutionary War service. The last additional warrants for military bounty lands were issued in 1858. Lands on such warrants were no longer allowed to be located after 1863.

The applications for bounty land warrants, often containing extensive personal information, should be requested from Military Records, National Archives, 700 Pennsylvania Ave. NW, Washington, DC 20408-0001. Most of the War of 1812 bounty land claims are indexed in National Archives microcopy M848 War of 1812 Military Bounty Land Warrants.

HOMESTEAD APPLICATIONS

Homestead lands were essentially given away to individuals, over age twenty-one and heads of households, willing to develop the land. These lands were first granted under the Homestead Act of May 20, 1862. Each adult head of household could receive up to 160 acres of land worth no more than two hundred dollars, for a ten dollar fee. No one could receive land where someone else had a "preemptive claim," i.e., a claim based upon occupancy without having applied for a grant. An act of March 21, 1864, allowed federal veterans to receive homestead grants of relatives with preemptive rights. No Confederate veterans, or anyone who gave them aid or comfort, could apply for a homestead grant. Also, only United States citizens could apply for these lands; foreign-born applicants had to provide proof of naturalization. The act of June 21, 1866, limited, for two years, homesteads in Alabama, Arkansas, Florida, Louisiana, and Mississippi to no more than 80 acres per grant, but also reduced the administrative fee from ten to five dollars.

Requests for searches for the applications for homestead lands should be made to National Archives, 700 Pennsylvania Ave. NW, Washington, DC 20408-0001. These files often contain extensive personal information.

12. CENSUS RECORDS

STATE CENSUS RECORDS

Incomplete and fragmentary records of territorial censuses, tax lists, and state census returns survive for Alabama. Accelerated Indexing Systems International (AISI) published indexes to these scattered records from the state archives of Alabama and Mississippi for 1810, 1811–1819, 1820–1829, and 1831–1839. Names that appear in these indexes and the indexes for later federal censuses prepared by AISI are widely available commercially on CD-ROM computer disks and can also be accessed through the Ancestry.com web site on the Internet.

The state census records that survive are found in the Alabama Department of Archives and History. The 1820 state census has been published several times. It survives for Baldwin, Conecuh, Dallas, Franklin, Limestone, St. Clair, Shelby, and Wilcox Counties. For 1850 a state census survives for all counties and is available on microfilm from the Alabama Archives, as are the later state censuses. The 1855 state census survives for Autauga, Baldwin, Blount, Coffee, Franklin, Henry, Lowndes, Macon, Mobile, Montgomery, Perry, Pickens, Sumter, Tallapoosa, Tuscaloosa, and Wilcox Counties; it has a published index: Ronald Vern Jackson, *Alabama 1855 Census Index* (Bountiful, Utah: Accelerated Indexing Systems, 1981). A state census survives for all of Alabama's counties for 1866 and includes information on the number of men killed, wounded, and missing from each family during the Civil War. This census has no published index.

Many individual Alabama county school boards have school censuses for their respective counties, almost all from the twentieth century.

FEDERAL CENSUS RECORDS (GENERAL)

Federal censuses were taken in the United States every ten years, starting in 1790. Beginning with the 1850 census, each free person is listed individually in the census, with such additional information as place of birth, age, sex, and race (only white, black, or mulatto until 1870). Place of birth of parents and relationship to the head of the household appear for each person beginning in 1880. Census takers recorded information on households in the order in which they traveled about the county, thereby indicating neighbors (and potential relatives) by the order in which people appear in the census. Sometimes persons recorded as neighbors in the census prove to be in-laws.

Not all early federal census records survive. For example, any federal census records for Alabama or what became Alabama do not survive for 1790 to 1820. Alabama census records survive for 1830 to the present. To learn what survives for other states, see William Thorndale and William Dollarhide, *Map Guide to the U.S. Federal Censuses, 1790–1920* (Baltimore: Genealogical Publishing Company, 1987); Thomas Jay Kemp, *The American Census Handbook* (Wilmington, Del.: Scholarly Resources, 2000); and Ann B. Hamilton, *Researcher's Guide to United States Census Availability, 1790–1920* (Bowie, Md.: Heritage Books, 1992) for specific states and counties. The Thorndale and Dollarhide book is also useful for showing county boundaries during each census.

Census records are also far from infallible. Census takers frequently relied on secondhand information from neighbors rather than interviews with each family. Many names are misspelled in the census records. Some people were omitted from the census (especially southerners in the 1870 federal census), sometimes because they were traveling and other times because they lived in isolated areas. Conversely, some families were accidentally recorded twice in the census, even within the same county. Native Americans (Indians) prior to 1870 might be listed as black, white, mulatto, or not at all. Often persons mistakenly stated previous place of residence instead of place of birth to the census takers.

The National Archives and Records Administration, 700 Pennsylvania Ave. NW, Washington, DC 20408-0001, sells microfilm of the federal census records. Many libraries have the film for at least their county or state. Regional branches of the National Archives have complete sets of the microfilm for 1790 to 1920, and this film can also be borrowed through LDS family history centers. Soon these census records will be available as images on web sites on the Internet. The National Archives retained the originals of the surviving federal census records for 1790 to 1870. The Alabama Department of Archives and History has contemporary duplicate copies of the 1850 and 1870 Alabama censuses and the original of the 1880 Alabama census. The original manuscript records of the federal census records for 1890 and later have been destroyed. For additional information on records of the federal census, see Katherine H. Davidson and Charlotte M. Ashby, *Preliminary Inventory of the Records of the Bureau of the Census (Record Group 29)* (Washington, D.C.: National Archives, 1964); and Ann B. Hamilton, *Researcher's Guide to United States Census Availability, 1790–1920* (Bowie, Md.: Heritage Books, 1992).

Federal census records from 1940 to the present are closed except to individuals seeking documented information only on themselves. This information must be requested from Bureau of the Census, P.O. Box 1545, Jeffersonville, IN 47131. The Bureau of the Census will also provide information, for a fee, on anyone in the census from 1940 to 2000 when proof is provided that the person sought is dead.

The National Archives, 700 Pennsylvania Ave. NW, Washington, DC 20408-0001, has a number of related records that are open to the public, including the 1932 and 1934 manufacturers censuses; the fruit and nut growers census of 1930 (selected states); censuses of businesses for 1929 and 1933; and census schedules of local religious establishments for 1926 through 1928. For details of these records, see Katherine H. Davidson and Charlotte M. Ashby, *Preliminary Inventories Number 161 Records of the Bureau of the Census* (Washington, D.C.: National Archives, 1964).

CENSUS STATISTICS

Published statistics survive from all of the censuses, 1790–1990, even when original census records such as the 1820 Alabama federal census no longer exist. The statistics have been published by census and also used in such works as W. Craig Remington, *The Statistical Atlas of Alabama* (Tuscaloosa: Department of Geography, University of Alabama, 1994); *A Century of Population Growth from the First Census of the United States to the Twelfth, 1790–1900* (Washington, D.C.: Government Printing Office, 1909); Donald B. Dodd and Wynelle S. Dodd, *Historical Statistics of the South, 1790–1970* (University: University of Alabama Press, 1973); and *Historical Statistics of the United States, Colonial Times to 1970* (Washington, D.C.: Government Printing Office, 1975). The publications of the statistics, by census, are usually available at federal government document repositories, such as the Birmingham Public Library. For specific citations to the volumes published by census, see Suzanne Schulze, *Population Information in Nineteenth-Century Census Volumes* (Phoenix, Ariz.: Oryx Press, 1983); and Suzanne Schulze, *Population Information in Twentieth-Century Census Volumes: 1900–1940* (Phoenix, Ariz.: Oryx Press, 1985). For other sources for statistics, see the current edition of *Statistics Sources;* and Jean L. Sears and Marilyn K. Moody, *Using Government Information Sources* (Phoenix, Ariz.: Oryx Press, 1994).

INDEXES TO CENSUS RECORDS (GENERAL)

Until recent times, statewide indexes to census records were notoriously faulty and incomplete. Individual publications by county of census records are often more complete and accurate. Indexes to surviving census records list heads of households and, starting in 1850, people of different last names than the head of their respective households. The indexes for Alabama to 1870 have been published in book form and are on microfiche, computer CD-ROM disks, and the Ancestry.com web site on the Internet.

A nationwide index to the surviving Federal census records, 1790–1850, is available on microfiche and on the Ancestry.com web site. The 1880 census has been transcribed on computer CD-ROM disks that can be searched for any name electronically. Genealogy.com offers a nationwide index to the 1900 census on the Internet.

There are also limited soundex indexes to the censuses of 1880, 1890 (what little that survives of the 1890 census has a published nationwide index: Helen Swenson, *Index to 1890 Census* [St. Louis, Mo.: Ingmire, 1981]), and 1900 to 1930 available on microfilm. When handwritten, these latter indexes are called the soundex, and when typed they are called the miracode. All states have a soundex or a miracode for 1920, but not every state has these for every census for 1880 through 1910 and 1930. Soundex or miracode indexes have surnames arranged by a phonetic code rather than by the census takers' spellings. The 1880 soundex only indexes the families that had children under age eleven, although all families are included in the census itself. For more information on the soundex see Tony Burroughs, "The Original Soundex Instructions," *National Genealogical Society Quarterly* 89 (2001): 287–98.

SPECIFIC FEDERAL CENSUSES, 1830–1840

Through 1840, census takers recorded the names of the heads of free households, with statistical descriptions of the members of the households. Sometimes the statistics represented non-family members living in the household.

The 1830 federal census is the earliest that survives for the state of Alabama. It represents the population on June 1, 1830, and is reproduced on National Archives microfilm M19, rolls one to four. It is indexed statewide in Ronald Vern Jackson's *Alabama 1830 Census Index* (Bountiful, Utah: Accelerated Indexing Systems, 1976). Another source for the 1830 census is Carter G. Woodson's *Free Negro Heads of Families in the United States in 1830* (Washington, D.C.: Association for the Study of Negro Life and History, 1925), a copy of which is in the Southern History Collection of the Birmingham Public Library.

The 1840 federal census reflected the population on June 1, 1840. In a few instances, the individual pages were bound backwards, causing the statistics on one page to wrongly appear as belonging to the names on the previous page. This error was not caught when the pages were numbered or microfilmed. This census has several unique features, including a special column for listing Revolutionary War pensioners (or all Revolutionary soldiers in some counties.) The actual pensioners from that list have been published: *A Census of Pensioners for Revolutionary or Military Services;*

with Their Names, Ages, and Places of Residence (Washington, D.C.: Blair and Rives, 1841). The National Archives has statistical descriptions of agriculture, manufacturing, mining, etc. in 1840 and will soon provide these records on microfilm. The 1840 federal census for Alabama appears in National Archives microfilm M704, rolls one through sixteen, and is indexed statewide in Ronald Vern Jackson and Gary Ronald Teeples, *Alabama 1840 Census Index* (Bountiful, Utah: Accelerated Indexing Systems, 1977).

SPECIFIC FEDERAL CENSUS RECORDS, 1850–1890

Starting with the 1850 federal census, each free person is named, with such information as age, sex, race, etc. Place of birth is usually given only as state or country. The 1850 and 1860 censuses also have separate slave population schedules listing each slave owner or estate, with a description of the slaves (but no names of slaves).

The censuses for 1850 to 1880 include not only the above population schedules for each census but also other schedules for recording certain information of the calendar year before each census. These other schedules are widely available on microfilm at major Alabama libraries. These extra schedules include mortality (persons who died); agriculture (farmers); large scale manufacturers; and social statistics (county-wide community data).

The 1850 census represents the population on June 1, 1850, and the National Archives reproduces the population and slave schedules for Alabama as microfilm M432, rolls one through twenty-four. It has been indexed statewide as Ronald Vern Jackson, ed., *Alabama 1850 Census Index* (Salt Lake: Accelerated Indexing Systems, 1981); and *Alabama Slave Schedule Census Index* (Salt Lake: Accelerated Indexing Systems, 1988). Sometimes references in these indexes to Randolph County actually refer to Russell County. The 1850 mortality schedule of persons dying between June 1, 1849, and June 1, 1850, has been published by Marilyn Davis Hahn as *Alabama Mortality Schedule 1850* (Easley, S.C.: Southern Historical Press, 1983). The Alabama Department of Archives and History has made available on microfilm a contemporary state copy of the 1850 federal census records, along with the state census for 1850.

The 1860 census represents the population on June 1, 1860; the population and slave schedules for Alabama are found in National Archives microfilm M653, rolls one through thirty-six. These schedules are indexed statewide in Ronald Vern Jackson et al., *Alabama 1860 Census Index* (Bountiful, Utah: Accelerated Indexing Systems International, 1985); *Alabama 1860 Mortality Schedule* (Bountiful, Utah: Accelerated Indexing Systems International, 1983); and *Alabama 1860 Slave Schedule Census Index* (Salt Lake: Accelerated Indexing Systems, 1990). The mortality schedule, listing persons dying between June 1, 1859, and June 1, 1860, has also been published: Marilyn Davis Barefield, *Alabama Mortality Schedule 1860* (Easley, S.C.: Southern Historical Press, 1987).

The 1870 federal census represents the population on June 1, 1870, and the population schedule is reproduced for Alabama on National Archives microfilm M593, rolls one to forty-six. The 1870 federal census has a reputation for being exceptionally incomplete, unreadable in places, and for having pages bound and numbered out of order. The population schedule is indexed statewide in Bradley W. Steuart, *Alabama 1870 Census Index* (Bountiful, Utah: Heritage Quest, 2000); and Ronald Vern Jackson et al., *Alabama 1870 Federal Census Index* (Salt Lake: Accelerated Indexing Systems International, 1989). The Steuart index contains far more names than the other index, including all males age fifty or older and all females age seventy or older, as well as personal information on each person listed; it has also been made available on computer CD-ROM by Heritage Quest.

The Alabama Department of Archives and History has a contemporary copy of much of the 1870 census of Alabama and from that has compiled a special "family" index. Widely available on microfilm, this index covers Autauga, Baker, Baldwin, Barbour, Bibb, Blount, Bullock, Calhoun, Chambers, Chilton, Clarke, Colbert, Conecuh, Coosa, Crenshaw, Dale, Dallas, DeKalb, Elmore, Escambia, Etowah, Geneva, Green, Hale, Henry, Houston, Jackson, Jefferson, Lauderdale, Lowndes, and Macon Counties.

The 1880 federal census represented the population on June 1, 1880. Among the information included for the first time was, for each person, place of birth of parents and relationship to the head of the household. For Alabama the population schedule for this census is reproduced as National Archives microfilm T9, rolls one through thirty-five. A soundex index to heads of households with children under age ten is National Archives microfilm T734. The Alabama Department of Archives and History has the original of, and has microfilmed, a special schedule, of the 1880 census, of persons in confinement, known as the "Defective, Dependent, and Delinquent Classes" schedule.

The Genealogical Society of Utah has prepared a transcript of the 1880 federal census for the whole United States. These CD-ROM computer disks contain almost all of the information from the census and can be searched by any name, electronically.

Almost all of the 1890 census was severely damaged in a fire in 1921 and thrown out sometime after 1933. Ashes of a few pages of the 1890 census for Perry County, Alabama, survive and are included in National Archives microfilm M407, roll one. It is indexed in Helen Swenson's *Index to 1890 Census of the United States* (St. Louis, Mo.: Ingmire, 1981). For the background on this census, see Kelle Blake, " 'First in the Path of the Firemen': The Fate of the 1890 Population Census," *Prologue: The Quarterly of the National Archives and Records Administration* 28 (1996): 64–81. The 1890 Civil War federal veterans census also does not survive for Alabama.

SPECIFIC FEDERAL CENSUS RECORDS, 1900–1930

Some special notes on using federal census records on microfilm, 1900–1930, appears below. For a list of the abbreviations used in the 1900 census, see page 84 of *Catalogue of 1900 Federal Population Census Data* (Washington, D.C.: National Archives Trust, 1982). For abbreviations used in the 1910 federal census, see pages 40–42 of *The 1910 Federal Population Census* (Washington, D.C.: National Archives Trust, 1982). The National Archives destroyed all original records of the 1900 through 1940 federal censuses in 1953, although it retained microfilm copies; see Kellee Green, "The Fourteenth Numbering of the People: The 1920 Federal Census," *Prologue: The Quarterly of the National Archives and Records Administration* 23 (1991): 140.

For the 1900 (National Archives microcopy T623, Alabama is reels number 1 to 44) and 1910 (National Archives microcopy T624, Alabama is reels number 1 to 37) federal censuses the census was to represent the population on June 1. For the 1920 census, the population was recorded for April 1, 1920. The censuses of 1900 and 1920 give for each person listed name, relationship to head of household, age (in 1900, the month of birth), place of birth, marital status, number of children (if female), and naturalization information. These censuses have soundex and/or miracode indexes on microfilm (1900 for Alabama is National Archives microcopy T1030, reels number 1 to 180; 1910 for Alabama is T624, reels number 1 to 37).

Alabama institutions, including asylums, prisons, poor farms, etc., for 1900 are listed in National Archives microcopy T1083, reel 1. (Alabama's state convict records to 1952 are at the Alabama Department of Archives and History. Records of inmates of state hospitals must be requested from the respective hospitals. However, the Alabama Department of Archives and History does have county probate court reports on mentally ill persons sent to Bryce Hospital, 1870–1895.)

The federal census for Alabama for January 1, 1920, is available on National Archives microcopy T1262, and the soundex index is National Archives microcopy M1557. Contrary to some printed accounts, the 1920 census only seldom includes information on village and province of birth.

The 1930 federal census will be released to the public on April 1, 2002. Alabama and its surrounding states have soundex indexes to this census.

The 1930 soundex for Alabama has two parts: an index for Jefferson, Mobile, and Montgomery counties (reels 128–98) and an index for the rest of the state. The "sheet" number in the 1930 soundex for Alabama is actually the household number in the census. Enumeration district numbers are expressed as county code–enumeration district. For information on the 1930 census, see Thomas Jay Kemp, *The 1930 Census: A Reference and Research Guide* (Salt Lake: Heritage Quest, 2002).

13. OTHER SPECIAL FEDERAL SOURCES

THE NATIONAL ARCHIVES AND RECORDS ADMINISTRATION

The National Archives and Records Administration (NARA), Washington, DC 20408-0001, has responsibility for the historical records of the federal government of the United States and its predecessor, the Continental Congress. Most of the federal records are kept in the National Archives' Washington facilities, although the most frequently used of this material has published finding aids and widely available microfilm copies. Local federal records are maintained at regional archives such as the National Archives Southeast Region (currently at, but soon to move from, 1557 St. Joseph Avenue, East Point, GA 30344), which includes Alabama in its jurisdiction. The following are important general guides to the holdings of the National Archives, including records relating to Alabama. These guides are widely available and most of them are accessible through the National Archives' web site on the Internet. Unless stated otherwise, the National Archives Trust published the work. Other guides are cited in other chapters elsewhere, under specific subject headings; also see the current printed catalog of National Archives microfilms.

Burton, Dennis A., et al. *A Guide to Manuscripts in the Presidential Libraries*. College Park, Md.: Research Materials Corporation, 1985.

Coren, Robert W., et al. *Guide to the Records of the United States Senate at the National Archives, 1789–1989.* 1989.

National Archives and Records Administration. *Guide to Federal Records in the National Archives of the United States.* 3 vols. 1995.

———. *Guide to Genealogical Research in the National Archives.* 1983.

———. *Military Service Records: A Select Catalog of National Archives Microfilm Publications.* (1985).

Schamel, Charles E., et al. *Guide to the Records of the United States House of Representatives at the National Archives, 1789–1989.* 1989.

Wehmann, Howard H. *A Guide to Pre-Federal Records in the National Archives.* 1989.

Valuable articles on research in federal records regularly appear in NARA's magazine, *Prologue: The Quarterly of the National Archives and Records Administration.* Some examples of these articles include Kenneth W. Heger, "Strategies for Reconstructing Careers of Foreign Service Officers, 1869–1887," 31 (1999): 74–83; and David A. Pfeiffer, "Archivist's Perspective: Riding the Rails up Paper Mountain: Researching Railroad Records in the National Archives," 31 (1999): 52–61; Trevor K. Plante, "U.S. Marines in the Boxer Rebellion," 284–89; and Jeanne Carnnella Schmitzer, "Genealogy Notes: Far from Home: American Citizens in the United States Military and Territorial Census Records," 29 (1997): 70–73.

NATIONAL ARCHIVES SOUTHEAST REGION

The National Archives maintains regional federal archives across the country. For all of these institutions, see Lorett Dennis Szucs, *The Archives: Guide to the National Archives Field Branches* (Salt Lake City, Utah: Ancestry, 1988).

The National Archives Southeast Region (NASR; formerly known as the Federal Records Center, the National Archives Atlanta Branch, and other names), currently at, but soon to move from, 1557 St. Joseph Avenue, East Point, GA 30344, maintains the specific federal historical government records for Alabama, Florida, Georgia, Kentucky, Mississippi, North Carolina, South Carolina, and Tennessee. Use of the microfilm readers requires an appointment, made by calling (404) 763-7477.

The regional holdings include the United States (federal) and Confederate district and circuit court records, starting in 1790, for the NASR's area. Prior to 1860, most federal court records involved debt suits between parties in different states, smuggling, and robbery of the mail. In almost all states, merchants did business with manufacturers and other companies in northern states, generating a number of interstate federal civil suits over debt. Federal court records are particularly rich in detailed bankruptcy suits in the late 1830s and 1840s. During the Civil War, Confederate courts replaced the federal courts in Alabama and other southern states. The records of those courts include extensive files on confiscation of locally and northern-owned property as well as suits by northern companies for debts owed by southern companies then under sequestration. Following the Civil War, cases involving moonshining, untaxed tobacco, and civil rights violations became common; see the special regional archives and federal court records issue of *Prologue: The Quarterly of the National Archives and Records Administration* 21, no. 3 (1989), and, for suggestions on the use of the printed directories of these records, see Emily Anne Croom, *The Genealogist's Companion and Sourcebook* (Cincinnati: Betterway Books, 1994), 127–29; and Stephen Elias and Susan Levinkind, *Legal Research: How to Find and Understand the Law* (Berkeley, Calif.: Nolo Press, 1997).

Other regional federal records at the NASR include federal direct tax lists, 1864–1870s; records of the Tennessee Valley Authority; and historical holdings of the Marshal Space Flight Center at Huntsville. On microfilm, this institution has regional indexes to passenger lists and Confederate service records; Native American records; and selected documents of the Bureau of Refugees, Freedmen and Abandoned Lands. The NASR also has some holdings that cover the entire country, such as World War I draft records; the population schedules of the federal censuses for 1790 through 1920; some indexes to military records, 1775–1848; and the Revolutionary War pension claims.

Aside from the printed catalogs to all of the NASR's original records and microfilm holdings, this institution also offers free handouts on such topics as its holdings on genealogical, American Indian, and African American family research. A support group for the National Archives Southeast Region is the Friends of the Federal Archives-Southeast Region, dedicated to making the NASR better known and to raising money for purchasing more National Archives microfilm. This group can be contacted care of the National Archives Southeast Region.

OTHER SOURCES

Most major libraries, including the Birmingham Public Library and the University of Alabama at Tuscaloosa, are U.S. government document centers. Twenty-three universities, colleges, and public libraries in Alabama are federal government records repositories. Federal publications and indexes have been placed in these collections for use by the general public. These facilities can provide information on many (but not all) government publications, past and present, and current addresses of federal agencies. Among the common holdings of these centers are legislative and executive printed documents as well as publications of federal laws and Supreme Court decisions. For more information on such sources, see Marilyn K. Moody, *Using Government Information Sources* (Phoenix, Ariz.: Oryx Press, 1994).

For a discussion of the basics to using resources at a U.S. government document center, see Emily Anne Croom, *The Genealogist's Companion and Sourcebook* (Cincinnati: Betterway Books, 1994), 123–29. For guides to researching federal and state laws, see Charles E. Schamel, "Untapped Resources: Private Claims and Legislation in the Records of the U.S. Congress," *Prologue: The Quarterly of the National Archives and Records Administration* 27 (1995): 45–58; and John Corbin, *Find the Law in the Library* (Chicago: American Library Association, 1989). For individual claims, also see *Digested Summary and Alphabetical List of Private Claims Which Have Been Presented to the House of Representatives* [1789–1851] (Washington, D.C.: Government Printing Office, 1853).

Many of the records of the Federal Bureau of Investigation are open to research. To learn how to access these files, see Yigal Rechtman, "The FBI for Genealogy? Really? Yes!" *Genealogical Helper* (November–December 1998): 42–43; and Gerald K. Haines and David A. Langbart, *Unlocking the Secrets of the FBI* (Wilmington, Del.: Scholarly Resources, 1997).

The Birmingham Public Library has microfilm of federal patent records. Full texts of patents, 1790 to present, can also be accessed to some degree at the U.S. Patent and Trademark Office web site: http://www.uspto.gov/patft/index.html.

14. CITY, COUNTY, AND COMMUNITY SOURCES

The best guides to modern local government in Alabama are David L. Martin, *Alabama's State and Local Governments*, 3rd ed. (Tuscaloosa: University of Alabama Press, 1994); William H. Stewart, *The Alabama State Constitution: A Reference Guide* (Westport, Conn.: Greenwood Press, 1994); and James D. Thomas and William H. Stewart, *Alabama Government and Politics* (Lincoln: University of Nebraska Press, 1988). The Alabama Department of Archives and History has an incomplete card catalog of information on legislation incorporating towns and cities.

CITY DIRECTORIES AND RELATED MUNICIPAL SOURCES

Many indexed maps, gazetteers, etc. exist providing information on past and present locations of Alabama towns and cities. The best such work is W. Craig Remington and Thomas J. Kallsen, *Historical Atlas of Alabama*, vol. 1, *Historical Locations by County* (Tuscaloosa: Department of Geography, University of Alabama, 1997). For other such works and a list of Sanborn Fire Insurance maps for individual Alabama towns and cities, see chapter 3 in this volume, "Maps and Places."

The Works Projects Administration in 1937 compiled a three-volume collection of historical sketches of early Alabama towns and communities. Included in these unpublished typescripts are memoirs of Auburn, Autauga County, Autaugaville, Blount County, Bullock County, Cahaba, Chambers, Dale County, Demopolis, Elmore County, Eutaw, Furman, Greene County, Lawrence County, Limestone County, Midway, Mobile, Montgomery, Opelika, Pickens County, Pike County, Randolph County, Selma, Shelby County, Sumter County, Tuscaloosa, West Alabama, and the iron industry. The Birmingham Public Library has this, called "Sketches of Alabama Towns and Counties: A Collection." Carl Elliott published a similar compilation for his region in his *Annals of Northwest Alabama,* 5 vols. (Northport, Ala.: Hermitage Press, 1965–1987). For other such works, see chapter 2 in this volume, "Books, Bibliographies, Periodicals, Newspapers, and Manuscripts." A bibliography of sources on individual urban areas is Catherine L. Brown's *The Urban South: A Bibliography* (New York: Greenwood Press, 1989).

As opposed to whole towns, city directories often identify residence and other personal information that supplement federal censuses and other records. Most Alabama county seats have at their respective public libraries at least some sort of modern city directories for recent times. Guides to extant city directories for the entire United States, including Alabama, are Dorothea N. Spear's *Bibliography of American Directories through 1860* (Westport, Conn.: Greenwood Press, 1978); and *City Directories of the United States, 1860–1901: Guide to the Microfilm Collections by Research Publications* (Woodbridge, Conn.: Research Publications, 1983). The Library of Congress and many local libraries also have old telephone directories. No bibliographies or catalogs of these holdings exist. At the Library of Congress, searches are made of these directories by locality. For more information consult *Telephone and City Directories in the Library of Congress: A Finding Guide* (Washington, D.C.: Library of Congress, 1994).

Listed below are the city directories found in the Alabama Department of Archives and History, as listed on its web site. For other local directories, consult the respective city's or town's public library.

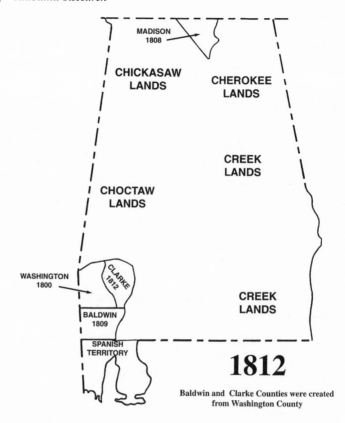

1812

Baldwin and Clarke Counties were created
from Washington County

Taken from the Alabama Historical Quarterly

Alabama Counties, 1812

Albertville/Boaz
1959, 1961, 1966, 1967, 1969, 1971, 1973, 1974
Alexander City
1957, 1961, 1963, 1965, 1967, 1969
Andalusia
1955, 1957, 1959, 1962, 1964, 1968, 1973, 1975, 1976, 1977, 1978
Anniston
1913/1914, 1940, 1942, 1945, 1948/1949, 1951, 1955/1956, 1957, 1958, 1959, 1961,
1962, 1963, 1965, 1966, 1967, 1969, 1971, 1972, 1973, 1974, 1975, 1976, 1977, 1978,
1979
Arab
1968

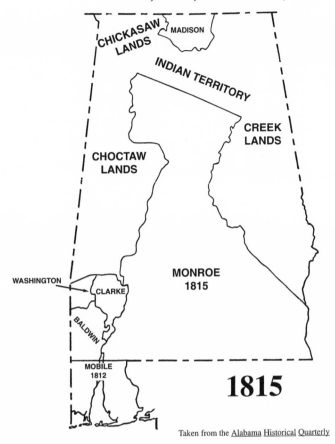

Taken from the Alabama Historical Quarterly

Alabama Counties, 1815

Atmore
1961, 1963/1964, 1968, 1972, 1973
Bay Minette
1963, 1965, 1967, 1971, 1973, 1976, 1978
Bessemer
1907, 1913/1914, 1916/1917, 1920/1921, 1938, 1940, 1946, 1948, 1951, 1953, 1955,
1957, 1959, 1960, 1961, 1963
Birmingham
1888, 1889, 1890, 1891, 1893, 1895, 1896, 1900, 1901, 1903, 1904, 1905, 1907, 1908,
1909, 1910, 1911, 1912, 1913, 1914, 1915, 1916, 1917, 1918, 1919, 1920/1921, 1922,
1923, 1924, 1925, 1926, 1927, 1928, 1929, 1930, 1931, 1932, 1934, 1935, 1937, 1938,

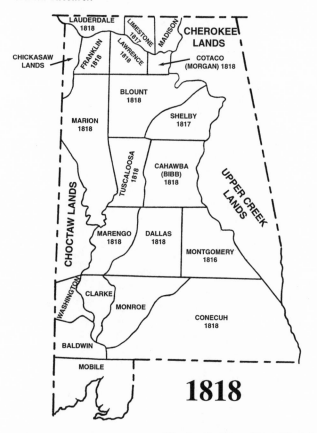

Taken from the <u>Alabama</u> <u>Historical</u> <u>Quarterly</u>

Alabama Counties, 1818

1939, 1941, 1944, 1946, 1947/1948, 1950/1951, 1952, 1953, 1954, 1956, 1957, 1959, 1960, 1961, 1962, 1963, 1964, 1965, 1966, 1967, 1968, 1969, 1970, 1971, 1972, 1973, 1974, 1975, 1976, 1977, 1978, 1979, 1980, 1981, 1982, 1983
    Brewton
1958, 1959, 1962, 1965, 1967, 1969, 1971, 1973, 1975, 1976, 1978
    Clanton
1966, 1972, 1974, 1977
    Cullman
1958, 1959, 1961, 1963, 1965, 1968, 1971, 1972, 1973, 1974, 1975, 1977, 1978
    Decatur
1913/1914, 1917/1918, 1958, 1969

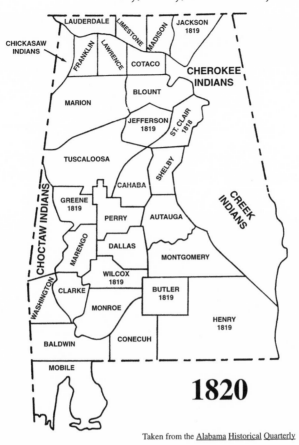

Taken from the <u>Alabama</u> <u>Historical</u> <u>Quarterly</u>

Alabama Counties, 1820

Demopolis
1959, 1961, 1963, 1965, 1967, 1969, 1971, 1973, 1975, 1976
Dothan
1951, 1953, 1955, 1958, 1959, 1960, 1962, 1963, 1964, 1965, 1966, 1969, 1971, 1978
Enterprise
1957, 1964, 1966, 1969, 1971, 1973, 1975, 1976, 1978
Eufaula
1961, 1963, 1965, 1967, 1969, 1971, 1974, 1976
Fairhope/Daphne
1965, 1967
Flomaton/South Flomaton/Century/Jay
1965, 1967, 1969, 1972, 1974

Alabama Counties, 1823

Florence/Sheffield/Tuscumbia/Muscle Shoals
1913/1914, 1920/1921, 1959, 1960, 1962, 1963, 1964, 1965, 1966, 1967, 1968, 1969, 1970, 1971/1972, 1973, 1974, 1975, 1976, 1977, 1978
Fort Payne
1969
Gadsden/Attalla
1947/1948, 1951, 1952, 1954, 1955, 1958, 1959, 1960, 1962, 1963, 1965, 1968, 1969, 1971, 1972, 1973, 1974, 1975, 1976, 1977, 1978, 1979
Girard
(Phenix City and Girard were often included in the city directories of Columbus, Georgia, as early as the 1870s.)

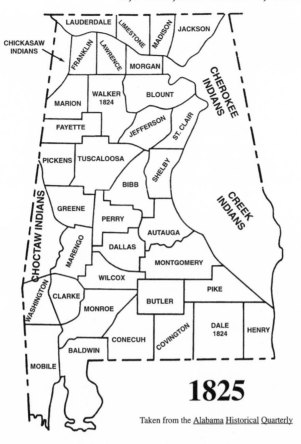

1825

Taken from the <u>Alabama</u> <u>Historical</u> <u>Quarterly</u>

Alabama Counties, 1825

Greensboro/Marion/Marion Junction/Uniontown
1957, 1958, 1959, 1960, 1962, 1975
    Huntsville
1859/1860, 1896, 1929/1930, 1955, 1957, 1959, 1960, 1961, 1962, 1963, 1964, 1965,
1968, 1969, 1971, 1972, 1973, 1974, 1975, 1976, 1977, 1978, 1979, 1981
    Jackson
1968
    Jasper
1955/1956, 1961
    Mobile
1837, 1839, 1842,1850/1851, 1852, 1855, 1859, 1861, 1867, 1869/1870, 1870–1872,

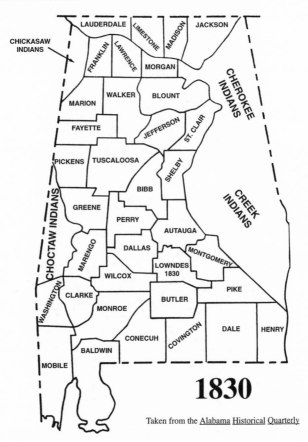

Alabama Counties, 1830

1873, 1874, 1875, 1876, 1877, 1878, 1879, 1880, 1881, 1882, 1883, 1884, 1885/1886, 1887, 1888, 1889, 1890, 1891, 1892, 1893, 1894, 1895, 1896, 1897, 1898, 1899, 1900, 1901, 1902, 1903, 1905, 1906, 1907, 1908, 1909, 1910, 1911, 1912, 1913, 1914, 1915, 1916, 1918, 1920, 1922, 1924, 1926, 1927, 1928, 1929, 1930, 1931, 1932, 1933, 1935, 1936, 1937, 1938, 1939, 1940, 1941, 1942, 1944/1945, 1946, 1947/1948, 1949/1950, 1951, 1952, 1953, 1954, 1955, 1956, 1958, 1959, 1960, 1961, 1962, 1963, 1964, 1965/ 1966, 1967, 1968, 1969, 1971, 1972, 1973, 1974, 1975, 1976, 1977, 1978, 1979, 1980, 1981, 1982, 1983, 1984

Monroeville/Frisco City

1965, 1967, 1972, 1974

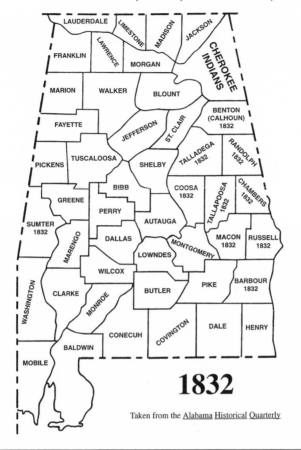

1832

Taken from the <u>Alabama</u> <u>Historical</u> <u>Quarterly</u>

Alabama Counties, 1832

Montgomery

1859/1860, 1866, 1873, 1880/1881 (all photocopied), 1883/1884, 1887, 1891, 1893, 1895, 1897, 1898, 1899, 1901, 1902, 1903, 1904, 1905, 1906, 1907, 1908, 1909, 1910, 1912, 1913, 1914, 1915, 1916, 1917, 1919, 1920, 1922, 1923, 1925, 1926, 1928, 1929, 1931, 1933, 1935, 1937, 1939, 1940, 1941, 1942, 1945, 1946, 1947/1948, 1950, 1951/ 1952, 1953, 1954, 1956, 1957, 1958, 1959, 1960, 1961 (2 parts), 1962, 1963 (2 parts), 1964, 1965, 1967, 1968 (2 parts), 1969 (2 parts), 1970 (2 parts), 1972 (2 parts), 1973 (2 parts), 1974 (2 parts), 1975 (2 parts), 1976 (2 parts), 1977 (2 parts), 1978 (2 parts), 1979 (2 parts), 1980 (2 parts), 1981(2 parts), 1984 (2 parts), 1985 (2 parts), and 1986 (2 parts), 1987–1990, 1992, 1996

1840

Taken from the Alabama Historical Quarterly

Alabama Counties, 1840

Opelika/Auburn
1960, 1962, 1964, 1966, 1968, 1972, 1974
Ozark
1960, 1962, 1964, 1966, 1968, 1972, 1974
Pell City
1968, 1972, 1977
Phenix City/Columbus
1941, 1946, 1947, 1950, 1951, 1952, 1953, 1954, 1955, 1957, 1958, 1959, 1960, 1961,
1962, 1963, 1964, 1965, 1966, 1967, 1968, 1969, 1971, 1972, 1974, 1975, 1976, 1977,

1850

Taken from the <u>Alabama</u> <u>Historical</u> <u>Quarterly</u>

Alabama Counties, 1850

1978. (Phenix City and Girard were often included in the city directories of Columbus, Georgia, as early as the 1870s.)

Prattville

1962, 1964, 1967, 1969, 1971, 1972, 1974, 1975, 1976, 1979, 1980

Prichard

1956, 1957, 1958, 1959, 1960, 1961, 1963, 1964, 1965, 1966, 1968, 1969, 1970, 1971, 1972, 1973, 1974, 1975, 1977, 1978

Saraland

1966

Alabama Counties, 1870

Scottsboro
1967
Selma
1880/1881, 1904, 1913/1914, 1916/1917, 1920/1921, 1939, 1945, 1947/1948, 1950,
1954, 1955, 1957, 1959, 1967, 1969, 1971, 1972, 1974, 1975, 1976, 1979
Sylacauga
1956, 1960
Talladega
1948, 1957, 1959, 1961, 1963, 1966, 1968, 1970, 1973, 1975, 1976, 1977, 1978

Taken from the Alabama Historical Quarterly

Alabama Counties, 1903

Tuscaloosa
1913, 1914, 1916, 1917, 1950, 1954, 1955, 1956, 1957, 1958, 1959, 1960, 1962, 1963,
1965, 1966, 1967, 1968, 1969, 1971, 1973, 1974, 1975, 1976, 1978
Tuskegee
1965, 1968, 1973, 1977
The Valley
1965, 1967, 1971, 1973, 1975
West Point
1962
Wetumpka
1975, 1977

ALABAMA

Court House Sites

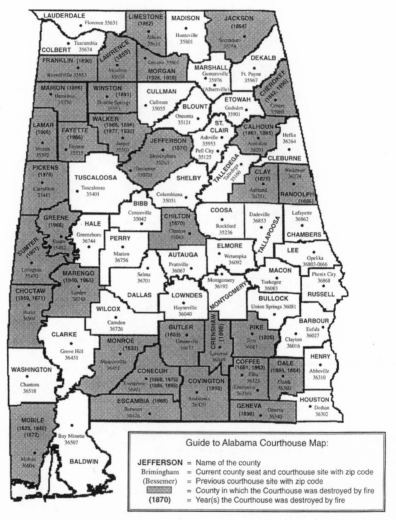

Guide to Alabama Courthouse Map:

JEFFERSON = Name of the county
Brimingham = Current county seat and courthouse site with zip code
(Bessemer) = Previous courthouse site with zip code
▨ = County in which the Courthouse was destroyed by fire
(1870) = Year(s) the Courthouse was destroyed by fire

Courtesy: Alabama Department of Archives and History   Research: Robert S. Davis, Jr.   Map Design: Gus Welborn

Alabama Court House Sites

COUNTY COURTHOUSES IN ALABAMA

County	Courthouse Address	Phone	Fax
Autauga	Court & 4th Streets · Prattville, AL 36067	334–361–3725	334–361–3740
Baldwin	P.O. Box 488 · Bay Minette, AL 36507	334–937–9561	334–580–2500
Barbour	#1 Court Square · Clayton, AL 36106	334–775–8371	
Bibb	Centreville, AL 35042	205–926–3108	205–926–3119
Blount	220 Second Ave · Oneonta, AL 35121	205–625–4222	205–625–4206
Bullock	217 N Prane SL · Union Springs, AL 36089	334–738–2250	
Butler	700 Court Square · Greenville, AL 36037	334–382–3512	334–382–5489
Calhoun	1702 Noble St., Suite 103 · Anniston, AL 36201	205–236–3521	205–237–6956
Chambers	LaFayette, AL 36862	334–964–4380	334–864–4387
Cherokee	100 Maine St. · Centre, AL 35960	205–927–3669	205–927–3669
Chilton	501 2nd Ave. · Clanton, AL 35045	205–755–1551	205–280–7204
Choctaw	117 S Mulberry, Suite 9 · Butler, AL 36904	205–459–2417	205–459–4666
Clarke	P.O. Box 548 · Grove Hill, AL 36451	334–275–3507	334–275–8517
Clay	P.O. Box 1120 · Ashland, AL 36251	205–354–2198	205–354–2197
Cleburne	406 Vickery St. · Heflin, AL 36264	205–463–5655	205–463–7780
Coffee	230 N. Court Ave. · Elba, AL 36323	334–897–2211	334–997–2028
Colbert	201 N. Main St. · Tuscumbia, AL 35674	205–386–8500	205–386–8510
Conecuh	P.O. Box 347 · Evergreen, AL 36401	334–378–1221	334–578–7002
Coosa	P.O. Box 218 · Rockford, AL 35136	205–377–2420	205–377–2524
Covington	Court Square · Andalusia, AL 36420	334–222–3613	334–222–2859
Crenshaw	301 S. Glenwood Ave. · Luverne, AL 36049	334–335–6568	334–335–3616
Cullman	500 2nd Ave. SW/Rm. 202 · Cullman, AL 35055	205–739–3530	205–739–3525
Dale	Court Square · Ozark, AL 36360	334–774–2754	334–774–0468
Dallas	P.O. Box 997 · Selma, AL 36702	334–874–2500	334–874–2553
DeKalb	111 Grand Ave. SW, Suite 200 · Fort Payne, AL 35967	205–845–8500	205–845–9502
Elmore	P.O. Box 280 · Wetumpka, AL 36092	334–567–1139	334–567–1144
Escambia	P.O. Box 848 · Brewton, AL 36427	334–867–0297	
Etowah	800 Forrest Ave. · Gadsden, AL 35901	205–549–5313	205–546–1149
Fayette	P.O. Box 819 · Fayette, AL 35555	205–932–4510	205–932–4370
Franklin	P.O. Box 1028 · Russellville, AL 35653	205–332–1210	205–332–8855
Geneva	P.O. Box 430 · Geneva, AL 36340	334–684–2275	
Greene	P.O. Box 656 · Eutaw, AL 35462	205–372–3349	205–372–0499
Hale	P.O. Box 396 · Greensboro, AL 36744	334–624–4257	
Henry	101 W. Court Sq-Suite A · Abbeville, AL 36310	334–585–3257	334–585–5006
Houston	P.O. Box 6406 · Dothan, AL 36302	334–677–4700	334–794–6633
Jackson	Courthouse · Scottsboro, AL 35768	205–574–9294	205–574–9318
Jefferson	716 N 21st St. · Birmingham, AL 35263	205–325–5311	205–325–4885
Lamar	P.O. Box 3380 · Vernon, AL 35592	205–695–9119	205–695–9253
Lauderdale	P.O. Box 1059 · Florence, AL 35631	205–760–5750	205–760–5703
Lawrence	750 Main St., Suite 1 · Moulton, AL 35650	205–974–0663	205–974–3188
Lee	P.O. Box 666 · Opelika, AL 36803–0666	334–745–9767	334–742–9478
Limestone	County Courthouse · Athens, AL 35611	205–233–6400	205–233–6474
Lowndes	P.O. Box 65 · Hayneville, AL 36040	334–548–2331	334–548–5101
Macon	County Courthouse · Tuskegee, AL 36083	334–724–2611	334–724–2512
Madison	100 Northside Sq. · Huntsville, AL 35801	205–532–3300	205–532–6977
Marengo	P.O. Box 4807 15 · Linden, AL 36748	334–295–2200	334–295–2254
Marion	132 Military St. S · Hamilton, AL 35570	205–921–3172	
Marshall	424 Blount Ave. · Guntersville, AL 35976	205–571–7701	205–571–7701
Mobile	205 Government St. · Mobile, AL 36644	334–690–8606	334–690–4770
Monroe	P.O. Box 8 · Monroeville, AL 36461	334–743–4107	334–575–7934
Montgomery	P.O. Box 1667 · Montgomery, AL 36102	334–832–4960	334–832–2533
Morgan	P.O. Box 668 · Decatur, AL 35602	205–351–4600	205–351–4738
Perry	P.O. Box 478 · Marion, AL 36756	334–683–2200	334–683–2201
Pickens	P.O. Box 4600 · Carrollton, AL 35447	205–367–2020	205–367–2025
Pike	P.O. Box 1147 · Troy, AL 36081	334–566–6374	334–566–0142
Randolph	P.O. Box 2490 · Wedowee, AL 36278	205–357–4933	205–357–2790
Russell	P.O. Box 969 · Phenix City, AL 36868	334–298–6426	334–298–0844
St. Clair	129 Fifth Ave. · Ashville, AL 35953	205–594–2120	205–594–2110
Shelby	P.O. Box 467 · Columbiana, AL 35051	205–669–3713	205–669–3714
Sumter	P.O. Box 70 · Livingston, AL 35470	205–652–2731	205–652–9439
Talladega	P.O. Box 755 · Talladega, AL 35161	205–362–1357	205–761–2147
Tallapoosa	125 N. Broadnax St. · Dadeville, AL 36853	205–825–4266	
Tuscaloosa	714 Greensboro Ave. · Tuscaloosa, AL 35401	205–349–3870	
Walker	P.O. Box 1447 · Jasper, AL 35501	205–384–7281	205–384–7005
Washington	P.O. Box 146 · Chantom, AL 36518	334–947–2208	334–947–3677
Wilcox	100 Broad St. · Camden, AL 36726	334–682–4883	334–682–9484
Winston	P.O. Box 147 · Double Springs, AL 35553	205–489–5026	205–489–5135

County Courthouses in Alabama, Addresses

COUNTY RECORDS (GENERAL)

An act of the Mississippi Territory in 1799 created, in each county, a five-man Orphans Court for maintenance of most county records in what became Alabama. This body recorded marriage licenses and bonds; property transfers (including deeds); and probate (estate) documents, including wills, administrations, and guardianships. In 1821, the state of Alabama reduced the Orphans Court from five justices to one justice and transferred maintenance of other county government functions to the newly created four-man county court. An act in 1850 changed the name of the Orphans Court to the Court of Probate, the same title used today.

Other county offices in Alabama maintain public records of historical and genealogical value. In addition to the probate court, the county court survives today as Alabama's boards of county commissioners and county small-claims courts. Major civil and all criminal court actions have been the responsibility of the individual county circuit courts since 1799. The state also operated district (usually one county per district) chancery courts for trying equity cases from 1839 to 1915. County school boards began in 1901, and any surviving school censuses taken by individual school boards can be sought at the individual county school boards.

NOTES ON ACCESSING LOCAL GOVERNMENT RECORDS

Almost any other kind of record can also be found in the courthouses of Alabama, but knowing where to look may prove problematic. Many Alabama counties have special county archives separate from the county offices. The Madison County Archives, for example, is part of the Huntsville Public Library. However, some counties have lost records in courthouse fires and by other means. Sometimes records of residents in "burned out" counties can be found in adjoining counties and even in counties in adjoining states.

The Alabama Department of Archives and History has microfilm of the most important early county records for most counties (see below). This microfilm and other county records can also be identified and borrowed through LDS family history centers. Microfilm of the county records of

Houston, Mobile, and Morgan Counties are not available through either of the above.

Many county records have been published, although often such information as marriage bond data does not appear when marriage licenses are abstracted and published. For an in-depth bibliography and list of local research sources, see Marcia K. Smith Collier, *Alabama County Data and Resources*, 2nd ed., (Titus, Ala.: The Author, 1999). For county records abstracts in periodicals, consult current editions of the *PERiodical Resource Index* (PERSI). A statewide list of Alabama wills is found in Alabama Society Daughters of the American Revolution, *Index to Alabama Wills, 1808–1870* (Montgomery: The Author, 1955).

Many people had no property at the time of death and therefore had no probate. Other people gave away their estates before they died. Sometimes the heirs did not bother with the paperwork. In many instances estate proceedings were never completed. In a few counties, general indexes to estate records were compiled, but for most counties a researcher must check the individual volumes of the estate records. Orphans Court or Court of Probate minute books sometimes contain information not found elsewhere on individual estates. For background on American estate records in general, see Carole Shammas et al., *Inheritance in America from Colonial Times to the Present* (New Brunswick, N.J.: Rutgers University Press, 1997).

Before modern times an estate would sometimes be probated in a county other than where the deceased resided. Deeds and other property records, however, are recorded in the county where the property lay at the time the record was recorded, not necessarily the county where the owner resided or the county where the land lay at the time that the deed was signed (some deeds were recorded as much as fifty years or more, and several county boundary changes, after being signed).

Local Alabama property records can include mortgages, deeds, deeds of gifts, powers of attorney, depositions, and even wills and emancipations recorded in what are usually titled "deed books." In most Alabama counties, the individual volumes are indexed and there is a cumulative index to grantors (direct) and grantees (indirect or reverse) for all of the volumes. However, usually these indexes are only to the deeds and not to the other documents frequently recorded in the deed books. When the property is sold for taxes or debt, the sheriff rather than the owner is usually indexed as the grantor. Some Alabama counties have indexes to deeds by township and range line number, the same numbers used throughout Alabama's history for purposes of designating locations of land. Deeds and other land records were only recorded when the landowner feared that there could be a challenge to a title. For background on land records, see E. Wade Hone, *Land and Property Research in the United States* (Salt Lake City: Ancestry, 1997).

Court records can be difficult to use, although they often contain valuable personal information found nowhere else, such as individual naturalizations (to 1906). The minute books are often not indexed and, in any event, sometimes give the barest details on a case. In an indictment for murder, the date of death of the victim is usually given in the minutes. Except for depositions from witnesses unable to appear in court (interrogatories), recorded testimony from court cases did not usually exist until the 1880s, and then only for cases where death existed as a potential punishment. The court case files, when they survive in local courthouses, are often unorganized and unavailable for use by the public from lack of storage space.

Autauga County

Autauga County was created November 21, 1818, from Montgomery County and originally included parts of today's Chilton and Elmore Counties. It gave land to Cahawba (now Bibb) County on December 13, 1819, and took land from the same on December 13, 1820. It gave land to Shelby County on January 12 and December 28, 1827, and took control over a large unorganized area of east central Alabama (including most or all of present-day Calhoun, Chambers, Clay, Cleburne, Coosa, Randolph, Talladega, and Tallapoosa Counties and part of Elmore) from March 1, 1827, to January 29, 1829. Autauga County gave land to Elmore County (December 1866) and to Baker (now Chilton) County (December 30, 1868, and December 15, 1869). The address of the courthouse is Court and 4th Streets, Prattville, AL 36067. Lands were granted through the St. Stephens (to 1819), Cahaba or Greenville (1819–1866), and Montgomery (1866–1927) land offices; see chapter 11 in this volume, "Federal Land Records."

A number of indexes to county probate records are being prepared for publication and are currently available on computer now at the Autauga County Public Library. Other sources include Larry W. Nobles, *Marriage Records of Autauga County* (Prattville, Autauga Genealogical Society, 1990); and Daniel S. Gray, *Autauga County: The First Hundred Years, 1818–1918* (Prattville; Autauga County Public Library, 1972). For extensive bibliographies, see the sources cited in chapter 2 in this volume, "Internet, Books, Bibliographies, Periodicals, Newspapers, and Manuscripts," but especially Collier, *Alabama County Data and Resources*, 2nd ed.; and Barefield, *Researching in Alabama*, rev. ed. For current addresses of historical societies, web sites, and public libraries, see the Internet web site of the Alabama Department of Archives and History. A county heritage book is being prepared for publication.

Listed below are the records available on microfilm, or as original records, at the Alabama Department of Archives and History. The list comes from the archives' inventories. Some gaps in records and scattered issues of newspapers are not indicated. The archives' newspaper microfilm can be borrowed on interlibrary loan through local public libraries. Specific newspapers are listed at the web site of the Alabama Department of Archives and History. Other records are available at the county courthouse. For other vital records, see the next chapter. Many county records, including some not listed below, can be borrowed on interlibrary loan through LDS family history centers.

> Bonds of administrators, executors, and guardians, 1830–1899
> Chancery Court minutes, 1859–1916
> Complete record, Chancery Court, c. 1872–1904
> Constitution, roll, and minutes, Southern Rights Association, c. 1850–c. 1851
> Cotton mill record, 1908–1915 (Lists children employed at Prattville Cotton Mill, includes many birth dates)
> Deeds and mortgages, c. 1819–1903
> Direct index, Chancery Court, c. 1859–c. 1930
> Fee book, c. 1824–c. 1827
> Fund in Aid of Soldiers Families, 1862–1863
> General index to estates, 1849–c. 1940
> Marriages, 1839–1950
> Military discharges, 1919–1946

Minutes in equity, 1904–1927
Naturalization records, 1905
Newspapers, 1853–1882, 1886–1996
Orphans and Probate Court minutes, 1823–1929
Pensions for Confederate veterans and widows, c. 1900–c. 1920s
Poll tax record, c. 1902–c. 1930
Registration book of voters, 1908, 1910, 1912, 1914, 1918
Reports of probate, 1825–1933
Reverse index, Chancery Court, c. 1859–c. 1930
Roll of Confederate soldiers, c. 1889–c. 1911 (Record of the Association of
    Confederate Veterans of Autauga County, Camp William W. Wadsworth,
    No. 491, United Confederate Veterans)
Vital records (births and deaths, 1908–1916)
Volunteers Aid Fund, 1862–1862
Will records, 1868–1927

Baine County

Baine County was created on December 7, 1866, from Blount, Calhoun, Cherokee, DeKalb, Marshall, and St. Clair Counties. It gave up land or changed boundaries with Blount, DeKalb, Marshall, and St. Clair Counties on February 19, 1867, before being abolished on December 3, 1867. The western part of Baine County was returned to Blount County. Of the rest of it, most of the former Baine County would be used to create Etowah County on December 1, 1868.

Baker County

See Chilton County.

Baldwin County

Baldwin County was created from Washington County, Mississippi Territory, on December 21, 1809, and gained land from Greene County on February 7, 1818. It took land from Conecuh and Monroe Counties on December 13, 1819; lost land during the border adjustment with Mississippi on May 29, 1820; exchanged with Mobile and lost territory to Monroe County on December 16, 1820; gained land from Mobile County on December 21, 1832; and lost land to Escambia and Monroe Counties on December 10, 1868. The address of the courthouse is P.O. Box 1488, Bay Minette, AL 36507. Federal lands were granted through the St. Stephens (to 1867), Mobile (1867–1879), and Montgomery (1879–1927) land offices; see chapter 11 in this volume, "Federal Land Records."

Several books have been published about places, families, and communities in Baldwin County. The county marriages, 1800–1900, have been published, as have the death records for 1886–1894 and deed book A (1809–1820). Other sources include Charles E. Bryant, *The Tensaw Country North of the Ellicott Line, 1800–1860: Baldwin County, Alabama* (Bay Minette: Lavender Press, 1998); and Kay Nuzum, *A History of Baldwin County* (n.p., 1970). For extensive bibliographies, see the sources cited in chapter 2 in this volume, "Internet, Books, Bibliographies, Periodicals, Newspapers, and Manuscripts," but especially Collier, *Alabama County Data and Resources* (2nd ed.), and Barefield, *Researching in Alabama* (rev. ed.). For current addresses of historical societies, web sites, and public libraries, see the Internet web site of the Alabama Department of Archives and History. A county heritage book is being prepared for publication.

Listed below are the records available on microfilm or as original records at the Alabama Department of Archives and History; the list comes from the archives' inventories. Some gaps in records and scattered issues of newspapers are not indicated. The archives' newspaper microfilm can be borrowed on interlibrary loan through local public libraries. Specific newspapers are listed at the web site of the Alabama Department of Archives and History. Other records are available at the county courthouse. For other vital records, see the next chapter. Many county records, including some not listed below, can be borrowed on interlibrary loan through LDS family history centers.

Direct index to Orphans and Probate Court records, 1810–1925
Direct index to deeds, 1905–1935
Reverse index to deeds, 1810–1911
Deed records, 1809–1901
General index to Orphans Court and Probate Court records, 1820–1930
Marriages, 1810–1935
Newspapers, 1896–1996
Orphans and Probate Court records, 1822–1929

Orphans and Probate Court minutes, 1822–1928
Tax assessor, assessment record of personal property, 1849
Vital records (births and deaths, 1886–1919)
Will records, 1809–1909

Barbour County

Barbour County was created from Pike County on December 18, 1832, and lost ground to Henry County (January 17, 1844) and to Bullock County (December 5, 1866) before exchanging territory with Bullock County (February 8, 1867). In later years, Barbour County exchanged small tracts of land with Bullock and Russell Counties. The address of the courthouse is #1 Court Square, Clayton, AL 36106. Lands were granted through the St. Stephens (to 1833), Cahaba or Greenville (1819–1822), Sparta or Elba (1822–1867), and Montgomery (1834–1927) land offices; see chapter 11 in this volume, "Federal Land Records."

Many nineteenth-century marriage records, newspaper abstracts, and census and estate records have been published for Barbour County; also see Helen F. Foley's *1833 State Census for Barbour County, Alabama* (Eufaula: The Author, 1976). Other sources include Anne Kendrick Walker, *Backtracking in Barbour County: A Narrative of the Last Alabama Frontier* (Richmond, Va.: Dietz Press, 1941); and Mattie Thomas Thompson, *History of Barbour County, Alabama* (n.p., 1939). For extensive bibliographies, see the sources cited in chapter 2 in this volume, "Internet, Books, Bibliographies, Periodicals, Newspapers, and Manuscripts," but especially Collier, *Alabama County Data and Resources* (2nd ed.); and Barefield, *Researching in Alabama* (rev. ed.). For current addresses of historical societies, web sites, and public libraries, see the Internet web site of the Alabama Department of Archives and History. A county heritage book is being prepared for publication.

Listed below are the records available on microfilm or as original records at the Alabama Department of Archives and History; the list comes from the archives' inventories. Some gaps in records and scattered issues of newspapers are not indicated. The archives' newspaper microfilm can be borrowed on interlibrary loan through local public libraries. Specific newspapers are listed at the web site of the Alabama Department of Ar-

chives and History. Other records are available at the county courthouse. For other vital records see the next chapter. Many county records, including some not listed below, can be borrowed on interlibrary loan through LDS family history centers.

Administrator's record, 1873–1943
Apprenticeships, 1867–1919
Child labor affidavits, c. 1908–c. 1914
Record of Confederate veterans, (1880s)
Conveyance record, 1874–1882 (contains deeds and mortgages)
Deed record, 1833–1903
Dower record, 1872–1886
Executors and will record, c. 1870s–c. 1899
General index, direct, 1877–c. 1900
General index, reverse, 1877–c. 1900
Guardians record, 1873–1941
Index to estates, wills, petitions, adoptions, bonds, marriage licenses, 1888–c. 1927
Marriages, 1874–1928
Minutes, 1833–1928
Newspapers, 1846–1850, 1869–1994
Orphans and Probate Court records, 1835–1924
Tax abstracts, 1881, 1887, 1890, 1895, 1896
Vital records (births, 1891–1899; births and deaths, 1906–1923)
Alphabetical registration of voters, 1912
Registration book of voters, 1910–1911

Benton County

See Calhoun County.

Bibb County

Created as Cahawba County from Montgomery County on February 7, 1818, Bibb County originally contained a large part of today's Chilton and Shelby Counties. On November 20, 1818, it gained from Dallas and Montgomery Counties while giving up territory to Shelby and Tuscaloosa Counties. On December 13, 1819, Cahawba County gained land from Autauga County and lost land to Perry County. Renamed Bibb County on December 4, 1820, it gave up land to Autauga County nine days later. On December 20, 1820, Bibb County gained from Tuscaloosa County and unorganized territory, while exchanging land with Perry County. It exchanged or gained land from Perry County (December 17, 1821, and January 3, 1828), exchanged ground with Tuscaloosa County (January 15, 1831), gained territory from Shelby County (January 18, 1832), lost land to Baker County (now Chilton County, December 30, 1868), and exchanged land with Shelby County (October 1, 1899, and March 2, 1907). The address of the courthouse is 103 Davidson Drive, Centreville, AL 35042. Lands were granted through the Huntsville (to 1821), St. Stephens (to 1819), Demopolis (1833–1866), Tuscaloosa (1822–1866), Cahaba or Greenville (1819–1866), and Montgomery (1866–1927) land offices; see chapter 11 in this volume, "Federal Land Records."

Several selective local histories have been done on Bibb County subjects as well as a county heritage book. Other records in print include early census and marriage records as well as the cemetery records. For the general history of the county, see Ulysses Huey Abrams, *A History of Early Bibb County, Alabama, 1820–1870* (n.p., 1981); and Rhoda Coleman Ellison, *Bibb County Alabama: The First Hundred Years, 1818–1918* (Tuscaloosa: University of Alabama Press, 1984). For extensive bibliographies, see the sources cited in chapter 2 in this volume, "Internet, Books, Bibliographies, Periodicals, Newspapers, and Manuscripts," but especially Collier, *Alabama County Data and Resources* (2nd ed.); and Barefield, *Researching in Alabama* (rev. ed.). For current addresses of historical societies, web sites, and public libraries, see the Internet web site of the Alabama Department of Archives and History.

Listed below are the records available on microfilm or as original records at the Alabama Department of Archives and History; the list comes from the archives' inventories. Some gaps in records and scattered issues of newspapers are not indicated. The archives' newspaper microfilm can be borrowed on interlibrary loan through local public libraries. Specific newspapers are listed at the web site of the Alabama Department of Archives and History. Other records are available at the county courthouse. For other vital records, see the next chapter. Many county records, including some not listed below, can be borrowed on interlibrary loan through LDS family history centers.

Administrators records and accounts, 1821–1942
Confederate pension records
Deeds and mortgages, 1824–1898
Marriages, 1818–1933
Military discharge record, 1921–1956
Naturalization record/declaration of intention, 1907–1912
Newspapers, 1860, 1879–1996
Orphans and Probate Court records, 1818–1930
Pension record, c. 1905
Record of registered voters, 1920–1951
Tax assessment records, 1851–1858, 1867
Vital records (births and deaths, 1900–1919)
Will records, 1900–1935

Blount County

As created on February 6, 1818, from Montgomery County, Blount County originally included all of the territory of present-day Cullman and most of today's Blount, Jefferson, and Winston Counties, with parts of modern Etowah, Marshall, and Walker Counties. Blount County gave land to Jefferson County in 1819 and to what would later be Hancock (Winston) County in 1822. Land was lost to Morgan County and gained from Morgan and Jackson Counties in 1832. Territory went to the creation of Marshall County in 1836; to Baine County in 1866 (regained in 1867); to Etowah County in 1868; and to Cullman County in 1877, 1887, 1893, and 1901. Minor boundary changes also occurred. The address of the courthouse and county archives is 220 Second Ave., Oneonta, AL 35121. Land was granted through the Huntsville Land Office until 1905, then through the Montgomery Land Office until it closed in 1927; see chapter 11 in this volume, "Federal Land Records."

For this county, census records, 1830–1880, have been published as well as the marriages and some early estate records. The county has two heritage books. The cemetery records were compiled by Elbert Johnston. A census of families of Confederate soldiers has also been published. Another source is Gaylon D. Johnson's *Before the German Settlement of 1873: The Land and*

People That Became Cullman County (Cullman: Gregath Company, 1980). For extensive bibliographies, see the sources cited in chapter 2 in this volume, "Internet, Books, Bibliographies, Periodicals, Newspapers, and Manuscripts," but especially Collier, *Alabama County Data and Resources* (2nd ed.); and Barefield, *Researching in Alabama* (rev. ed.). For current addresses of historical societies, web sites, and public libraries, see the Internet web site of the Alabama Department of Archives and History. Blount County is included in *Alabama Family History and Genealogy News*, published by the North Central Alabama Genealogical Society, Box 13, Cullman, AL 35056–0013. The Northeast Alabama Genealogical Society, P.O. Box 674, Gadsden, AL 35902, publishes *Northeast Alabama Settlers*. Historical and genealogical research files can be found in the county archives in the basement of the courthouse and at the nearby Blount County Museum in Oneonta.

Listed below are the records available on microfilm or as original records at the Alabama Department of Archives and History; the list comes from the archives' inventories. Some gaps in records and scattered issues of newspapers are not indicated. The archives' newspaper microfilm can be borrowed on interlibrary loan through local public libraries. Specific newspapers are listed at the web site of the Alabama Department of Archives and History. Other records are available at the county courthouse in the basement county archives. Many county records, including some not listed below, can be borrowed on interlibrary loan through LDS family history centers. The Family and Regional History Program, Wallace State College, Hanceville, Alabama, and the Birmingham Public Library have microfilm of many of the county records.

> Administrators record, 1870–1916
> Census of Confederate soldiers, 1907
> Index to deeds, 1818–1900
> Direct index to deeds, 1818–1900
> Reverse index to deeds, 1818–1900
> Deed record, 1830–1901
> Dower record, 1874–1926
> Guardians record, 1917–1941
> General record, 1893–1940 (contains miscellaneous filings such as contracts,

ex parte, bonds, and probate matters. Vols. 3 and 4 also contain World
War I military discharges.)
Marriages, 1820–1912
Newspapers, 1879–1995
Orphans and Probate Court minutes, 1820–1933
Partial and final settlement record, 1870–1883
Probate docket and fee book, 1871–1882
Real estate sale record, 1871–1896
Settlement record, 1874–1914
Sale record of personal property, 1870–1900
Vital records (births, 1919–1924; births and deaths, 1905–1912; and deaths,
1914–1924)
Will record, 1872–1933

Bullock County

This county was formed on December 5, 1866, from Barbour, Macon,
Montgomery, and Pike Counties and has only had minor boundary
changes since. The address of the courthouse is 217 N. Prane Street, Union
Springs, AL 36089. Lands were granted through the St. Stephens (to 1819),
Cahaba or Greenville (1819–1866), Sparta or Elba (1822–1867), and Mont-
gomery (1834–1927) land offices; see chapter 11 in this volume, "Federal
Land Records."

For information on this county's past, see Bullock County Historical
Society, *Collections and Recollections of Bullock County History* (n.p.: The
Author, 1977). For extensive bibliographies, see the sources cited in chapter
2 in this volume, "Internet, Books, Bibliographies, Periodicals, Newspapers, and Manuscripts," but especially Collier, *Alabama County Data and
Resources* (2nd ed.); and Barefield, *Researching in Alabama* (rev. ed.). For
current addresses of historical societies, web sites, and public libraries, see
the Internet web site of the Alabama Department of Archives and History.
A county heritage book is being prepared for publication.

Listed below are the records available on microfilm or as original
records at the Alabama Department of Archives and History; the list comes
from the archives' inventories. Some gaps in records and scattered issues
of newspapers are not indicated. The archives' newspaper microfilm can
be borrowed on interlibrary loan through local public libraries. Specific

newspapers are listed at the web site of the Alabama Department of Archives and History. Other records are available at the county courthouse. For other vital records, see the next chapter. Many county records, including some not listed below, can be borrowed on interlibrary loan through LDS family history centers.

> Administrators appointment record, 1867–1872
> Child labor affidavits, 1908
> Deed records, 1867–1908
> Dower record, 1893–1898
> Estate settlement record, 1867–1870
> Executors record, 1867–1886
> Guardians record, 1867–1922
> Land book, 1898–1901
> Land sold for taxes, 1878–1885
> Marriages, 1867–1954
> Newspapers, 1866–1996
> Vital records (births and deaths, 1909–1913; deaths, 1911; births, 1913; births,
>   1920–1935; deaths, 1920–1931)

Butler County

Butler County was created on December 13, 1819. from Conecuh, Dallas, and Monroe Counties. It originally included part of the western areas of today's Crenshaw County. Aside from minor boundary changes, it lost land to the creation of Crenshaw County on November 24, 1866. The address of the courthouse is 700 Court Square, Greenville, AL 36037. Lands were granted through the St. Stephens (to 1819), Cahaba or Greenville (1819–1866), and Montgomery (1866–1927) land offices; see chapter 11 in this volume, "Federal Land Records."

The Birmingham Public Library and some other Alabama libraries have transcripts of Butler County cemetery records. Published sources include cemetery records, an index to probate records, and obituaries. For historical background, see Michael Jackson Daniel, "Red Hills and Piney Woods: A Political History of Butler County, Alabama, in the Nineteenth Century," (Ph.D. diss., University of Alabama, 1985); John Buckner Little, *History of Butler County, Alabama, 1815–1885* (1885; reprint, with index, n.p., 1971). For extensive bibliographies, see the sources cited in chapter 2 in this volume, "Internet, Books, Bibliographies, Periodicals, Newspapers, and Manuscripts," but especially Collier, *Alabama County Data and Resources* (2nd ed.); and Barefield, *Researching in Alabama* (rev. ed.). For current addresses of historical societies, web sites, and public libraries, see the Internet web site of the Alabama Department of Archives and History. A county heritage book is being prepared for publication.

Listed below are the records available on microfilm or as original records at the Alabama Department of Archives and History; the list comes from the archives' inventories. Some gaps in records and scattered issues of newspapers are not indicated. The archives' newspaper microfilm can be borrowed on interlibrary loan through local public libraries. Specific newspapers are listed at the web site of the Alabama Department of Archives and History. Other records are available at the county courthouse. For other vital records, see the next chapter. Many county records, including some not listed below, can be borrowed on interlibrary loan through LDS family history centers.

> Estate record, 1853–1929
> Deed and mortgage record, c. 1853–1904
> Marriages, 1853–1928
> Newspapers, 1859–1861, 1866–1995
> Probate minutes, 1853–c. 1933
> Tax assessment record for personal property, 1849
> Tract book, 1817–1850s
> Sixteenth section lands, c. 1840–1853 (includes school student lists)
> Vital records: births, 1886–1891; births and deaths, 1894–1920
> Lists of registered voters, c. 1920–c. 1934
> Will record, 1880–1936

Cahawba County

See Bibb County.

Calhoun County

Created on December 18, 1832, as Benton County, the original boundaries of what was renamed Calhoun County included today's Calhoun County and parts of modern Cleburne, Etowah, and Talladega Counties.

On December 23, 1836, the new county gained land from Cherokee County but lost land to Talladega County. Aside from many minor border changes, Calhoun County gave up area to the creation of Cleburne County on December 6, 1866, and to Etowah County on December 1, 1868. The address of the courthouse is 1702 Noble Street, Suite 103, Anniston, AL 36201. Lands were granted through the Montevallo or Mardisville Land Office until 1872; the Huntsville Land Office, 1872–1905; and the Montgomery Land Office, 1872–1927; see chapter 11 in this volume, "Federal Land Records."

For Calhoun County, cemetery, census, and marriage records as well as a county heritage book have been published. For extensive bibliographies, see the sources cited in chapter 2 in this volume, "Internet, Books, Bibliographies, Periodicals, Newspapers, and Manuscripts," but especially Collier, *Alabama County Data and Resources* (2nd ed.); and Barefield, *Researching in Alabama* (rev. ed.). For current addresses of historical societies, web sites, and public libraries, see the Internet web site of the Alabama Department of Archives and History.

Special sources exist for Calhoun County research. The Public Library of Anniston, 108 E. 10th Street, Anniston, AL 36201, has funeral notices (1946–1998); files on families, individuals, and subjects; photographs; newspapers (1900–); Anniston city directories (1887–); and private manuscript collections, as well as an extensive genealogical book collection. The Northeast Alabama Genealogical Society, P.O. Box 674, Gadsden, AL 35902, publishes *Northeast Alabama Settlers*.

Listed below are the records available on microfilm or as original records at the Alabama Department of Archives and History; the list comes from the archives' inventories. Some gaps in records and scattered issues of newspapers are not indicated. The archives' newspaper microfilm can be borrowed on interlibrary loan through local public libraries. Specific newspapers are listed at the web site of the Alabama Department of Archives and History. Other records are available at the county courthouse. For other vital records, see the next chapter. Many county records, including some not listed below, can be borrowed on interlibrary loan through LDS family history centers.

> Administrator's record, 1871–1927
> Census, 1880

Deeds and mortgages, 1886–1901
Estate case files, 1848–1873
Executor's record, 1872–1927
Guardians' record, 1871–1927
Newspapers, 1851–1856, 1884–1885, 1887–1899, 1904–1996
Probate records, 1879–1929
Probate minutes, 1864–1931
Record of election results, 1974–1976
Tax assessment book, 1893–1894
Lists of registered voters, 1906–1942
Will record, 1891–1936

Chambers County

Created from Montgomery and Shelby Counties on December 18, 1832, this county gave land to the creation of Lee County on December 5, 1866, and had minor boundary changes afterwards. The address of the courthouse is #2 LaFayette St., LaFayette, AL 36862. Lands were granted through the Montgomery Land Office (1834–1927); see chapter 11 in this volume, "Federal Land Records."

The tract book, some cemetery records, and marriages, as well as a county heritage book, have been published for this county. John Peavy Wright has published the 1840, 1850, and 1860 federal censuses with genealogical notes as *The People of Chambers County*. Another source is Bobby L. Lindsey's *"The Reason for the Tears": A History of Chambers County, Alabama, 1832–1900* (West Point, Ga.: The Author, 1971). For extensive bibliographies, see the sources cited in chapter 2 in this volume, "Internet, Books, Bibliographies, Periodicals, Newspapers, and Manuscripts," but especially Collier, *Alabama County Data and Resources* (2nd ed.); and Barefield, *Researching in Alabama* (rev. ed.). For current addresses of historical societies, web sites, and public libraries, see the Internet web site of the Alabama Department of Archives and History. The Cobb Memorial Library, 3419 20th Avenue, Valley, AL 36854, has local newspapers (1916–), city directories (1965–), maps, cemetery records, genealogical and biographical files, and obituaries (1988–). They also have some resources for research in neighboring Troup County, Georgia. Other nearby libraries with Chambers County holdings include the Troup County Archives in LaGrange,

Georgia; the Bradley Library in Columbus, Georgia; Chattahoochee Valley
Community College in Phenix City, Alabama; and Auburn University Special Collections and Archives.

Listed below are the records available on microfilm or as original records at the Alabama Department of Archives and History; the list comes
from the archives' inventories. Some gaps in records and scattered issues
of newspapers are not indicated. The archives' newspaper microfilm can
be borrowed on interlibrary loan through local public libraries. Specific
newspapers are listed at the web site of the Alabama Department of Archives and History. Other records are available at the county courthouse.
For other vital records, see the next chapter. Many county records, including some not listed below, can be borrowed on interlibrary loan through
LDS family history centers. The Cobb Memorial Archives, 3419 20th Avenue, Valley, AL 36854, collects historical material on the Chambers County
area.

> Administrator's record, 1923–1926
> Appraisement record, 1871–1907
> Chattel mortgage record, 1839–1945
> Confederate pension records, 1876–1898
> Deeds and mortgages, 1834–1899
> Estate case files, 1840–1860
> Estate records, 1834–1846 (includes Native American landholders)
> Executor's record, 1871–1927
> Fee book, 1836–1837
> Inventory record, 1834–1924
> Marriages, 1838–1950 (some years missing)
> Military discharge records, 1918–1919
> Miscellaneous court records:
>> Applications for bonds for tavern licenses, 1850–1886
>> Business licenses issued, 1876–1877
>> Special election for justice of the peace, 1860
>> Results and voters list, 1860
>> Fee book, 1867
>> Orphans Court records, 1833–1842
>> Vouchers, 1819–1893
> Miscellaneous records, 1907–1927
> Newspapers, 1843, 1873–1878, 1885–1892, 1894–1895, 1897, 1899, 1921–1925,
>   1938–1996

Orphans Court records, 1833–1856
Probate Court minutes, 1850–1926
Settlement record, 1841–1926
Tax assessment records, 1842, 1920–1927
Voter register, 1912
Will records, 1895–1927

Cherokee County

Cherokee County was created from Jackson, Benton (Calhoun), and St. Clair Counties on January 6, 1836. It lost land to DeKalb County on January 16, 1844, and to the creation of Etowah County on December 1, 1868. Minor changes in boundaries have occurred over the years. The address of the courthouse is 100 Maine Street, Centre, AL 35960. Lands were granted through the Montevallo or Mardisville Land Office until 1872, then the Huntsville Land Office to 1905, and finally through the Montgomery Land Office until it closed in 1927; see chapter 11 in this volume, "Federal Land Records."

Marriages have been published for 1821 to 1898, and cemetery and census records as well, for Cherokee County. Several books on this county's history have been published, including Mrs. Frank Ross Stewart's five-volume *Cherokee County History, 1836–1956*. Robert P. Lindley has published *Cherokee County, Alabama, Information Abstracted from the Jacksonville Republican, 1837–1860* (n.p., 1997) as well as a county heritage book. For extensive bibliographies, see the sources cited in chapter 2 in this volume, "Internet, Books, Bibliographies, Periodicals, Newspapers, and Manuscripts," but especially Collier, *Alabama County Data and Resources* (2nd ed.); and Barefield, *Researching in Alabama* (rev. ed.). For current addresses of historical societies, web sites, and public libraries, see the Internet web site of the Alabama Department of Archives and History.

Some special resources for Cherokee County exist. The Cherokee County Public Library, 310 Mary Street, Centre, AL 35960, has local newspapers and genealogical files. The Northeast Alabama Genealogical Society, P.O. Box 674, Gadsden, AL 35902, publishes *Northeast Alabama Settlers*. The Cherokee County Genealogical Society, Box 90, Spring Garden, AL 36275, publishes a newsletter.

Listed below are the records available on microfilm or as original records at the Alabama Department of Archives and History; the list comes from the archives' inventories. Some gaps in records and scattered issues of newspapers are not indicated. The archives' newspaper microfilm can be borrowed on interlibrary loan through local public libraries. Specific newspapers are listed at the web site of the Alabama Department of Archives and History. Other records are available at the county courthouse. For other vital records, see the next chapter. Many county records, including some not listed below, can be borrowed on interlibrary loan through LDS family history centers.

> Deed records, 1892–1901
> Marriages, 1928–1952
> Military discharge records, 1919–1959
> Newspapers, 1882–1883, 1887–1990
> Probate minutes, 1882–1929
> Probate records, 1885–1932
> Lists of registered voters, 1919–1920
> Will records, 1948–1952

Chilton County

As Baker County, it was created from Autauga, Bibb, Dallas, and Shelby Counties on December 30, 1868, but lost territory to Shelby County in 1873. It was renamed Chilton County on December 17, 1874, and gained ground from Dallas County in 1875. The address of the courthouse is 100 Maine Street, Centre, AL 35960. Lands were granted through the Huntsville (to 1821), St. Stephens (to 1819), Cahaba or Greenville (1819–1866), Tuscaloosa (1822–1866), Demopolis (1833–1866), and Montgomery (1866–1927) land offices; see chapter 11 in this volume, "Federal Land Records."

Among the county records in print for Chilton County there are cemetery, census, Confederate service, death (1908–1919), and newspaper abstracts (1898–1945). A county heritage book has been done. Other sources include Cecil Little, *Chilton County, Alabama: Index to Probate Court Records, Abstracts of County Newspapers, County Confederate Veterans Book 1, 1868–1924* (Clanton: The Author, 1990); and T. E. Wyatt, *Chilton County and Her People* (Montevallo, Ala.: The Author, 1976). For extensive bibliographies, see the sources cited in chapter 2 in this volume, "Internet, Books, Bibliographies, Periodicals, Newspapers, and Manuscripts," but especially Collier, *Alabama County Data and Resources* (2nd ed.); and Barefield, *Researching in Alabama* (rev. ed.). For current addresses of historical societies, web sites, and public libraries, see the Internet web site of the Alabama Department of Archives and History. For research on Chilton County, see Chilton County Historical Society and Archives, Chilton-Clanton Public Library, P.O. Box 644, Clanton, AL 35045.

Listed below are the records available on microfilm or as original records at the Alabama Department of Archives and History; the list comes from the archives' inventories. Some gaps in records and scattered issues of newspapers are not indicated. The archives' newspaper microfilm can be borrowed on interlibrary loan through local public libraries. Specific newspapers are listed at the web site of the Alabama Department of Archives and History. Other records are available at the county courthouse. For other vital records, see the next chapter. Many county records, including some not listed below, can be borrowed on interlibrary loan through LDS family history centers.

> Administrators' record, 1870–1906
> Deed records, 1888–1902
> Dower record, 1874–1878
> Estate record/minutes of Probate Court, 1870–1884
> Executors' record, 1870–1874
> Exemption record to widows and orphans, 1890–1901
> Final settlement record, 1879–1904
> Guardians' records, 1871–1904
> Inventory and appraisement record, 1871–1903
> Military discharge record, 1919–1946
> Minutes Probate Court/Probate Court record, 1881–1928
> Miscellaneous records, 1916–1946
> Newspapers, 1893, 1895, 1897–1912, 1920–1994
> Partial settlement record, 1870–1903
> Poll tax record, 1901–c. 1940s
> Record of pensions, 1908
> Will record, 1921–1940

Choctaw County

Choctaw County was created on December 29, 1847, from Sumter and Washington Counties. The address of the courthouse is 117 S. Mulberry, Suite 9, Butler, AL 36904. Lands were granted through the St. Stephens (to 1833), Demopolis (1833–1866), and Montgomery (1866–1927) land offices; see chapter 11 in this volume, "Federal Land Records."

This county's cemetery records have been published; also see Ann Harwell Gay, *Choctaw Names and Notes* (Meridian, Miss.: The Author, 1993); and Choctaw County Historical Society, *Church Histories of Choctaw County, Alabama* (n.p., 1980). For extensive bibliographies, see the sources cited in chapter 2 in this volume, "Internet, Books, Bibliographies, Periodicals, Newspapers, and Manuscripts," but especially Collier, *Alabama County Data and Resources* (2nd ed.); and Barefield, *Researching in Alabama* (rev. ed.). For current addresses of historical societies, web sites, and public libraries, see the Internet web site of the Alabama Department of Archives and History. A county heritage book is being prepared for publication. The Choctaw County Public Library, 124 N. Academy Ave., Butler, AL 36904, has locally oriented collections of newspapers (1868–), manuscript collections, and files on individuals, families, and subjects. Other materials are found with the Choctaw County Historical Society in Butler and the Choctaw County Museum in Gilbertown.

Listed below are the records available on microfilm or as original records at the Alabama Department of Archives and History; the list comes from the archives' inventories. Some gaps in records and scattered issues of newspapers are not indicated. The archives' newspaper microfilm can be borrowed on interlibrary loan through local public libraries. Specific newspapers are listed at the web site of the Alabama Department of Archives and History. Other records are available at the county courthouse. For other vital records, see the next chapter. Many county records, including some not listed below, can be borrowed on interlibrary loan through LDS family history centers.

> Census record, 1880
> Deed record, 1871–1901
> Guardian's record, 1903–1927

Inventory record, 1871–1935
Marriages, 1871–1930
Military record, 1917
Newspapers, 1870–1873, 1876–1882, 1885–1886, 1890–1894, 1896, 1898–1995
Probate minutes, 1871–1932
Tax assessment record, 1849
Vital records (births and deaths, 1910?–1919)
Will record, 1871–1922

Claiborne County, Mississippi Territory

This county, created January 27, 1802, extended across today's central Alabama and Mississippi to Georgia, until the overlap with Washington County was clarified in 1807.

Clarke County

The original Clarke County was created from Washington County on December 10, 1812. It gained territory from Monroe and Wilcox Counties on January 26, 1829. The address of the courthouse is P.O. Box 548, Grove Hill, AL 36451. Lands were granted through the St. Stephens (to 1867), Demopolis (1833–1866), Tuscaloosa (1822–1866), Cahaba or Greenville (1819–1866), and Montgomery (1866–1927) land offices; see chapter 11 in this volume, "Federal Land Records."

Marriages and other records are found in Marilyn Davis Barefield's *Clarke County, Alabama, Records, 1814–1885.* (Greenville, S.C.: Southern Historical Press, 1983). The several histories of Clarke County include T. H. Ball, *Clarke County, Alabama and Its Surroundings* (Grove Hill, Ala.: The Author, 1882); John Simpson Graham, *History of Clarke County* (Birmingham, Ala.: Birmingham Printing Company, 1923); and Clarke County Historical Society, *Historical Sketches of Clarke County, Alabama* (Huntsville: Strode, 1977). A county heritage book is being prepared for publication. For extensive bibliographies, see the sources cited in chapter 2 in this volume, "Internet, Books, Bibliographies, Periodicals, Newspapers, and Manuscripts," but especially Collier, *Alabama County Data and Resources* (2nd ed.); and Barefield, *Researching in Alabama* (rev. ed.). For current addresses of historical societies, web sites, and public libraries, see the Internet web site of the Alabama Department of Archives and History. The Clarke County Historical Society, Box 789, Grove Hill, AL 36459, publishes a quarterly.

Listed below are the records available on microfilm or as original records at the Alabama Department of Archives and History; the list comes from the archives' inventories. Some gaps in records and scattered issues of newspapers are not indicated. The archives' newspaper microfilm can be borrowed on interlibrary loan through local public libraries. Specific newspapers are listed at the web site of the Alabama Department of Archives and History. Other records are available at the county courthouse. For other vital records, see the next chapter. Many county records, including some not listed below, can be borrowed on interlibrary loan through LDS family history centers.

> Cemetery records, 1840–1977 (Grove Hill Cemetery)
> Deed records, 1814–1883
> Deeds and mortgages, 1883–1901
> Direct and reverse indexes to records, 1820–1902 (indexes to deeds, mortgages, deeds of trust, gifts, title bonds, patents, and division of lands)
> Election officer warrants, 1945–1946
> Marriages, 1909–1916
> Newspapers, 1836–1837, 1845–1846, 1850, 1852, 1854, 1856–1994
> Plat books, 1897–1909, 1910, 1914
> Poll tax record, 1897–1913
> Probate and Orphans Court minutes, 1824–1928
> Probate records, 1876–1928
> Sheriffs' jail registers, 1871–1939
> Soldiers and sailors discharge records, 1926–1943
> Vital records (births and deaths 1914–1919)

Clay County

Created December 7, 1866, from Randolph and Talladega Counties, Clay County exchanged land repeatedly with Talladega County, 1867–1894. The address of the courthouse is P.O. Box 1120, Ashland, AL 36251. Lands were granted through the Montevallo or Mardisville Land Office until 1905 and then through the Montgomery Land Office until it closed in 1927; see chapter 11 in this volume, "Federal Land Records."

Marriage records, Confederate records, and cemetery inscriptions, as well as the indexes to the 1870 and 1880 censuses, have been published for Clay County. This county also has some social-community histories as well as a county heritage book. For extensive bibliographies, see the sources cited in chapter 2 in this volume, "Internet, Books, Bibliographies, Periodicals, Newspapers, and Manuscripts," but especially Collier, *Alabama County Data and Resources* (2nd ed.); and Barefield, *Researching in Alabama* (rev. ed.). For current addresses of historical societies, web sites, and public libraries, see the Internet web site of the Alabama Department of Archives and History.

The locally oriented research resources include the Ashland City Public Library, P.O. Box 296, Ashland, AL 36251. The Northeast Alabama Genealogical Society, P.O. Box 674, Gadsden, AL 35902, publishes *Northeast Alabama Settlers.*

Listed below are the records available on microfilm or as original records at the Alabama Department of Archives and History; the list comes from the archives' inventories. Some gaps in records and scattered issues of newspapers are not indicated. The archives' newspaper microfilm can be borrowed on interlibrary loan through local public libraries. Specific newspapers are listed at the web site of the Alabama Department of Archives and History. Other records are available at the county courthouse. For other vital records, see the next chapter. Many county records, including some not listed below, can be borrowed on interlibrary loan through LDS family history centers.

Applications for relief, 1893–1898
Census of Confederate veterans, 1907
Confederate pension record, 1922
Deed records, 1875–1908
Inventories and appraisements, 1879–1895
Lists of registered voters, 1906–1936
Marriages, 1872–1950
Newspapers, 1878–1994
Probate minutes, 1876–1899
Probate records, 1865–1875
Vital records (births, 1902–1920; deaths, 1920–1940)
Will records, 1867–1944

Cleburne County

Cleburne County was created from Calhoun, Randolph, and Talladega Counties on December 6, 1866. It lost land on the southwest end of the county to Talladega County on February 14, 1867. There were many minor boundary changes. The address of the courthouse is 406 Victory Street, Heflin, AL 36264. Lands were granted through the Montevallo or Mardis-ville Land Office until 1872; Huntsville Land Office, 1872–1905; and the Montgomery Land Office, 1872–1927; see chapter 11 in this volume, "Federal Land Records."

Wills and inventories (1868–1884), cemetery records, census records indexes (1870 and 1880), and Confederate sources have been published for this county. Historical material has been collected and published by Mrs. Frank Ross Stewart in *Alabama's Cleburne County*, 2 vols. (Centre, Ala.: Stewart University Press, 1983), as well as a county heritage book. For extensive bibliographies, see the sources cited in chapter 2 in this volume, "Internet, Books, Bibliographies, Periodicals, Newspapers, and Manuscripts," but especially Collier, *Alabama County Data and Resources* (2nd ed.); and Barefield, *Researching in Alabama* (rev. ed.). For current addresses of historical societies, web sites, and public libraries, see the Internet web site of the Alabama Department of Archives and History.

Listed below are the records available on microfilm or as original records at the Alabama Department of Archives and History; the list comes from the archives' inventories. Some gaps in records and scattered issues of newspapers are not indicated. The archives' newspaper microfilm can be borrowed on interlibrary loan through local public libraries. Specific newspapers are listed at the web site of the Alabama Department of Archives and History. Other records are available at the county courthouse. For other vital records, see the next chapter. Many county records, including some not listed below, can be borrowed on interlibrary loan through LDS family history centers.

Deed records, 1884–1902
Deeds and mortgages, 1881–1884
Register of deeds, 1867–1877
Marriages, 1915–1954

Newspapers, 1891–1995
Probate minutes, 1869–1944
Vital records (births, 1913–1916; deaths, 1913–1921)
Will records, 1906–1937
Wills and inventories, 1884–1910

Coffee County

Created from Dale County on December 29, 1841, this county lost land to Crenshaw County in 1866 and to the creation of Geneva County in 1866. The address of the courthouse is 230 N. Court St., Elba, AL 36323. Lands were granted through the St. Stephens (to 1833), Cahaba or Greenville (1819–1866), Sparta or Elba (1822–1867), and Montgomery (1866–1927) land offices; see chapter 11 in this volume, "Federal Land Records."

Cemetery and census records have been published for this county; also see Fred S. Watson's *Coffee Grounds: A History of Coffee County, Alabama, 1841–1970* (Anniston: The Author, 1970). A county heritage book is being prepared for publication. For extensive bibliographies, see the sources cited in chapter 2 in this volume, "Internet, Books, Bibliographies, Periodicals, Newspapers, and Manuscripts," but especially Collier, *Alabama County Data and Resources* (2nd ed.); and Barefield, *Researching in Alabama* (rev. ed.). For current addresses of historical societies, web sites, and public libraries, see the Internet web site of the Alabama Department of Archives and History. The Pea River Historical and Genealogical Society, P.O. Box 310628, Enterprise, AL 36331-0628, publishes *Pea River Trails*.

Listed below are the records available on microfilm or as original records at the Alabama Department of Archives and History; the list comes from the archives' inventories. Some gaps in records and scattered issues of newspapers are not indicated. The archives' newspaper microfilm can be borrowed on interlibrary loan through local public libraries. Specific newspapers are listed at the web site of the Alabama Department of Archives and History. Other records are available at the county courthouse. For other vital records, see the next chapter. Many county records, including some not listed below, can be borrowed on interlibrary loan through LDS family history centers.

Deeds and mortgages, 1851–1900
Inventory record, 1860–1906

Lists of registered voters, 1908, 1912–1914, 1920, 1926
Marriages, 1877–1933
Military discharge record, 1919–1953
Newspapers, 1901–1919, 1921–1996
Probate minutes (Elba Courthouse), 1861–1928
Vital records (births, 1904–1916; deaths, 1908–1916; births and deaths, 1916–
    1919; deaths, 1926–1927)
Will record, 1908–1937

Colbert County

Created from Franklin County on February 6, 1867, it was abolished on
November 29, 1867, and recreated on January 24, 1870. It gained land from
Lawrence County and lost territory to Franklin County in 1895. The address of the courthouse is 201 N. Main St., Tuscumbia, AL 35674. Land was
granted through the Huntsville Land Office until 1905, then through the
Montgomery Land Office until it closed in 1927; see chapter 11 in this volume, "Federal Land Records."

The county tract book and a county heritage book have been published;
also see R. L. James, *Colbertians: A History of Colbert County . . . before 1875*
(Florence: Natchez Trace Genealogical Society, 1980); and Nina Leftwich,
Two Hundred Years at Muscle Shoals . . . 1700–1900 (Tuscumbia: The Author, 1935). Another source for the county's history is Sandra McGrady
Sockwell's "The Place Names of Colbert and Lauderdale Counties, Alabama" (Ph.D. diss., University of Alabama, 1985). For extensive bibliographies, see the sources cited in chapter 2 in this volume, "Internet, Books,
Bibliographies, Periodicals, Newspapers, and Manuscripts," but especially
Collier, *Alabama County Data and Resources* (2nd ed.); and Barefield, *Researching in Alabama* (rev. ed.).

Several journals cover the history of this county. They include that of
the Tennessee Valley Historical Society, P.O. Box 149, Sheffield, AL 35660;
Tennessee Valley Genealogical Society, P.O. Box 1568, Huntsville, AL 35807;
and Natchez Trace Genealogical Society, Box 420, Florence, AL 35360. For
current addresses of historical societies, web sites, and public libraries, see
the Internet web site of the Alabama Department of Archives and History.

Listed below are the records available on microfilm or as original records at the Alabama Department of Archives and History; the list comes from the archives' inventories. Some gaps in records and scattered issues of newspapers are not indicated. The archives' newspaper microfilm can be borrowed on interlibrary loan through local public libraries. Specific newspapers are listed at the web site of the Alabama Department of Archives and History. Other records are available at the county courthouse. For other vital records, see the next chapter. Many county records, including some not listed below, can be borrowed on interlibrary loan through LDS family history centers.

> Administration and guardians' records, 1877–1890
> Deed records, 1887–1900
> Final record, 1881–1925
> Guardian and administrators bonds, 1906–1934
> Inventory record, 1893–1919
> Marriages, 1910–1963
> Military discharge record, 1919–1951
> Mortgages and liens, 1874–1900
> Newspapers, 1824–1827, 1836–1838, 1840–1842, 1872–1883, 1884–1885, 1889–1995
> Petitions and applications, 1889–1930
> Probate minutes, 1890–1930
> Wills, 1861–1939

Conecuh County

Created on February 13, 1818, from Monroe County, Conecuh County originally covered most of modern southern Alabama, the area east of present-day Monroe County and south of modern Montgomery County. In 1819, it lost land to Baldwin, Butler, and Henry Counties. Conecuh County also lost a large amount of territory to the creation of Escambia County in 1868 but gained some area from Covington County in 1874. The address of the courthouse is P.O. Box 347, Evergreen, AL 36401. Lands were granted through the St. Stephens (to 1833), Cahaba or Greenville (1819–1866), Sparta or Elba (1822–1867), and Montgomery (1866–1927) land offices; see chapter 11 in this volume, "Federal Land Records."

Among the Conecuh County records in print there are cemetery records, the 1818 tax list, the 1866 state census, and the 1870 federal census.

Other sources include Benjamin Franklin Riley, *History of Conecuh County, Alabama* (1881, reprint, with index, Blue Hill, Maine: Weekly Packet, 1964); and Mary E. Brantley, *Early Settlers along the Old Federal Road in Monroe and Conecuh Counties, Alabama* (Atmore: The Author, 1976). For extensive bibliographies, see the sources cited in chapter 2 in this volume, "Internet, Books, Bibliographies, Periodicals, Newspapers, and Manuscripts," but especially Collier, *Alabama County Data and Resources* (2nd ed.); and Barefield, *Researching in Alabama* (rev. ed.). The Evergreen-Conecuh Public Library, 201 Park St., Evergreen, AL 36401, does limited genealogical research. A county heritage book is being prepared for publication.

Listed below are the records available on microfilm or as original records at the Alabama Department of Archives and History; the list comes from the archives' inventories. Some gaps in records and scattered issues of newspapers are not indicated. The archives' newspaper microfilm can be borrowed on interlibrary loan through local public libraries. Specific newspapers are listed at the web site of the Alabama Department of Archives and History. Other records are available at the county courthouse. For other vital records, see the next chapter. Many county records, including some not listed below, can be borrowed on interlibrary loan through LDS family history centers.

> Administrators' record, 1881–c. 1892
> Alphabetical registration of voters, 1908, 1910, 1912, 1914, 1915–1916
> Chancery court minutes, 1902–1928
> Chancery court, final record, 1881–1925
> Deed records, 1866–1903
> Dower record, 1872–1883
> Executors' record, 1875–1916
> Final settlement record, 1871–1916
> Guardians' record, 1883–1918
> Marriages, 1866–1924
> Military discharge record, 1919–c. 1940s
> Newspapers, 1880–1888, 1892–1996
> Pension register, c. 1905–c. 1915
> Poll tax record, c. 1920–c. 1932
> Probate court minutes, 1900–1932
> Probate inventory record, 1867–1916

Probate order book, 1866–c. 1931
Tax assessment record, 1819
Vital records (deaths, 1881–1889; births, 1887–1889; deaths, 1895–1930; births, 1920–1933)

Coosa County

Coosa County was created on December 18, 1832, from Montgomery and Shelby Counties and gave significant territory to the creation of Elmore County in 1866. The address of the courthouse is P.O. Box 218, Rockford, AL 35136. Lands were granted through the Montgomery Land Office (1834–1927); see chapter 11 in this volume, "Federal Land Records."

For this county, the early wills, administrations, and marriage records have been published, as have the cemetery records. Other sources for research include Grover Eugene Pike, *Coosa County Cousins* (Birmingham: The Author, 1987); and George E. Brewer, *History of Coosa County* (Wetumpka: Wetumpka Printers, 1955). For extensive bibliographies, see the sources cited in chapter 2 in this volume, "Internet, Books, Bibliographies, Periodicals, Newspapers, and Manuscripts," but especially Collier, *Alabama County Data and Resources* (2nd ed.); and Barefield, *Researching in Alabama* (rev. ed.). A county heritage book has been published. The Coosa County Public Library, P.O. Box 128, Rockford, AL 35136, has genealogical vertical files; and the Coosa County Historical Society, Box 5, Rockford, AL 35156, publishes *Coosa Heritage.*

Listed below are the records available on microfilm or as original records at the Alabama Department of Archives and History; the list comes from the archives' inventories. Some gaps in records and scattered issues of newspapers are not indicated. The archives' newspaper microfilm can be borrowed on interlibrary loan through local public libraries. Specific newspapers are listed at the web site of the Alabama Department of Archives and History. Other records are available at the county courthouse. For other vital records, see the next chapter. Many county records, including some not listed below, can be borrowed on interlibrary loan through LDS family history centers.

Accounts, inventories, appraisements, c. 1842–c. 1897
Deed record, 1834–1904

Deed and mortgage record, 1881–1887
Index to Orphans Court record, 1834–1858
List of registered voters, 1908–1910, 1912–c. 1916
Miscellaneous records, 1909–1937
Newspapers, 1905–1921, 1930–1981
Orphans Court minutes, 1842–1855
Pension record, c. 1902–c. 1910
Probate Court minutes, 1855–c. 1928
Vital records (births, 1920–1945; deaths, 1937–?)
Will book, c. 1883–c. 1939

Cotaco County

See Morgan County.

Covington County

Created on December 7, 1821, from Henry County, the county gave land to the creation of Dale County in 1825 and to the creation of Crenshaw County in 1866. There were many minor boundary changes and it was briefly renamed Jones County in 1868. The address of the courthouse is Court Square, Andalusia, AL 36420. Lands were granted through the St. Stephens (to 1833), Cahaba or Greenville (1819–1866), Sparta or Elba (1822–1867), and Montgomery (1866–1927) land offices. See chapter 11 in this volume, "Federal Land Records"; and Wyley Donald Ward, *Original Land Sales and Grants in Covington County, Alabama* (Spartanburg, S.C.: Reprint Company, 1991).

The cemetery and census records for 1850 and 1860 have been published for Covington County. For other sources, see Wyley Donald Ward, *Early History of Covington County, Alabama, 1821–1871* (Huntsville, Ala.: The Author, 1976); and George Sidney Waits, *From the Halls of Montezuma: Sketches of Early Covington County and Andalusia, Alabama History* (Andalusia: The Author, 1991). For extensive bibliographies, see the sources cited in chapter 2 in this volume, "Internet, Books, Bibliographies, Periodicals, Newspapers, and Manuscripts," but especially Collier, *Alabama County Data and Resources* (2nd ed.); and Barefield, *Researching in Alabama* (rev. ed.). The Andalusia Public Library, 212 Three Notch Street, Andalusia, AL

36420, has newspapers (1895–), Andalusia city directories, and files on families, individuals, and subjects. The Covington County Historical Society, Box 1582, Andalusia, AL 36420, publishes a newsletter. A county heritage book is being prepared for publication.

Listed below are the records available on microfilm or as original records at the Alabama Department of Archives and History; the list comes from the archives' inventories. Some gaps in records and scattered issues of newspapers are not indicated. The archives' newspaper microfilm can be borrowed on interlibrary loan through local public libraries. Specific newspapers are listed at the web site of the Alabama Department of Archives and History. Other records are available at the county courthouse. For other vital records, see the next chapter. Many county records, including some not listed below, can be borrowed on interlibrary loan through LDS family history centers.

> Deed records, 1881–1902
> General index to estates, wills, c. 1896–1890
> Marriages, 1895–1931
> Military discharge record, c. 1932–c. 1950
> Newspapers, 1889–1897, 1901–1996
> Probate minutes, 1895–c. 1928
> Tract book, c. 1820s–c. 1940s
> Record of wills, 1896–1899
> Wills and deeds, 1882–c. 1895
> Vital records (births, 1909–1913; deaths, 1938–1941)
> List of registered voters, c. 1900–1901, 1902, 1903, 1904, 1910

Crenshaw County

Crenshaw County was created from Butler, Coffee, Covington, Lowndes, and Pike Counties on November 24, 1866. The address of the courthouse is 301 S. Glenwood Ave., Luverne, AL 36049. Lands were granted through the St. Stephens (to 1819), Cahaba or Greenville (1819–1866), and Montgomery (1866–1927) land offices; see chapter 11 in this volume, "Federal Land Records."

Listed below are the records available on microfilm at the Alabama Department of Archives and History; the list comes from the archives' inventories. Some gaps in records and scattered issues of newspapers are not indicated. The archives' newspaper microfilm can be borrowed on inter-library loan through local public libraries. Specific newspapers are listed at the web site of the Alabama Department of Archives and History. Other records are available at the county courthouse. For other vital records, see the next chapter. Many county records, including some not listed below, can be borrowed on interlibrary loan through LDS family history centers.

For extensive bibliographies, see the sources cited in chapter 2 in this volume, "Internet, Books, Bibliographies, Periodicals, Newspapers, and Manuscripts," but especially Collier, *Alabama County Data and Resources* (2nd ed.); and Barefield, *Researching in Alabama* (rev. ed.). The Crenshaw County Historical Society, Box 633, Luverne, AL 36049-0633, publishes a quarterly; and the Luverne Public Library, 300 E. 3rd Street, Luverne, AL 36049, has a genealogy room. A county heritage book is being prepared for publication.

> Administrators record, 1870–1930
> Deed record, 1868–1903
> Dower record, 1873–c. 1891
> Executors record, 1872–1917
> Final settlement record, 1883–1927
> Guardians record, 1871–1924
> Inventory record, c. 1868–1906
> Marriages, 1867–1936
> Newspapers, 1890–1894, 1897–1991
> Partial settlement record, 1871–1904
> Petition book (estates), 1867–1874
> Probate Court minutes, 1875–1886
> Probate docket, 1886–1930
> Probate docket and fee books, 1870–1874
> Probate fee book and guardians' *ad litem* record, 1917
> Probate minutes, 1871–1893
> Real estate sale record, 1871–1904
> Record of estate matters, 1900–1929
> Settlement book of estates, 1868–1874
> Will record, 1886–1954
> Variety record, 1893–c. 1934 (contains miscellaneous filings, such as con-
> tracts, removal of disabilities of nonage, claims of exemptions, incorpora-
> tions, and family histories)
> Voter registration record, c. 1902–c. 1933

Cullman County

Created from Blount, Marshall, Morgan, and Winston Counties on January 24, 1877, this county took significant territory from Blount County in 1887, 1893, and 1901. The address of the courthouse and county archives is 500 2nd Ave., Cullman, AL 35055. Land was granted through the Huntsville Land Office until 1905, then through the Montgomery Land Office until it closed in 1927; see chapter 11 in this volume, "Federal Land Records."

Cemetery records, marriages, censuses (1870–1900), naturalizations, a tax list (1889), deaths (1886–1908), births (1887–1907), and many church records have been published for Cullman County. Other sources include Gaylon D. Johnson, *Before the German Settlement of 1873: The Land and People That Became Cullman County* (Cullman: Gregath Company, 1980); Margaret Jean Jones, *Cullman County across the Years* (Cullman: The Author, 1975); and Margaret Jean Jones, *Combing Cullman County* (Cullman: The Author, 1972); as well as a county heritage book. For extensive bibliographies, see the sources cited in chapter 2 in this volume, "Internet, Books, Bibliographies, Periodicals, Newspapers, and Manuscripts," but especially Collier, *Alabama County Data and Resources* (2nd ed.); and Barefield, *Researching in Alabama* (rev. ed.).

Listed below are the records available on microfilm or as original records at the Alabama Department of Archives and History; the list comes from the archives' inventories. Some gaps in records and scattered issues of newspapers are not indicated. The archives' newspaper microfilm can be borrowed on interlibrary loan through local public libraries. Specific newspapers are listed at the web site of the Alabama Department of Archives and History. Other records and newspapers are available at the county courthouse in the basement county archives. Many county records, including some not listed below, can be borrowed on interlibrary loan through LDS family history centers. The Family and Regional History Program, Wallace State College, Hanceville, Alabama, and the Birmingham Public Library have microfilm of county records and newspapers, and some private papers relating to Cullman County history. The Cullman County Public Library, 200 Clark Street NE, Cullman, AL 35055, has a genealogy collection. *Alabama Family History and Genealogy News* is published by North Central Alabama Genealogical Society, Box 13, Cullman, AL 35056-0013.

> Deed records, 1870–1913
> Marriages, 1877–1951
> Newspapers, 1884–1886, 1888, 1890–1891, 1896–1996 (The Family and Regional History Program, Wallace State College, Hanceville, has a larger collection of Cullman County newspapers.)
> Probate minutes, 1888–1929
> Vital records (delayed births, 1878–1936; deaths, 1886–1919; births, 1894–1897; births, 1903–1904; births and deaths, 1911–1912)
> Will records, 1914–1919

Dale County

Created from Covington and Henry Counties on October 17, 1825, Dale County originally contained a large amount of today's Coffee (lost in 1841), Geneva (lost in 1868), and Houston (lost in 1903) Counties. The address of the county seat is Court Square, Ozark, AL 36360. Lands were granted through the St. Stephens (to 1833), Cahaba or Greenville (1819–1822), Sparta or Elba (1822–1867), and Montgomery (1867–1927) land offices; see chapter 11 in this volume, "Federal Land Records."

The marriages have been published for this county. Other information can be found in Fred S. Watson, *Forgotten Trails: A History of Dale County, Alabama, 1824–1966* (Birmingham: Banner Press, 1968); and Val L. McGee, *Claybank Memories: A History of Dale County, Alabama* (Ozark, Ala.: Dale County Historical Society, 1989). A county heritage book is being prepared for publication. For extensive bibliographies, see the sources cited in chapter 2 in this volume, "Internet, Books, Bibliographies, Periodicals, Newspapers, and Manuscripts," but especially Collier, *Alabama County Data and Resources* (2nd ed.); and Barefield, *Researching in Alabama* (rev. ed.). The Southeast Alabama Genealogical Society, Box 246, Dothan, AL 36202-0246, publishes *Wiregrass Roots* and *SEAGHS Magazine*. For current addresses of historical societies, web sites, and public libraries, see the Internet web site of the Alabama Department of Archives and History.

Listed below are the records available on microfilm or as original records at the Alabama Department of Archives and History; the list comes from the archives' inventories. Some gaps in records and scattered issues of newspapers are not indicated. The archives' newspaper microfilm can be borrowed on interlibrary loan through local public libraries. Specific newspapers are listed at the web site of the Alabama Department of Archives and History. Other records are available at the county courthouse. For other vital records, see the next chapter. Many county records, including some not listed below, can be borrowed on interlibrary loan through LDS family history centers.

> Deed record, 1884–1904
> Guardians' record, 1885–1924
> Inventory record, 1891–1918
> Marriages, 1884–1935
> Military discharge record, 1919–1942
> Newspapers, 1884–1997
> Probate settlement record, 1886–1923
> Probate court record, 1885–1930
> Probate orders and decrees, 1885–1897
> Lists of registered voters, 1894, 1914–1929 (males), 1920–1944 (females)
> Will record, 1921–1946

Dallas County

Dallas County was created on February 9, 1818, and originally contained significant parts of today's Baker or Chilton (1868–1875), Butler (1819), Marengo (1840), Perry (lost in 1822), and Wilcox (lost in 1819, 1822) Counties and swapped small tracts of land with Perry County for many years. The courthouse address is P.O. Box 997, Selma, AL 36701. Lands were granted through the St. Stephens (to 1819), Cahaba or Greenville (1819–1866), and Montgomery (1866–1927) land offices; see chapter 11 in this volume, "Federal Land Records."

The cemetery and marriage records have been published for this county, as has a list of persons in deed book A in 1829. For other sources, see Flora England, *Dallas County, Alabama, Genealogical Records*, 3 vols. (Selma: Sturdivant Museum Association, 1963). For extensive bibliographies, see the sources cited in chapter 2 in this volume, "Internet, Books, Bibliographies, Periodicals, Newspapers, and Manuscripts," but especially Collier,

Alabama County Data and Resources (2nd ed.); and Barefield, *Researching in Alabama* (rev. ed.). A county heritage book is being prepared for publication. The local genealogical society is the Central Alabama Genealogical Society, P.O. Box 125, Selma, AL 36702-0125. For current addresses of historical societies, web sites, and public libraries, see the Internet web site of the Alabama Department of Archives and History.

Listed below are the records available on microfilm or as original records at the Alabama Department of Archives and History; the list comes from the archives' inventories. Some gaps in records and scattered issues of newspapers are not indicated. The archives' newspaper microfilm can be borrowed on interlibrary loan through local public libraries. Specific newspapers are listed at the web site of the Alabama Department of Archives and History. Other records are available at the county courthouse. For other vital records, see the next chapter. Many county records, including some not listed below, can be borrowed on interlibrary loan through LDS family history centers.

> Administrators and guardians record, 1838–1873
> Administrators, guardians, and executors bonds and letters, 1873–1901
> Administrators and guardians accounts, inventories, appraisements, 1829–1927
> Child labor affidavits, 1908–1914
> Complete records of Orphans Court, 1836–1842
> Deed and mortgage record, 1823–1901
> Equity record, 1876–1879
> Equity minutes, 1876–1916
> Estate file index, c. 1818–1957
> History of Camp Catesby ap. R. Jones, No.317, United Confederate Veterans, c. 1900–c. 1930
> Marriages, 1818–1930
> Military discharge record, c. 1918–c. 1930
> Minors' disabilities of nonage, 1879–1951
> Newspapers, 1825, 1835–1841, 1853, 1860, 1862–1880, 1882–1886, 1888, 1897–1990
> Orphans Court minutes, 1818–1851
> Orphans and Probate Court record, 1844
> Paupers' record, 1905–1911
> Poll tax record, 1901–1944
> Probate Court minutes, 1851–1928

Record of sale of land for taxes, 1870–1874
Real estate sold for taxes, 1880–1917
Removal of disabilities, 1877–1912
Sheriffs' sale record, 1878–1890
Sale record, 1875–1880
Tax assessment record, 1851, 1870
Tract book, c. 1818–c. 1850s
Vital records: deaths, 1882–1888; births, 1920–1921; deaths, 1920–1923
Will record, 1821–1935

Decatur County

The county came into being from Jackson County on December 7, 1821, only to be abolished and returned to Jackson County on December 28, 1825.

Dekalb County

Created on January 9, 1836, from Jackson and St. Clair Counties, DeKalb County originally included part of modern Etowah County, which it gave up in 1868. Many boundary adjustments were made with Cherokee, Jackson, and Marshall Counties over the years. The address of the courthouse is 111 Grand Ave. SW, Fort Payne, AL 35967. Lands were granted through the Montevallo or Mardisville Land Office until 1905 and then through the Montgomery Land Office until it closed in 1927; see chapter 11 in this volume, "Federal Land Records."

The cemetery and marriage records have been published, as has Elizabeth S. Howard's *A Partial Who Was Who in DeKalb County*, 3 vols. (Collegedale, Tenn.: Landmarks of DeKalb County, 1978), as well as a county heritage book. For extensive bibliographies, see the sources cited in chapter 2 in this volume, "Internet, Books, Bibliographies, Periodicals, Newspapers, and Manuscripts," but especially Collier, *Alabama County Data and Resources* (2nd ed.); and Barefield, *Researching in Alabama* (rev. ed.). For current addresses of historical societies, web sites, and public libraries, see the Internet web site of the Alabama Department of Archives and History. The Northeast Alabama Genealogical Society, P.O. Box 674, Gadsden, AL 35902, publishes *Northeast Alabama Settlers*.

Listed below are the records available on microfilm or as original records at the Alabama Department of Archives and History; the list comes from the archives' inventories. Some gaps in records and scattered issues of newspapers are not indicated. The archives' newspaper microfilm can be borrowed on interlibrary loan through local public libraries. Specific newspapers are listed at the web site of the Alabama Department of Archives and History. Other records are available at the county courthouse. For other vital records, see the next chapter. Many county records, including some not listed below, can be borrowed on interlibrary loan through LDS family history centers.

> Appraisement and inventory records, c. 1867–1892
> Child labor affidavits from the Florence Hosiery Mill, Fort Payne, Ala., 1908–1915
> Deed records, 1835–1901
> Marriages, 1836–1927
> Orphans and Probate Court records, 1848–c. 1926
> Probate minutes, 1858–1929
> Probate final record, 1838–1868
> Registers of instruments, 1897–1900
> Naturalization records, 1890–1912
> Newspapers, 1902–1903, 1906–1915, 1923–1996
> Will records, 1906–1931
> Voter registration and poll tax records, c. 1901–c. 1960s
> Alphabetical lists of registered voters, 1902–1930

Elmore County

Elmore County was created in December 1866 from Autauga, Coosa, Montgomery, and Tallapoosa Counties and has had only minor boundary changes. The address of the courthouse is P.O. Box 280, Wetumpka, AL 36092. Lands were granted through the St. Stephens (to 1819), Cahaba or Greenville (1819–1866), and Montgomery (1834–1927) land offices; see chapter 11 in this volume, "Federal Land Records."

Newspaper abstracts, the 1870 census, and cemetery records have been published for Elmore County. For extensive bibliographies, see the sources cited in chapter 2 in this volume, "Internet, Books, Bibliographies, Periodicals, Newspapers, and Manuscripts," but especially Collier, *Alabama County Data and Resources* (2nd ed.); and Barefield, *Researching in Alabama* (rev. ed.). For current addresses of historical societies, web sites, and public libraries, see the Internet web site of the Alabama Department of Archives and History. The public library is the Elmore County Public Library, 212 South Main Street, Wetumpka, AL 36092. A county heritage book is being prepared for publication.

Listed below are the records available on microfilm or as original records at the Alabama Department of Archives and History; the list comes from the archives' inventories. Some gaps in records and scattered issues of newspapers are not indicated. The archives' newspaper microfilm can be borrowed on interlibrary loan through local public libraries. Specific newspapers are listed at the web site of the Alabama Department of Archives and History. Other records are available at the county courthouse. For other vital records, see the next chapter. Many county records, including some not listed below, can be borrowed on interlibrary loan through LDS family history centers.

Apprentice records, 1888–1913
Book of administrations, 1869–1881
Census records, 1880
Child labor affidavits, c. 1908–c. 1915
Confederate pension applications, c. 1883–c. 1914
Deeds, mortgages, and conveyance records, 1867–1907
Discharge records, 1919–1944
Letters of administration, 1881–1932
Letters of guardianship, 1882–1947
Letters testamentary, 1882–1941
Marriages, 1867–1929
Newspapers, 1847, 1867–1868, 1892–1893, 1895–1996
Probate Court minutes, 1891–c. 1935
Probate records, 1866–1928
Tax assessments, 1881
Vital records, register of births and deaths, 1909–1913
Lists of registered voters, 1908, 1910, 1912, 1914, 1916, 1919, 1920, 1922, 1924, 1925–1926
Will records, 1866–1949

Escambia County

Created from Baldwin and Conecuh Counties on December 10, 1868, Escambia County has had few and very minor border changes. The address of the courthouse is P.O. Box 848, Brewton, AL 36427. Lands were granted through the St. Stephens (to 1833), Cahaba or Greenville (1819–1822), Sparta or Elba (1822–1867), and Montgomery (1867–1927) land offices; see chapter 11 in this volume, "Federal Land Records."

For historical background on this county, see Annie C. Waters, *History of Escambia County, Alabama* (n.p.: The Author, 1983). For extensive bibliographies, see the sources cited in chapter 2 in this volume, "Internet, Books, Bibliographies, Periodicals, Newspapers, and Manuscripts," but especially Collier, *Alabama County Data and Resources* (2nd ed.); and Barefield, *Researching in Alabama* (rev. ed.). A county heritage book is being prepared for publication.

For current addresses of historical societies, web sites, and public libraries, see the Internet web site of the Alabama Department of Archives and History. The Brewton Public Library, 206 West Jackson Street, Brewton, AL 36426, has locally oriented genealogical files. The Escambia County Historical Society, Box 276, Brewton, AL 36427-0276, publishes the *Escambia County Historical Society Journal*.

Listed below are the records available on microfilm or as original records at the Alabama Department of Archives and History; the list comes from the archives' inventories. Some gaps in records and scattered issues of newspapers are not indicated. The archives' newspaper microfilm can be borrowed on interlibrary loan through local public libraries. Specific newspapers are listed at the web site of the Alabama Department of Archives and History. Other records are available at the county courthouse. For other vital records, see the next chapter. Many county records, including some not listed below, can be borrowed on interlibrary loan through LDS family history centers.

> Administrators, executors, and guardians record, 1871–1903
> Deed record, 1891–1901
> Discharge record, 1919–1931
> Final record, 1885–1929 (Chancery and Circuit Court)

Index to estate matters, 1900–1973
Marriages, 1879–1930
Military discharges, 1919–1931
Miscellaneous record, 1919–1931
Newspapers, 1882, 1883, 1884–1888, 1892–1996
Order books, 1869–1900
Orders and decrees, 1900–1930
Poll tax record, 1901–[1965]
Tax record, 1898
Tract book, c. 1819–c. 1900s
Will and deed record, 1869–1891
Will record, c. 1890–1925

Etowah County

Created from Blount, Calhoun, Cherokee, DeKalb, Marshall, and St. Clair Counties on December 1, 1868, Etowah County included some of the same area as the extinct county of Blaine. It has had minor border changes with Calhoun, DeKalb, and St. Clair Counties. The address of the courthouse is 800 Forrest Ave., Gadsden, AL 35901. Lands were granted through the Huntsville and Montevallo or Mardisville land offices until 1905 and then through the Montgomery Land Office until it closed in 1927; see chapter 11 in this volume, "Federal Land Records."

The Gadsden Public Library, 254 College Street, Gadsden, AL 35901, serves as a local research center. Its holdings include newspapers (1867–), Gadsden city directories (1907–), maps, obituary files, biographical files, photographs, and much more. The Northeast Alabama Genealogical Society, P.O. Box 674, Gadsden, AL 35902, operates the Nichols Memorial Library and publishes *Northeast Alabama Settlers*.

The cemetery, probate, 1870 census, marriage, and newspaper abstract records have been published, as has *A History of Etowah County, Alabama* (Birmingham: Etowah Centennial Commission, 1968) as well as a county heritage book. For extensive bibliographies, see the sources cited in chapter 2 in this volume, "Internet, Books, Bibliographies, Periodicals, Newspapers, and Manuscripts," but especially Collier, *Alabama County Data and Resources* (2nd ed.); and Barefield, *Researching in Alabama* (rev. ed.). For current addresses of historical societies, web sites, and public libraries, see the Internet web site of the Alabama Department of Archives and History.

Listed below are the records available on microfilm or as original records at the Alabama Department of Archives and History; the list comes from the archives' inventories. Some gaps in records and scattered issues of newspapers are not indicated. The archives' newspaper microfilm can be borrowed on interlibrary loan through local public libraries. Specific newspapers are listed at the web site of the Alabama Department of Archives and History. Other records are available at the county courthouse. For other vital records, see the next chapter. Many county records, including some not listed below, can be borrowed on interlibrary loan through LDS family history centers.

> Administrators' final record, 1887–c. 1907
> Birth certificates (delayed), 1944–1958
> Confederate pension records, c. 1890s
> Deed records, 1867–1902
> Final record, 1907–1929
> Index to Probate Court files, 1867–1946
> List of registered voters, 1902–1919
> Marriages, 1867–1928
> Military discharge records, 1931–1946
> Naturalization records, 1904–1906
> Newspapers, 1885, 1894–1924, 1946–1990
> Probate minutes, 1867–1930
> Will records, 1867–1939

Fayette County

Fayette County was created from Marion, Pickens, Tuscaloosa, and Walker Counties on December 20, 1824, and included a significant part of today's Lamar County until 1867/1868 and part of today's Walker County until 1843. However, the county gained large areas from Marion (1831, 1837) and Tuscaloosa (1832) Counties. The address of the courthouse is P.O. Box 819, Fayetteville, AL 35555. Lands were granted through the Huntsville (closed 1905) and Tuscaloosa (closed 1866) land offices, then through the Montgomery Land Office until it closed in 1927; see chapter 11 in this volume, "Federal Land Records."

Listed below are the records available on microfilm at the Alabama Department of Archives and History; the list comes from the archives' inventories. Some gaps in records and scattered issues of newspapers are not indicated. The archives' newspaper microfilm can be borrowed on interlibrary loan through local public libraries. Specific newspapers are listed at the web site of the Alabama Department of Archives and History. Other records are available at the county courthouse. For other vital records, see the next chapter. Many county records can be borrowed on interlibrary loan through LDS family history centers. For extensive bibliographies of material in print, see the sources cited in chapter 2 in this volume, "Internet, Books, Bibliographies, Periodicals, Newspapers, and Manuscripts," but especially Collier, *Alabama County Data and Resources* (2nd ed.); and Barefield, *Researching in Alabama* (rev. ed.). A county heritage book has recently been published. For current addresses of historical societies, web sites, and public libraries, see the Internet web site of the Alabama Department of Archives and History.

Listed below are the records available on microfilm or as original records at the Alabama Department of Archives and History; the list comes from the archives' inventories. Some gaps in records and scattered issues of newspapers are not indicated. The archives' newspaper microfilm can be borrowed on interlibrary loan through local public libraries. Specific newspapers are listed at the web site of the Alabama Department of Archives and History. Other records are available at the county courthouse. For other vital records, see the next chapter. Many county records, including some not listed below, can be borrowed on interlibrary loan through LDS family history centers.

Census records, 1880
Record of Confederate pensions, c. 1905
Deed records, 1848–1903
Marriages, 1866–1931
Military discharge record, 1919–1961
Newspapers, 1894–1962, 1977–1995
Probate Court minutes, 1851–1931
Probate Court record, 1887–1929
Vital records (register of births, 1884–1892; register of births and deaths, 1899–1912)
Voter registration record, 1908
Will record, 1888–1934

Feliciana County

This county was created from the Orleans Territory on October 7, 1810. The part in what became extreme southern Alabama was controlled by the Spanish and therefore never functioned as part of the county, except on paper.

Franklin County

Created on December 19, 1820, Franklin County originally included to-day's Colbert County, which it gave up in 1867 through 1870, although it regained some of this area in 1895. The address of the courthouse is P.O. Box 1028, Russellville, AL 35653. Land was granted through the Huntsville Land Office until 1905, then through the Montgomery Land Office until it closed in 1927; see chapter 11 in this volume, "Federal Land Records."

Books of miscellaneous information on Franklin County have been published, including Johnny Hester, *Facts and Fables of Franklin County* (n.p., n.d.); Robert L. James, *Distinguished Men, Women, and Families of Franklin County, Alabama* (n.p., n.d.); Mrs. Frank Ross Stewart, "Alabama's Franklin County," (D.Ed. diss., University of Alabama, 1988); as well as a county heritage book. The county tract book has also been published. For extensive bibliographies, see the sources cited in chapter 2 in this volume, "Internet, Books, Bibliographies, Periodicals, Newspapers, and Manuscripts," but especially Collier, *Alabama County Data and Resources* (2nd ed.); and Barefield, *Researching in Alabama* (rev. ed.). The Tennessee Valley Genealogical Society, P.O. Box 1568, Huntsville, AL 35807, publishes *Valley Leaves;* and the Natchez Trace Genealogical Society, Box 420, Florence, AL 35360, publishes *Natchez Trace Traveler.* For current addresses of historical societies, web sites, and public libraries, see the Internet web site of the Alabama Department of Archives and History.

Listed below are the records available on microfilm or as original records at the Alabama Department of Archives and History; the list comes from the archives' inventories. Some gaps in records and scattered issues of newspapers are not indicated. The archives' newspaper microfilm can be borrowed on interlibrary loan through local public libraries. Specific newspapers are listed at the web site of the Alabama Department of Ar-

chives and History. Other records are available at the county courthouse. For other vital records, see the next chapter. Many county records, including some not listed below, can be borrowed on interlibrary loan through LDS family history centers.

Deed records, 1890–1903
Final probate record, 1890–1929
Inventory and sales record, 1890–1918
Marriages, 1897–1901, 1915–1916, 1931–1938
Military discharge record, 1919–1944
Newspapers, 1899–1956, 1982–1996
Probate minutes, 1890–1930
Will record, 1890–1943

Geneva County

Geneva County was created on December 28, 1868, and gave up some ground to create Houston County in 1903. In 1879, the local people considered changing the name to Gordon County. The address of the courthouse is P.O. Box 430, Geneva, AL 36340. Lands were granted through the St. Stephens (to 1819), Cahaba or Greenville (1819–1822), Sparta or Elba (1822–1867), and Montgomery (1867–1927) land offices; see chapter 11 in this volume, "Federal Land Records."

Marriages, 1898–1930, have been published for Geneva County. For extensive bibliographies, see the sources cited in chapter 2 in this volume, "Internet, Books, Bibliographies, Periodicals, Newspapers, and Manuscripts," but especially Collier, *Alabama County Data and Resources* (2nd ed.); and Barefield, *Researching in Alabama* (rev. ed.). The Southeast Alabama Genealogical Society, Box 246, Dothan, AL 36202-0246, publishes *Wiregrass Roots* and *SEAGHS Magazine*. For current addresses of historical societies, web sites, and public libraries, see the Internet web site of the Alabama Department of Archives and History. A county heritage book is being prepared for publication.

Listed below are the records available on microfilm or as original records at the Alabama Department of Archives and History; the list comes from the archives' inventories. Some gaps in records and scattered issues of newspapers are not indicated. The archives' newspaper microfilm can be borrowed on interlibrary loan through local public libraries. Specific newspapers are listed at the web site of the Alabama Department of Archives and History. Other records are available at the county courthouse. For other vital records, see the next chapter. Many county records, including some not listed below, can be borrowed on interlibrary loan through LDS family history centers. The Emmas Knox Kenan Library, Geneva, AL 36340, has local newspapers.

> Administrators record, 1898–1926
> Deed records, 1898–1900
> Divorces, 1901–1917
> Dower record, 1906–1927
> Final settlement record, 1900–1929
> Guardians record, 1901–1928
> Military discharge record, c. 1931–1946
> Naturalization record, c. 1910
> Newspapers, 1866–1892, 1894, 1895–1896, 1897–1898, 1899–1902, 1914–1925,
>   1929–1996
> Probate minutes, 1901–1930
> Record of estates, 1908–1930
> Will record, 1883–1943

Greene County

Greene County, Mississippi Territory, was created on December 9, 1811, but lost its ground in present-day Alabama with the creation of the Alabama Territory in 1817. The present Greene County, Alabama, was created on December 13, 1819, and originally included today's Hale County, which it lost on January 30, 1867. It gained land from Pickens County in 1843 and 1867. The address of the courthouse is P.O. Box 656, Eutaw, AL 35462. Lands were granted through the Huntsville (to 1821), St. Stephens (to 1833), Demopolis (1833–1866), Tuscaloosa (1822–1866), and Montgomery (1866–1927) land offices; see chapter 11 in this volume, "Federal Land Records."

The 1840 and 1850 censuses and the cemetery records for this county have been published, as well as several books of miscellaneous records and information, including Mrs. S. M. Marshall, *Greene County, Alabama, Records* (Tuscaloosa: Willo Publications, 1960); *Snedecor's Greene County Directory [1855–1856]* (Eutaw, Ala.: Franklin Shacleford Moseley, 1957); and

Mary Morgan Glass, *A Goodly Heritage: Memories of Greene County* (Eutaw, Ala.: Greene County Historical Society, 1977). For extensive bibliographies, see the sources cited in chapter 2 in this volume, "Internet, Books, Bibliographies, Periodicals, Newspapers, and Manuscripts," but especially Collier, *Alabama County Data and Resources* (2nd ed.); and Barefield, *Researching in Alabama* (rev. ed.). A county heritage book is being prepared for publication. For current addresses of historical societies, web sites, and public libraries, see the Internet web site of the Alabama Department of Archives and History. The James C. Poole Memorial Library, 219 Prairie Avenue, Eutaw, AL 35462, has genealogical files.

Listed below are the records available on microfilm or as original records at the Alabama Department of Archives and History; the list comes from the archives' inventories. Some gaps in records and scattered issues of newspapers are not indicated. The archives' newspaper microfilm can be borrowed on interlibrary loan through local public libraries. Specific newspapers are listed at the web site of the Alabama Department of Archives and History. Other records are available at the county courthouse. For other vital records, see the next chapter. Many county records, including some not listed below, can be borrowed on interlibrary loan through LDS family history centers.

> Census, 1880
> Deed records, 1819–1901
> Military discharge record, 1919–1949
> Newspapers, 1854–c. 1861, 1864–1923, 1927–1996
> Probate Court directory, n.d.
> Orphans and Probate Court minutes, 1837–1852, 1854–1929
> Orphans and Probate Court records, 1822–1928
> Tax assessment records, 1832, 1848, 1849, 1851
> Will records, 1890–1935

Hale County

Hale County was created from Greene, Marengo, Perry, and Tuscaloosa Counties on January 30, 1867. The address of the courthouse is P.O. Box 396, Greensboro, AL 36744. Lands were granted through the St. Stephens (to 1833), Demopolis (1933–1866), Tuscaloosa (1822–1866), Cahaba or

Greenville (1819–1866), and Montgomery (1866–1927) land offices; see chapter 11 in this volume, "Federal Land Records."

Marriages, 1867–1920, and an undated tax record have been published for this county. For extensive bibliographies, see the sources cited in chapter 2 in this volume, "Internet, Books, Bibliographies, Periodicals, Newspapers, and Manuscripts," but especially Collier, *Alabama County Data and Resources* (2nd ed.); and Barefield, *Researching in Alabama* (rev. ed.). For current addresses of historical societies, web sites, and public libraries, see the Internet web site of the Alabama Department of Archives and History. A county heritage book is being prepared for publication. The address of the public library is Hale County Public Library, 1105 Main Street, PO. Box 399, Greensboro, AL 36744-1503.

Listed below are the records available on microfilm or as original records at the Alabama Department of Archives and History; the list comes from the archives' inventories. Some gaps in records and scattered issues of newspapers are not indicated. The archives' newspaper microfilm can be borrowed on interlibrary loan through local public libraries. Specific newspapers are listed at the web site of the Alabama Department of Archives and History. Other records are available at the county courthouse. For other vital records, see the next chapter. Many county records, including some not listed below, can be borrowed on interlibrary loan through LDS family history centers.

> Confederate pension record, c. 1900s
> Deed records, 1867–1902
> Dog tax abstract book, 1917
> Inventory record, 1867–1868
> Marriages, 1867–1936
> Military discharge records, 1920–1965
> Newspapers, 1843–1855, 1857–1994
> Probate minutes, 1867–1928
> Probate records, 1867–1939
> Registration and poll tax record, 1920–1939
> Tax abstracts, 1920–1924
> Vital records (register of births, 1881–1896, 1919–1935; record of deaths, 1920–1930; register of births and deaths, 1918–1919)
> Voter registration book, 1912
> Will record, 1867–1938

Hancock County

See Winston County.

Henry County

Created on December 13, 1819, Henry County originally included parts or all of today's Barbour, Bullock, Coffee, Covington, Crenshaw, Dale, Geneva, Henry, and Houston Counties. It gave up ground to Covington and Pike Counties on December 7, 1821; to Dale in 1825 and 1826; to Geneva on December 26, 1868; and to Houston on February 9, 1903. It gained land from Pike on December 28, 1831, and from Barbour on January 17, 1844. The address of the courthouse is 101 W. Court Square, Abbeville, AL 36310. Lands were granted through the St. Stephens (to 1833), Cahaba or Greenville (1819–1822), Sparta or Elba (1822–1867), and Montgomery (1834–1927) land offices; see chapter 11 in this volume, "Federal Land Records."

Census, cemetery, and marriage records have been published on this county, as well as local histories and collections of family sketches. A county heritage book is being prepared for publication. For extensive bibliographies, see the sources cited in chapter 2 in this volume, "Internet, Books, Bibliographies, Periodicals, Newspapers, and Manuscripts," but especially Collier, *Alabama County Data and Resources* (2nd ed.); and Barefield, *Researching in Alabama* (rev. ed.). For current addresses of historical societies, web sites, and public libraries, see the Internet web site of the Alabama Department of Archives and History. The Southeast Alabama Genealogical Society, Box 246, Dothan, AL 36202-0246, publishes *Wiregrass Roots*. The Abbeville Memorial Library, 301 Kirkland Street, Abbeville, AL 36310, has local newspapers, photographs, historical-biographical vertical files, maps, and other materials.

Listed below are the records available on microfilm or as original records at the Alabama Department of Archives and History; the list comes from the archives' inventories. Some gaps in records and scattered issues of newspapers are not indicated. The archives' newspaper microfilm can be borrowed on interlibrary loan through local public libraries. Specific newspapers are listed at the web site of the Alabama Department of Archives and History. Other records are available at the county courthouse.

For other vital records, see the next chapter. Many county records, including some not listed below, can be borrowed on interlibrary loan through LDS family history centers.

> Apprentice records, 1867–1888
> Deed records, 1824–1900
> Divorces, 1899–1925
> Fee book, 1870–1892
> List of registered voters, c. 1902–c. 1944
> Marriages, 1821–1923
> Newspapers, 1870–1874, 1901–1909, 1917–1996
> Orphans and Probate Court records, 1839–1929
> Poll tax record, c. 1901–c. 1940
> Probate Court minutes, 1853–1855
> Tax assessment records, 1882
> Vital records (register of births, 1895–1922; register of deaths, 1895–1906)

Houston County

Houston County was created February 9, 1903, from Dale, Geneva, and Henry Counties. The address of the courthouse is P.O. Box 6406, Dothan, AL 36302. Lands were granted through the St. Stephens (to 1833), Cahaba or Greenville (1819–1822), Sparta or Elba (1822–1867), and Montgomery (1867–1927) land offices; see chapter 11 in this volume, "Federal Land Records."

For Houston County, marriages, 1903–1936, have been published; also see Fred S. Watson, *Hub of the Wiregrass: A History of Houston County, Alabama, 1903–1972* (Anniston, Ala.: Higginbotham, 1972). A county heritage book is being prepared for publication. For extensive bibliographies, see the sources cited in chapter 2 in this volume, "Internet, Books, Bibliographies, Periodicals, Newspapers, and Manuscripts," but especially Collier, *Alabama County Data and Resources* (2nd ed.); and Barefield, *Researching in Alabama* (rev. ed.). For current addresses of historical societies, web sites, and public libraries, see the Internet web site of the Alabama Department of Archives and History. The Southeast Alabama Genealogical Society, Box 246, Dothan, AL 36202-0246, publishes *Wiregrass Roots*.

Although Alabama's most recently created county, Houston does have some resources for research. The Houston-Love Memorial Library, 212 West Burdeshaw Street, P.O. Box 1369, Dothan, AL 36302, has local newspapers (1906–), maps, photographs, and files on individuals, families, and subjects. The Alabama Department of Archives and History has jury lists for 1911 and 1976 for this county as well as newspapers for 1883, 1887 to 1902, and 1907 to 1999 (several issues missing).

Jackson County

Jackson County, Mississippi Territory, created December 12, 1812, gave up its western land with the creation of the Alabama Territory in 1817. Modern Jackson County was created on December 13, 1819, as an original county. It gave land to Madison County in 1826 and 1836. It also lost land to the creation of Cherokee, DeKalb, and Marshall Counties in 1836. Jackson and DeKalb Counties have made numerous border adjustments. The address of the courthouse is P.O. Box 128, Scottsboro, 35768. Lands were granted through the Huntsville and Montevallo or Mardisville land offices until 1905 and then through the Montgomery Land Office until it closed in 1927; see chapter 11 in this volume, "Federal Land Records."

The census, index to probate records, marriages, tract book, and other early records as well as local collections of family histories have been published for Jackson County. A county heritage book has been published. For extensive bibliographies, see the sources cited in chapter 2 in this volume, "Internet, Books, Bibliographies, Periodicals, Newspapers, and Manuscripts," but especially Collier, *Alabama County Data and Resources* (2nd ed.); and Barefield, *Researching in Alabama* (rev. ed.). The Tennessee Valley Genealogical Society, P.O. Box 1568, Huntsville, AL 35807, publishes *Valley Leaves;* and the Jackson County Historical Society, Box 1494, Scottsboro, AL 35768, publishes *Jackson County Chronicles.* The Scottsboro Public Library, 1002 South Broad Street, Scottsboro, AL 35768, has local newspapers (1868–) and files on persons, families, and subjects.

Listed below are the records available on microfilm or as original records at the Alabama Department of Archives and History; the list comes from the archives' inventories. Some gaps in records and scattered issues of newspapers are not indicated. The archives' newspaper microfilm can be borrowed on interlibrary loan through local public libraries. Specific newspapers are listed at the web site of the Alabama Department of Archives and History. Other records are available at the county courthouse. For other vital records, see the next chapter. Many county records, including some not listed below, can be borrowed on interlibrary loan through LDS family history centers.

Deed records, 1834–1901
Divorces, 1900–1930
Marriages, 1851–1929
Military discharge records, 1932–c. 1956
Newspapers, 1878–1995 (several issues missing)
Orphans and Probate Court records, 1820–1830
Probate minutes, 1856–1927
Vital records (births, 1920–1934)
Voter registration records, 1908–1909
Will records, 1855–1929

Jefferson County, Mississippi Territory

Jefferson County, Mississippi Territory, was created on April 2, 1799, and lost its area in today's Alabama with the creation of Washington County on June 4, 1800.

Jefferson County (Alabama)

Modern Jefferson County was created from Blount, St. Clair, and Shelby Counties on December 13, 1819. It lost land to the creation of Walker County in 1823 but gained territory from Shelby County (1833, 1841, 1861, 1871, 1884). Minor boundary changes have taken place with Blount, Shelby, St. Clair, and Tuscaloosa Counties. The address of the county seat is 716 N 21st Street, Birmingham, AL 35263. Lands were granted through the Huntsville (closed 1905) and Tuscaloosa (closed 1866) land offices, then through the Montgomery Land Office until it closed in 1927; see chapter 11 in this volume, "Federal Land Records"; and "Disposition of the Public Lands in Jefferson County, Alabama," 2 vols. (Birmingham: Works Projects Administration, 1937). A copy of the latter typescript is at the Birmingham Public Library.

The several source books on Jefferson County, different books of marriages, cemetery, estate, and land records, have been published; none include all records for any particular period. Several books of biographical sketches and historical information, usually centered around the history of Birmingham, have also been published. A county heritage book is being prepared for publication. For extensive bibliographies, see the sources cited in chapter 2 in this volume, "Internet, Books, Bibliographies, Periodicals, Newspapers, and Manuscripts," but especially Collier, *Alabama County Data and Resources* (2nd ed.); and Barefield, *Researching in Alabama* (rev. ed.). For current addresses of historical societies, web sites, and public libraries, see the Internet web site of the Alabama Department of Archives and History. The Birmingham Genealogical Society, Box 2432, Birmingham, AL 35201, publishes *Pioneer Trails*.

Listed below are the records available on microfilm or as original records at the Alabama Department of Archives and History; the list comes from the archives' inventories. Some gaps in records and scattered issues of newspapers are not indicated. The archives' newspaper microfilm can be borrowed on interlibrary loan through local public libraries. Specific newspapers are listed at the web site of the Alabama Department of Archives and History. Other records are available at the county courthouse, next door to the main branch of the Birmingham Public Library.

The Birmingham Public Library has microfilm of the Jefferson County records, including some microfilms available nowhere else. Researchers should be aware that county records are divided between those created by the Birmingham courthouse and the Bessemer courthouse. Many county records, including some not listed below, can be borrowed on interlibrary loan through LDS family history centers.

> Administrators final settlement record (Bessemer division), 1916–1929
> Administrators record, 1870–1928
> Administrators record (Bessemer division), 1916–1928
> Apprentice record, 1885–1915
> Deed records, 1820–1901
> Dower record, 1872–1891
> Estate case file (Virgil L. Long), 1908–1911
> Estray record, 1823–1880

Executors record, 1871–1881
Final record, 1880–c. 1928
Final record (Bessemer division), 1916–1930
Final settlement record, 1888–1928
Final settlement record (Bessemer division), 1921–1942
General administrators' record, 1880–c. 1948
General index to estates, c. 1898–c. 1933
Guardians record, 1870–1928
Guardians record (Bessemer division), 1916–1931
Index to deeds and mortgages, c. 1812–1902
Inventory record, 1871–1928
Marriages, 1818–1928
Newspapers, 1874–1884, 1888–1912, 1920–1995
Partial final settlement record, 1870–1886
Probate minutes, 1851–1928
Probate minutes (Bessemer division), 1916–1930
Orphans and Probate Court record, 1818–1855, 1850–1868
Will record, 1856–1928
Will record (Bessemer division), 1916–1929

Jones County

See Covington County.

Lamar County

Lamar County was created from Fayette and Marion Counties on February 4, 1867, as Sanford County. The name was changed on February 8, 1877. The address of the county seat is P.O. Box 3380, Vernon, AL 35592. Lands were granted through the Huntsville (closed 1905) and Tuscaloosa (closed 1866) land offices, then through the Montgomery Land Office until it closed in 1927; see chapter 11 in this volume, "Federal Land Records."

Some cemetery and early marriage records have been published for Lamar County. A county heritage book has been published. For extensive bibliographies, see the sources cited in chapter 2 in this volume, "Internet, Books, Bibliographies, Periodicals, Newspapers, and Manuscripts," but especially Collier, *Alabama County Data and Resources* (2nd ed.); and Barefield, *Researching in Alabama* (rev. ed.). The Mary Wallace Cobb Memorial Library, P.O. Box 357, Vernon, AL 35592, has newspapers (1896–) and genealogical files. The Lamar County Genealogical and Historical Society, Box 357, Vernon, AL 35592, publishes *Links to Lamar*.

Listed below are the records available on microfilm or as original records at the Alabama Department of Archives and History; the list comes from the archives' inventories. Some gaps in records and scattered issues of newspapers are not indicated. The archives' newspaper microfilm can be borrowed on interlibrary loan through local public libraries. Specific newspapers are listed at the web site of the Alabama Department of Archives and History. Other records are available at the county courthouse. For other vital records, see the next chapter. Many county records, including some not listed below, can be borrowed on interlibrary loan through LDS family history centers.

> Administrators' record, 1908–1916
> Apprentice record, c. 1908–1929
> Census record, 1880
> Confederate pension record, c. 1900s–c. 1920s
> Deed records, 1867–1904
> Estates, 1868–c. 1870
> Index to estates, c. 1889–c. 1939
> Marriages, 1867–1923
> Newspapers, 1875–1880, 1886–1952 (missing several issues), 1982–1995
> Order books, 1873–c. 1934
> Probate minutes, 1917–1985
> Vital records (births, 1919–1922; deaths, 1919–1937)
> Voters' registers, 1901–1919
> Will record, 1878–1961

Lauderdale County

Lauderdale County was created on February 6, 1818, from Cherokee and Chickasaw Indian lands. The address of the county seat is P.O. Box 1059, Florence, AL 35631. Land was granted through the Huntsville Land Office until 1905, then through the Montgomery Land Office until it closed in 1927; see chapter 11 in this volume, "Federal Land Records."

Cemetery, marriage, and Civil War service records have been published for Lauderdale County as well as death notices for 1890–1930 (Lauderdale and surrounding counties) and a county heritage book. Another source is

Sandra McGrady Sockwell's "The Place Names of Colbert and Lauderdale Counties, Alabama" (Ph.D. diss., University of Alabama, 1985). For extensive bibliographies, see the sources cited in chapter 2 in this volume, "Internet, Books, Bibliographies, Periodicals, Newspapers, and Manuscripts," but especially Collier, *Alabama County Data and Resources* (2nd ed.); and Barefield, *Researching in Alabama* (rev. ed.).

Several journals cover the history of this county. They include that of the Tennessee Valley Historical Society, P.O. Box 149, Sheffield, AL 35660; Tennessee Valley Genealogical Society, P.O. Box 1568, Huntsville, AL 35807; and Natchez Trace Genealogical Society, Box 420, Florence, AL 35360. For current addresses of historical societies, web sites, and public libraries, see the Internet web site of the Alabama Department of Archives and History.

The Florence-Lauderdale Public Library, 218 North Wood Avenue, Florence, AL 35630, has materials for local research. The library's holdings include newspapers for Colbert (1872–1969), Franklin (1824–1920), and Lauderdale (some as early as 1820s but extensive for 1840 to present) Counties; genealogical and biographical files; maps; and funeral notices (1824–1945, 1985–1997).

Listed below are the records available on microfilm or as original records at the Alabama Department of Archives and History; the list comes from the archives' inventories. Some gaps in records and scattered issues of newspapers are not indicated. The archives' newspaper microfilm can be borrowed on interlibrary loan through local public libraries. Specific newspapers are listed at the web site of the Alabama Department of Archives and History. Other records are available at the county courthouse. For other vital records, see the next chapter. Many county records, including some not listed below, can be borrowed on interlibrary loan through LDS family history centers.

> County court minutes, 1825–1868
> Deed and mortgage records, 1887–1901
> Estate record, 1920–1924
> Inventory record, 1911
> Marriages, 1929–1952
> Military discharge record, 1918–1939
> Newspapers, 1860–1996
> Probate minutes, 1850–1916

Lawrence County

Created on February 6, 1818, from Montgomery County, Lawrence County gave territory to Colbert County on February 6, 1895. The address of the county seat is 750 Main Street, Moulton, AL 35650. Land was granted through the Huntsville Land Office until 1905, then through the Montgomery Land Office until it closed in 1927; see chapter 11 in this volume, "Federal Land Records."

Several books of cemetery, marriage, and newspaper abstracts have been published for this county; also see Dorothy Gentry, *Life and Legend of Lawrence County, Alabama* (Tuscaloosa: The Author, 1962), and the county heritage book. For extensive bibliographies, see the sources cited in chapter 2 in this volume, "Internet, Books, Bibliographies, Periodicals, Newspapers, and Manuscripts," but especially Collier, *Alabama County Data and Resources* (2nd ed.); and Barefield, *Researching in Alabama* (rev. ed.). The Tennessee Valley Genealogical Society, P.O. Box 1568, Huntsville, AL 35807, publishes *Valley Leaves;* and the Lawrence County Historical Commission, P.O. Box 728, Moulton, AL 35650-0728, publishes *Old Lawrence Reminiscences.*

Listed below are the records available on microfilm or as original records at the Alabama Department of Archives and History; the list comes from the archives' inventories. Some gaps in records and scattered issues of newspapers are not indicated. The archives' newspaper microfilm can be borrowed on interlibrary loan through local public libraries. Specific newspapers are listed at the web site of the Alabama Department of Archives and History. Other records are available at the county courthouse. For other vital records, see the next chapter. Many county government and other historical resources for this county are found in the Lawrence County Archives, P.O. Box 728, 698 Main Street, Moulton, AL 35650, e-mail: lchc35650@aol.com. Some county records and the archives' newspaper microfilm, including some not listed below, can be borrowed on interlibrary loan through LDS family history centers.

> Confederate pension records, 1893–1935
> Deed records, 1819–1932
> Divorces, 1859–1925

Inventory record, 1846–1866
Inventories and wills, 1891–1934
Marriages, 1818–1935
Military discharge record, 1943–1949
Miscellaneous record, 1924–1929
Newspapers, 1855–1858, 1867–1996 (missing several issues)
Official bond book, 1818–1824
Orphans and Probate Court minutes, 1825–1941
Probate Court record, 1885–1928
Tax assessment records, 1849–1863, 1864, 1866
Voter registration and poll list, c. 1911–c. 1925
Vital records (deaths, 1881–1908)

Lee County

Lee County was created from Chambers, Macon, Russell, and Tallapoosa Counties on December 5, 1866. It exchanged land with Russell
County on September 30, 1932. The address of the county seat is P.O. Box
666, Opelika, AL 36803-0666. Lands were granted through the Montgomery Land Office (1834–1927); see chapter 11 in this volume, "Federal Land
Records."

For this county, marriage records, 1867–1903, have been published; also
see Alexander Nunn, *Lee County and Her Forbearers* (n.p., 1984). A county
heritage book is being prepared for publication. For extensive bibliographies, see the sources cited in chapter 2 in this volume, "Internet, Books,
Bibliographies, Periodicals, Newspapers, and Manuscripts," but especially
Collier, *Alabama County Data and Resources* (2nd ed.); and Barefield, *Researching in Alabama* (rev. ed.). For current addresses of historical societies,
web sites, and public libraries, see the Internet web site of the Alabama
Department of Archives and History. The Lee County Historical Society,
P.O. Box 206, Loachapoka, AL 36865, publishes *Trails in History*.

The Lewis Cooper Jr. Memorial Library, P.O. Box 125, Opelika, AL
36803-0125, has a locally oriented genealogical collection. Its holdings include newspapers (1890–) and vertical files on individuals and subjects.

Listed below are the records available on microfilm or as original
records at the Alabama Department of Archives and History; the list comes
from the archives' inventories. Some gaps in records and scattered issues

of newspapers are not indicated. The archives' newspaper microfilm can be borrowed on interlibrary loan through local public libraries. Specific newspapers are listed at the web site of the Alabama Department of Archives and History. Other records are available at the county courthouse. For other vital records, see the next chapter. Many county records, including some not listed below, can be borrowed on interlibrary loan through LDS family history centers.

Deed and mortgage records, 1863–1901
Marriages, 1867–1950
Newspapers, 1859–1860, 1861–1862, 1868–1869, 1875–1886, 1947–1969, 1982–1996
Tax assessment list, 1880
Will records, 1861–1898

Limestone County

Limestone County was created February 6, 1818, from Madison County and gained land from Limestone County on November 27, 1821. The address of the courthouse is 310 W. Washington Street, Athens, AL 35611-2561. Land was granted through the Huntsville Land Office until 1905, then through the Montgomery Land Office until it closed in 1927; see chapter 11 in this volume, "Federal Land Records."

Cemetery, census, probate, land, birth, and death records have been published for this county, chiefly through the efforts of the Limestone County Archives, 310 W. Washington Street, Athens, AL 35611. A county heritage book has been published. For extensive bibliographies, see the sources cited in chapter 2 in this volume, "Internet, Books, Bibliographies, Periodicals, Newspapers, and Manuscripts," but especially Collier, *Alabama County Data and Resources* (2nd ed.); and Barefield, *Researching in Alabama* (rev. ed.). For current addresses of historical societies, web sites, and public libraries, see the Internet web site of the Alabama Department of Archives and History.

Limestone County has several institutions for area research, including the Limestone County Archives, 310 W. Washington Ave., Athens, AL 35611; Athens Public Library, 411 E. South Street, Athens, AL 35611; Houston Memorial Library and Museum, 101 N. Houston Street, Athens, AL 35611; and Athens State College Library and Archives, Athens, AL 35611.

Listed below are the records available on microfilm or as original records at the Alabama Department of Archives and History; the list comes from the archives' inventories. Some gaps in records and scattered issues of newspapers are not indicated. The archives' newspaper microfilm can be borrowed on interlibrary loan through local public libraries. Specific newspapers are listed at the web site of the Alabama Department of Archives and History. Other records are available at the county courthouse. For other vital records, see the next chapter. Many county records, including some not listed below, can be borrowed on interlibrary loan through LDS family history centers. Historical records of the area are collected by the Limestone County Archives, 310 Washington Street, Athens, AL 35611.

> Census, 1866
> Deed records, 1818–1887
> Marriages, 1832–1928
> Newspapers, 1867–1870, 1880–1889, 1892–1893, 1899–1900, 1968, 1982–1990
> Tax assessment list, 1882
> Vital records (births, 1881–1887; deaths, 1881–1895; births and deaths, 1881–1895)
> Will records, 1826–1897

Lowndes County

Created on January 20, 1830, from Butler, Dallas, Montgomery, Pike, and Wilcox Counties, Lowndes County gave land to Butler and Crenshaw Counties (November 24, 1866). The address of the county seat is P.O. Box 65, Hayneville, AL 36040. Lands were granted through the St. Stephens (to 1819), Cahaba or Greenville (1819–1866), and Montgomery (1866–1927) land offices; see chapter 11 in this volume, "Federal Land Records."

Historical sites' surveys for Lowndes County have been published. For extensive bibliographies, see the sources cited in chapter 2 in this volume, "Internet, Books, Bibliographies, Periodicals, Newspapers, and Manuscripts," but especially Collier, *Alabama County Data and Resources* (2nd ed.); and Barefield, *Researching in Alabama* (rev. ed.). For current addresses of historical societies, web sites, and public libraries, see the In-

ternet web site of the Alabama Department of Archives and History. A
county heritage book is being prepared for publication.

Listed below are the records available on microfilm or as original
records at the Alabama Department of Archives and History; the list comes
from the archives' inventories. Some gaps in records and scattered issues
of newspapers are not indicated. The archives' newspaper microfilm can
be borrowed on interlibrary loan through local public libraries. Specific
newspapers are listed at the web site of the Alabama Department of Archives and History. Other records are available at the county courthouse.
For other vital records, see the next chapter. Many county records, including some not listed below, can be borrowed on interlibrary loan through
LDS family history centers.

> Administrators records, 1870–1944
> Census of Confederate veterans, 1907
> Confederate pension record, 1899
> County commission minutes, 1830–1851
> Deed records, 1885–l900
> Estate case files, c. 1830–1910
> Executors record, 1870–1945
> Fee book, c. 1860
> Guardians record, 1870–1910
> Inventory book, 1830–1867
> Land and property (16th section), 1830–1871
> Land sold for taxes, 1869–1879
> List of registered voters, 1901–1914, 1920–1933 (men), 1920–1922 (women)
> Military discharge record, c. 1919–c. 1943
> Minutes and record of final settlement, 1870–1906
> Newspapers, 1860, 1880–1884, 1892–1922, 1929–1993
> Oaths of allegiance, 1865
> Oaths and bonds of office holders, 1867–1929
> Partitioned land, c. 1842–1852
> Paupers record, 1881–1902
> Pension record, c. 1920–1935
> Petition record, c. 1860–1901
> Poll tax record, 1875–1930
> Orphans and Probate Court case files, 1848–1898
> Orphans and Probate Court minutes, 1830–1935
> Orphans and Probate record (estate of Bolling Smith), 1835

Record of sales of real estate, 1875–1897
Register of conveyances, 1882–1885
Register of voters, 1867, 1902–1931
Tally list statement, 1896
Tax assessment record, 1849, 1877
Tract book, 1817–1856
Vital records (births, 1881–1905, 1919–1935; delayed birth certificates, 1879–
    1911; deaths, 1920–1924; births and deaths, 1881–1905, 1910–1919)
Will records, 1862–1869, 1899–1940

Macon County

Macon County was created from Montgomery and Pike Counties on December 18, 1832. It gained land from Montgomery County on January 1, 1834; from Pike County on December 20, 1837; and from Tallapoosa County on February 2, 1846. Macon County lost land to Tallapoosa County on January 27, 1845, and to the creation of Bullock and Lee Counties on December 5, 1866. The address of the county seat is P.O. Box 659, Tuskegee, AL 36083. Lands were granted through the Montgomery Land Office (1834–1927); see chapter 11 in this volume, "Federal Land Records."

A historical sites' survey has been published for Macon County. For extensive bibliographies, see the sources cited in chapter 2 in this volume, "Internet, Books, Bibliographies, Periodicals, Newspapers, and Manuscripts," but especially Collier, *Alabama County Data and Resources* (2nd ed.); and Barefield, *Researching in Alabama* (rev. ed.). For current addresses of historical societies, web sites, and public libraries, see the Internet web site of the Alabama Department of Archives and History. A county heritage book is being prepared for publication.

Listed below are the records available on microfilm or as original records at the Alabama Department of Archives and History; the list comes from the archives' inventories. Some gaps in records and scattered issues of newspapers are not indicated. The archives' newspaper microfilm can be borrowed on interlibrary loan through local public libraries. Specific newspapers are listed at the web site of the Alabama Department of Archives and History. Other records are available at the county courthouse. For other vital records, see the next chapter. Many county records, including some not listed below, can be borrowed on interlibrary loan through LDS family history centers.

> Census records, 1880
> Deed records, 1836–1902
> Marriages, 1834–1931
> Military discharge record, 1933–1955
> Newspapers, 1849–1992
> Orphans and Probate Court record, 1838–1852
> Orphans and Probate files, c. 1837–c. 1903
> Orphans and Probate minutes, 1834–1841, 1850–1930
> Vital records (deaths, 1920–1937)
> Will record, 1851–1923

Madison County

Created on December 13, 1808, as an original county, Madison County gained land from Jackson County (1826, 1836) and lost ground to Marshall County (1837). The address of the county seat is 100 Northside Square, Huntsville, AL 35801. Land was granted through the Huntsville Land Office until 1905, then through the Montgomery Land Office until it closed in 1927; see chapter 11 in this volume, "Federal Land Records."

Cemetery, marriage, and some probate records have been published as well as a county heritage book. Several historical works have been done, centered around the history of Huntsville. For extensive bibliographies, see the sources cited in chapter 2 in this volume, "Internet, Books, Bibliographies, Periodicals, Newspapers, and Manuscripts," but especially Collier, *Alabama County Data and Resources* (2nd ed.); and Barefield, *Researching in Alabama* (rev. ed.). For current addresses of historical societies, web sites, and public libraries, see the Internet web site of the Alabama Department of Archives and History. The Tennessee Valley Genealogical Society, P.O. Box 1568, Huntsville, AL 35807, publishes *Valley Leaves;* and the Huntsville-Madison County Historical Society, P.O. Box 666, Huntsville, AL 35804, publishes *Historic Huntsville Review.*

Listed below are the records available on microfilm or as original records at the Alabama Department of Archives and History; the list comes from the archives' inventories. Some gaps in records and scattered issues of newspapers are not indicated. The archives' newspaper microfilm can be borrowed on interlibrary loan through local public libraries. Specific newspapers are listed at the web site of the Alabama Department of Archives and History. Other records are available at the county courthouse. For other vital records, see the next chapter. The earliest county records are in the Madison County Archives on the third floor of Huntsville-Madison County Public Library. Many county records, including some not listed below, can be borrowed on interlibrary loan through LDS family history centers.

> Census, 1880
> Deed records, 1810–1886
> Estate case files, 1818
> Marriages, 1809–1928
> Newspapers, 1817–1818, 1823–1862, 1870–1887, 1895–1996
> Orphans and Probate Court records, 1810–1858
> Sexton's records, 1867–1963 (contains records of internment in the City
>   Cemetery and Maple Hill Cemetery, Huntsville)
> Vital records (births and deaths, 1881–1912, incomplete)
> Will records, 1853–1927

Marengo County

Marengo County was created on February 6, 1818, as an original county and included parts of today's Greene, Hale, and Perry Counties. It lost ground to Greene, Perry, and Wilcox Counties on December 13, 1819, and to the creation of Hale County on January 30, 1867. The address of the county seat is P.O. Box 4807, Linden, AL 36748. Lands were granted through the St. Stephens (to 1833), Demopolis (1833–1866), Cahaba or Greenville (1819–1866), and Montgomery (1866–1927) land offices; see chapter 11 in this volume, "Federal Land Records."

Marriages have been published for this county, as well as sketches of early families and history. Another source is W. C. Tharin's *Tharin's Marengo County Directory for 1860–61* (Demopolis, Ala.: Marengo County Historical Society, 1973). A county heritage book is being prepared for publication. For extensive bibliographies, see the sources cited in chapter 2 in this volume, "Internet, Books, Bibliographies, Periodicals, Newspapers, and Manuscripts," but especially Collier, *Alabama County Data and Resources* (2nd ed.); and Barefield, *Researching in Alabama* (rev. ed.). For current addresses of historical societies, web sites, and public libraries, see the Internet web site of the Alabama Department of Archives and History. The public library is Marengo County Public Library, P.O. Box 519, Linden, AL 36748.

Listed below are the records available on microfilm or as original records at the Alabama Department of Archives and History; the list comes from the archives' inventories. Some gaps in records and scattered issues of newspapers are not indicated. The archives' newspaper microfilm can be borrowed on interlibrary loan through local public libraries. Specific newspapers are listed at the web site of the Alabama Department of Archives and History. Other records are available at the county courthouse. For other vital records, see the next chapter. Many county records, including some not listed below, can be borrowed on interlibrary loan through LDS family history centers.

> Apprentice records, 1867–c. 1870
> Cotton mill record, c. 1911–c. 1914
> Deed records, 1820–1901
> Guardians letter, 1870–1964
> Marriages, 1818–1936
> Military discharge record, c. 1919–c. 1935
> Miscellaneous record, 1823–1923
> Newspapers, 1873–1876, 1879–1996
> Poll list, c. 1895–c. 1896
> Orphans and Probate Court minutes, 1820–1919
> Registration book of voters, 1908, 1910, 1912, 1914, 1915–16, 1920
> Vital records (births and deaths, 1906–1909; births, 1910–1913; deaths, 1910–1913)
> Will record, 1898–1936

Marion County

Created on February 13, 1818, from Tuscaloosa County, Marion County originally included parts of today's Cullman, Fayette, Lamar, Walker, and Winston Counties, as well as part of eastern Mississippi. It lost land to the creation of Walker County (1823), to Fayette County (1824, 1831, 1837, 1867), and to Sanford or Lamar County (1868). The address of the county seat is 132 Military Street S., Hamilton, AL 35570. Land was granted through the Huntsville Land Office until 1905, then through the Montgomery Land Office until it closed in 1927; see chapter 11 in this volume, "Federal Land Records."

Cemetery, marriage, federal land, and Civil War service records have been published for Marion County. A county heritage book has been published. For extensive bibliographies, see the sources cited in chapter 2 in this volume, "Internet, Books, Bibliographies, Periodicals, Newspapers, and Manuscripts," but especially Collier, *Alabama County Data and Resources* (2nd ed.); and Barefield, *Researching in Alabama* (rev. ed.). For current addresses of historical societies, web sites, and public libraries, see the Internet web site of the Alabama Department of Archives and History.

Listed below are the records available on microfilm or as original records at the Alabama Department of Archives and History; the list comes from the archives' inventories. Some gaps in records and scattered issues of newspapers are not indicated. The archives' newspaper microfilm can be borrowed on interlibrary loan through local public libraries. Specific newspapers are listed at the web site of the Alabama Department of Archives and History. Other records are available at the county courthouse. For other vital records, see the next chapter. Many county records, including some not listed below, can be borrowed on interlibrary loan through LDS family history centers.

> Census of Confederate soldiers, 1907
> Deed records, 1887–1901
> Estate record, 1887–1922
> Final estate record, 1885–1935
> Marriages, 1930–1958
> Military discharge record, 1920–1953
> Newspapers, 1887, 1889–1959, 1992–1996
> Orphans or guardians record, 1907–1922
> Plat book, c. 1912
> Probate minutes, 1897–1923
> Vital records (births and deaths, 1909–1917; deaths, 1920–1934; births, 1920–1931)

Marshall County

Marshall County was created from Blount and Jackson Counties on January 6, 1836, and gained from Morgan County on December 15, 1840, as well as from DeKalb County on February 2, 1858. It lost land to the creation of Etowah County on December 1, 1868, and to the creation of Cullman County on January 24, 1877. The address of the county seat is 424 Blount Ave., Guntersville, AL 35976. Lands were granted through the Huntsville and Montevallo or Mardisville land offices until 1905 and then through the Montgomery Land Office until it closed in 1927; see chapter 11 in this volume, "Federal Land Records."

Census (to 1900), cemetery, and marriage records have been published for this county. A county heritage book has been published. For extensive bibliographies, see the sources cited in chapter 2 in this volume, "Internet, Books, Bibliographies, Periodicals, Newspapers, and Manuscripts," but especially Collier, *Alabama County Data and Resources* (2nd ed.); and Barefield, *Researching in Alabama* (rev. ed.). For current addresses of historical societies, web sites, and public libraries, see the Internet web site of the Alabama Department of Archives and History. The Tennessee Valley Genealogical Society, P.O. Box 1568, Huntsville, AL 35807, publishes *Valley Leaves*.

For local research there is the Guntersville Public Library, 1240 O'Brig Ave., Guntersville, AL 35976. This library has newspapers (1880–), some city directories, TVA maps, and files on persons, families, and subjects. The Northeast Alabama Genealogical Society, P.O. Box 674, Gadsden, AL 35902, publishes *Northeast Alabama Settlers*.

Listed below are the records available on microfilm or as original records at the Alabama Department of Archives and History; the list comes from the archives' inventories. Some gaps in records and scattered issues of newspapers are not indicated. The archives' newspaper microfilm can be borrowed on interlibrary loan through local public libraries. Specific newspapers are listed at the web site of the Alabama Department of Archives and History. Other records are available at the county courthouse. For other vital records, see the next chapter. Many county records, including some not listed below, can be borrowed on interlibrary loan through

LDS family history centers. The Family and Regional History Program at Wallace State College, Hanceville, Alabama, has Marshall County records on microfilm.

> Census, 1880
> Deed records, 1836–1902
> Estate index, c. 1836–c. 1950s
> Final record, 1836–c. 1930
> Lists of registered voters, 1867, c. 1902–c. 1946
> Marriages, 1849–1928
> Military assessment record, 1860
> Newspapers, 1852–1855, 1881–1996
> Orphans and Probate Court minutes, 1836–1931
> Probate records, 1854–1861
> Vital records (births, 1920–1937; deaths, 1920–1935)
> Will records, 1904–1937

Mobile County

Mobile County was created from territory claimed by the United States on August 1, 1812, as part of the Mississippi Territory. It lost territory to the creation of Hancock and Jackson Counties in Mississippi. Mobile County also lost ground to Baldwin County (1820) and Washington County (1829). The address of the county seat is 205 Government Street, Mobile, AL 36644. Federal lands were granted through the St. Stephens (to 1867), Mobile (1867–1879), and Montgomery (1879–1927) land offices; see chapter 11 in this volume, "Federal Land Records."

Birth, cemetery, death, divorce, marriage, naturalization, passenger list, (some) probate, and (some) land grant records have been published for Mobile County. Many books of biographical sketches and historical background have been published, centered around the city of Mobile. A county heritage book is being prepared for publication. For extensive bibliographies, see the sources cited in chapter 2 in this volume, "Internet, Books, Bibliographies, Periodicals, Newspapers, and Manuscripts," but especially Collier, *Alabama County Data and Resources* (2nd ed.); and Barefield, *Researching in Alabama* (rev. ed.). The Mobile Genealogical Society, P.O. Box 6224, Mobile, AL 36660-6224, publishes *Deep South Genealogical Quarterly*.

For current addresses of historical societies, web sites, and public libraries, see the Internet web site of the Alabama Department of Archives and History.

Several research facilities have extensive collections on the Mobile area. These libraries and archives include Mobile Public Library, Local History and Genealogy Division, 701 Government Street, Mobile, AL 36602; Special Collections and West Florida Archives, John C. Pace Library, University of West Florida, 11000 University Parkway, Pensacola, FL 32514-5750; Mobile County Probate Court Records Department, P.O. Box 7, 109 Government Street, Room 111, Mobile, AL 36601-0007; Museum of the City of Mobile, 355 Government Street, Mobile, AL 36602; Historic Mobile Preservation Society Archives, 300 Oakleigh Place, Mobile, AL 36604; and Mobile Historic Development Commission, 1 St. Louis Centre, Suite 1001, P.O. Box 1827, Mobile, AL 36633. Specifically for the Mobile Municipal Archives, 457 Church Street, Mobile, AL 36602, see Clifton Dale Foster, Tracey J. Berezansky, E. Frank Roberts, and Edwin K. Harkins, *A Guide to the Mobile Municipal Archives,* rev. ed. (Mobile: Mobile Municipal Archives, 1999). For the University of South Alabama Archives, USA Springhill Avenue, Room 0722, Mobile, AL 36688, see *A Guide to the Collections of the University of South Alabama Archives* (Mobile: University of South Alabama Archives, 1990).

The Alabama Department of Archives and History has a tax assessment record, 1849; and newspapers for 1840–1849, 1869–1872, 1874–1876, 1900–1934, and 1939–1994. The following records, and some not listed below, can be borrowed on microfilm through LDS family history centers. Other records are found in the Mobile County courthouse. The Mobile County Probate Court has also begun microfilming and indexing local records for 1715 to 1850.

> Deeds and mortgages, 1813–1886
> Marriages, 1823–1930
> Military discharges, 1919–1931
> Orphans and Probate Court minutes, 1814–1930
> Probate Court records (1814–1930?)
> Tax lists, 1879–1915
> Wills, 1813–1930

Monroe County

Monroe County was created as an original county on June 29, 1815, and originally included the central half of modern Alabama. It lost territory to create Montgomery (1816), Dallas (1818), Conecuh (1818), Butler (1819), and Wilcox (1819) Counties. Monroe lost territory to Clarke County in 1843. The address of the county seat is P.O. Box 8, Monroeville, AL 36461. Lands were granted through the St. Stephens (to 1833), Cahaba or Greenville (1819–1866), Sparta or Elba (1822–1867), and Montgomery (1866–1927) land offices; see chapter 11 in this volume, "Federal Land Records."

For some historical background, see Mary E. Brantley, *Early Settlers along the Old Federal Road in Monroe and Conecuh Counties, Alabama* (Atmore: The Author, 1976). A county heritage book is being prepared for publication. For extensive bibliographies, see the sources cited in chapter 2 in this volume, "Internet, Books, Bibliographies, Periodicals, Newspapers, and Manuscripts," but especially Collier, *Alabama County Data and Resources* (2nd ed.); and Barefield, *Researching in Alabama* (rev. ed.). For current addresses of historical societies, web sites, and public libraries, see the Internet web site of the Alabama Department of Archives and History.

Listed below are the records available on microfilm or as original records at the Alabama Department of Archives and History; the list comes from the archives' inventories. Some gaps in records and scattered issues of newspapers are not indicated. The archives' newspaper microfilm can be borrowed on interlibrary loan through local public libraries. Specific newspapers are listed at the web site of the Alabama Department of Archives and History. Other records are available at the county courthouse. For other vital records, see the next chapter. Many county records, including some not listed below, can be borrowed on interlibrary loan through LDS family history centers.

> Administrators' and executors' settlement book, 1873–1880
> Apprentice record, 1866–1871
> Bonds of executors and administrators, 1858–1867
> Chancery Court minutes, 1909–1919
> Court case files, 1846–1860s
> Fee books, 1844–1875

Inventory record, 1833–c. 1916

Military discharge record, 1920–1956

Newspapers, 1860–1861, 1867, 1870, 1878–1996

Official bond books, Probate Court order book, 1816–1821

Orphans and Probate Court order book, 1833–1854

Probate Court minutes, 1854–1933

Register of Confederate soldiers, c. 1915

Register of voters, 1908–1926

Tax assessment record, 1854

Tract book, 1817–c. 1900s

Will record, 1906–1930

Wills and deeds, 1881–1907

Montgomery County

Originally created from Monroe County on December 6, 1816, Montgomery County at first covered more than a quarter of Alabama. In February 1817, however, it gave land to create Blount, Cahawba or Bibb, Dallas, Franklin, Lawrence, Shelby, and Tuscaloosa Counties. It lost land to Autauga (1818, 1827), Cahawba or Bibb (1818), Bullock (1866), Dallas (1819), Elmore (1866), Lowndes (1830), Shelby (1831), Pike (1832), and Wilcox (1819) Counties. The address of the county seat is P.O. Box 1667, Montgomery, AL 36102. Lands were granted through the St. Stephens (to 1819), Cahaba or Greenville (1819–1866), and Montgomery (1866–1927) land offices; see chapter 11 in this volume, "Federal Land Records."

Early marriages and wills have been published for this county. Some books of biographical information centered around the city of Montgomery have been published. A county heritage book is being prepared for publication. For extensive bibliographies, see the sources cited in chapter 2 in this volume, "Internet, Books, Bibliographies, Periodicals, Newspapers, and Manuscripts," but especially Collier, *Alabama County Data and Resources* (2nd ed.); and Barefield, *Researching in Alabama* (rev. ed.). The Montgomery County Genealogical Society, Box 1829, Montgomery, AL 36102, publishes *MGS Quarterly*. For current addresses of historical societies, web sites, and public libraries, see the Internet web site of the Alabama Department of Archives and History. Records of Oakwood Cemetery and files on many Montgomery families are found in the microfilm of the surname files at the Alabama Department of Archives and History. Several books have been published on Montgomery and the Civil Rights movement. For the earlier history of the city, see Wayne Flynt, *Montgomery: An Illustrated History* (Woodland Hills, Calif.: Windsor Publications, 1980); and William Warren Rogers Jr., *Confederate Home Front: Montgomery during the Civil War* (Tuscaloosa: University of Alabama Press, 1999).

Listed below are the records available on microfilm or as original records at the Alabama Department of Archives and History; the list comes from the archives' inventories. Some gaps in records and scattered issues of newspapers are not indicated. The archives' newspaper microfilm can be borrowed on interlibrary loan through local public libraries. Specific newspapers are listed at the web site of the Alabama Department of Archives and History. Other records are available at the county courthouse. For other vital records, see the next chapter. Many county records, including some not listed below, can be borrowed on interlibrary loan through LDS family history centers. Historical government records for this county are kept by the Montgomery County Archives, P.O. Box 195, 100 S. Lawrence Street, Montgomery, AL 36195-0223.

Abstract of records of chattel mortgages, 1888–1903

Administrators' appointment record, 1817, 1870–1912

Administrators' record, 1870–1899

Annual errors in [tax] assessment, 1896–1918

Annual lists of insolvents, 1896–1918

Bond record, 1844

Chattel mortgage record, 1868

City council minutes (Montgomery), 1820–1873

City ordinances (Montgomery), 1820–1850

Claims dockets, 1828–1869

Commissioners court minutes, 1818–1837

Convicts sentenced to hard labor, 1872

Court case files, 1820–1868

County commission minutes, 1980–1987

County court minutes, 1822, 1828–1839

County court case files, 1877–1941

Deed records, 1857, c. 1869–1901, 1890–1907

Deeds and mortgages index, 1883–1884

Dower records, 1872–1883

Estate case files, 1838–1946

Estray record, 1865–1866

Executors' record, 1870–1899

Exemption record, 1888–1893

Fee books, 1873–1901

Guardians' record, 1831–1937

Insolvents lists, 1896–1918

Inventory record, 1819–1953

Marriages, 1817–1951

Military discharge record, 1919–c. 1944

Minute book, 1821–1896

Minutes and record of final settlement, 1831–1935

Miscellaneous record, 1862, 1868

Mortgage record, 1860

Municipal incorporation records, 1895–1933

Newspapers, 1825–1997

Oaths of allegiance, 1865

Official bond books, 1817–1937

Plat books, [c. 1909–c 1920]

Poll tax records, 1901–1907

Orphans and Probate Court minutes, 1817–1928

Orphans and Probate Court case files, 1820s–1940s

Orphans and Probate dockets and fee books, 1802–1942

Orphans and Probate judge letter book, 1819–1880

Record book, 1836

Record of conveyances, c. 1820–1869 (early deed records)

Record of estates, c. 1824–1838

Record of licensed practitioners of medicine, 1878–1922

Register order book, 1852–1865

Sheriff feeding prisoners account books, 1922–1926

Sheriff jail registers, 1878–1935

Sixteenth section lands book, 1833–1855

Slave jail register, 1860–1862

Tax assessment record, 1872–1873, 1930–1936, 1955–1956, 1958

Tax collector's daily cash receipts reports, 1862–1863

Vital records (births, 1908–1917; delayed birth certificates, 1944–1950s; deaths, 1908–1912)

Voter lists, 1902–1908, 1912–1920, 1922–1932, 1935–1965

Will record, 1820–1932

Morgan County

Morgan County was created on February 6, 1818, as Cotaco County. The name was changed on June 14, 1821. It lost land to Marshall County on December 14, 1840, and Cullman County on January 24, 1877. The address of the county seat is P.O. Box 668, Decatur, AL 35602. Land was granted through the Huntsville Land Office until 1905, then through the Montgomery Land Office until it closed in 1927; see chapter 11 in this volume, "Federal Land Records."

Marriage, newspaper abstract, cemetery, and census records have been published, as well as a county heritage book. For extensive bibliographies, see the sources cited in chapter 2 in this volume, "Internet, Books, Bibliographies, Periodicals, Newspapers, and Manuscripts," but especially Collier,

Alabama County Data and Resources (2nd ed.); and Barefield, *Researching in Alabama* (rev. ed.). For current addresses of historical societies, web sites, and public libraries, see the Internet web site of the Alabama Department of Archives and History.

The Alabama Department of Archives and History has on microfilm the newspapers for 1887 to 1896 and 1898 to 1996 (missing some issues). Historical records for this area are kept by the Morgan County Archives, 624 Bank Street NE, Decatur, AL 35601.

Pascagoula County

Created on January 4, 1811, this county in Orleans Territory was abolished on April 30, 1812.

Perry County

Perry County was created on December 13, 1819, from Cahawba or Bibb, Dallas, Marengo, and Tuscaloosa Counties. It lost ground to Greene and Tuscaloosa Counties on December 20, 1820; to Hale County on January 30, 1867; and to Dallas County on February 18, 1867. The address of the county seat is P.O. Box 478, Marion, AL 36756. Lands were granted through the St. Stephens (to 1819), Cahaba or Greenville (1819–1866), and Montgomery (1866–1927) land offices; see chapter 11 in this volume, "Federal Land Records."

Sources for Perry County include W. Stuart Harris, *Perry County Heritage* (n.p., 1991); Flora Dainwood England, comp., *Perry County Record* (Marion, Ala.: The Compiler, 1955–1965); and a county heritage book. For extensive bibliographies, see the sources cited in chapter 2 in this volume, "Internet, Books, Bibliographies, Periodicals, Newspapers, and Manuscripts," but especially Collier, *Alabama County Data and Resources* (2nd ed.); and Barefield, *Researching in Alabama* (rev. ed.). For current addresses of historical societies, web sites, and public libraries, see the Internet web site of the Alabama Department of Archives and History.

Listed below are the records available on microfilm or as original records at the Alabama Department of Archives and History; the list comes from the archives' inventories. Some gaps in records and scattered issues of newspapers are not indicated. The archives' newspaper microfilm can be borrowed on interlibrary loan through local public libraries. Specific newspapers are listed at the web site of the Alabama Department of Archives and History. Other records are available at the county courthouse. For other vital records, see the next chapter. Many county records, including some not listed below, can be borrowed on interlibrary loan through LDS family history centers.

Administrators and executors
bonds, 1841–1850
Administrators records,
1870–1916
Abstract of records of chattel
mortgages, 1895–1901
Applications for [voter]
registration questionnaire and
oath, 1951–1952
Bonds of executors and
administrators, c. 1820s–1940s
Census record, 1880
Chattel mortgage record, c.
1825–1945
Child labor affidavits, 1908–1914
Claims docket, 1852–1910
Confederate pension record,
1895–1914
County court case files,
1823–1879, 1919–1941
Court case files, 1823–1948
Deed record, c. 1821–1945
Delinquent tax docket, 1878–1899
Election results, 1823–1930
Estate case files, 1822–1914
Estray record, 1830–1907
Executors record, 1870–1913
Exemption record, 1877–1936
Fee books, 1855–1903
Final settlements, 1871
Guardians record, 1870–1916
Inventory record, 1823–1871

Jail registers, 1876–1930
Land books, 1884–1927
Lists of registered voters, 1859,
1875–1920
Lot book, 1916–1919
Marriages, 1820–1936
Military discharge record,
1920–1961
Minutes and record of partial
settlement, 1868–1871
Minute books, 1849–1914
Miscellaneous receipts,
1831–1932
Miscellaneous records, 1830–1930
Mortgage and deed record, 1887
Mortgage record, c. 1825–1945
Newspapers, 1871–1887,
1889–1994
Oaths of allegiance, 1868
Official bond books, c.
1820s–1940s
Partial settlements, 1871
Penitentiary convict record, 1913
Plat books, 1898–1923
Poll lists, 1892–1914
Poll tax record, 1876, 1879–1895,
1897, 1901–1909, 1911–1917,
1919–1926, 1928, 1930–1931
Prenuptial examination health
reports, 1926–1936
Orphans and Probate Court case
files, 1820–1940

Orphans and Probate Court
minutes, 1821–1919
Orphans and Probate dockets
and fee books, 1845–1905
Probate minutes and inventories,
1919–1929
Road tax record and receipts,
1925–1930
Sale record of personal property
from an estate, 1870–1871
Sheriff jail registers, 1876–1930

Tax abstracts, 1875–1927
Tax assessment records,
1848–1941
Tax sale record, 1870–1881
Vital records (births and deaths,
1912–1930)
Voter registration oaths,
1908–1930, 1930s–1940s,
1951–1952
Will records, 1821–1932

Pickens County

On December 19, 1820, Pickens County was created from Marion and Tuscaloosa Counties. It lost territory to the creation of Fayette County on December 20, 1824, and to Greene County on February 14, 1843, and January 30, 1867. The address of the county seat is P.O. Box 4600, Carrollton, AL 35447. Lands were granted through the Huntsville (closed 1905) and Tuscaloosa (closed 1866) land offices, then through the Montgomery Land Office until it closed in 1927; see chapter 11 in this volume, "Federal Land Records."

Marriages, cemetery records, and newspaper abstracts have been published for Pickens County, as well as several histories, including Nelson F. Smith, *History of Pickens County* (1856; reprint, with index, Spartanburg, S.C.: Southern Historical Press, 1980); James F. Clanahan, *The History of Pickens County, Alabama* (Carrollton, Ala.: Clanahan Publication, 1964); James Dolphus Johnson Jr., *Early Settlers of Pickens County, Alabama* (Cullman: Gregath Publishing, 1992); and *Pickens County, Alabama: History and Families* (Humboldt, Tenn.: Rose Publishing Company, 1998). A county heritage book has also been published. For extensive bibliographies, see the sources cited in chapter 2 in this volume, "Internet, Books, Bibliographies, Periodicals, Newspapers, and Manuscripts," but especially Collier, *Alabama County Data and Resources* (2nd ed.); and Barefield, *Researching in Alabama* (rev. ed.). For current addresses of historical societies, web sites, and public libraries, see the Internet web site of the Alabama Department of Archives and History.

Listed below are the records available on microfilm or as original records at the Alabama Department of Archives and History; the list comes from the archives' inventories. Some gaps in records and scattered issues of newspapers are not indicated. The archives' newspaper microfilm can be borrowed on interlibrary loan through local public libraries. Specific newspapers are listed at the web site of the Alabama Department of Archives and History. Other records are available at the county courthouse. For other vital records, see the next chapter. Many county records, including some not listed below, can be borrowed on interlibrary loan through LDS family history centers.

Census record, 1880
Confederate pension
    applications, c. 1900–c. 1920s
Deed records, 1876–1902
Final record, chancery court, c.
    1851–1876
List of registered voters, c.
    1908–c. 1931
Marriages, 1876–1910
Military discharges, 1920–c. 1945
Minutes, chancery court,
    1843–1929

Newspapers, 1849–1861,
    1866–1887, 1889–1899,
    1905–1907, 1918–1996
Poor house record, c. 1876–c.
    1915
Probate minutes, 1869–c. 1918
Probate files, c. 1876–c. 1930s
Substitute records, 1876–c. 1927
Vital records (births and deaths,
    1909–1917; births, 1919–1941;
    deaths, 1920–1942)
Will record, 1907–1954

Pike County

Created from Henry and Montgomery Counties on December 7, 1821, Pike County had significant boundary changes with Butler, Covington, Dale, Lowndes, and Montgomery Counties from 1824 to 1830. It lost land to Henry County (1831); gained territory from Montgomery County (1832); and lost ground to Barbour, Macon, and Russell Counties (1832). Pike County lost territory to Macon (1837), Crenshaw (1866, 1877) and Bullock (1866) Counties. The address of the county seat is P.O. Box 1147, Troy, AL 36081. Lands were granted through the St. Stephens (to 1833), Cahaba or Greenville (1819–1866), Sparta or Elba (1822–1867), and Montgomery (1866–1927) land offices; see chapter 11 in this volume, "Federal Land Records."

For extensive bibliographies, see the sources cited in chapter 2 in this volume, "Internet, Books, Bibliographies, Periodicals, Newspapers, and

Manuscripts," but especially Collier, *Alabama County Data and Resources* (2nd ed.); and Barefield, *Researching in Alabama* (rev. ed.). For current addresses of historical societies, web sites, and public libraries, see the Internet web site of the Alabama Department of Archives and History. A county heritage book is being prepared for publication.

The Troy Public Library, 300 N. Three Notch Street, Troy, AL 36081, has extensive local research holdings. The library's collection includes newspapers, some Troy city directories, county records microfilm, maps, photographs, and files on families, individuals, and subjects.

Listed below are the records available on microfilm or as original records at the Alabama Department of Archives and History; the list comes from the archives' inventories. Some gaps in records and scattered issues of newspapers are not indicated. The archives' newspaper microfilm can be borrowed on interlibrary loan through local public libraries. Specific newspapers are listed at the web site of the Alabama Department of Archives and History. Other records are available at the county courthouse. For other vital records, see the next chapter. Many county records, including some not listed below, can be borrowed on interlibrary loan through LDS family history centers.

Administrators, executors, and
  guardians deeds, 1895–1928
Administrators record, 1889–1933
Administrators settlement
  record, 1893–1931
Appraisement record, 1871–1916
Confederate soldiers, c. 1860s–c.
  1990
Deed records, 1886–1901
Dower record, 1875–1905
Final settlement record, 1877–c.
  1923
Inventory record, 1833–1844
Inventory and appraisement
  record, 1845–c. 1911
List of registered voters, 1902
Military discharge record, c.
  1919–c. 1930s

Newspapers, 1855–1868,
  1870–1996
Orphans Court minutes,
  1844–1853
Partial settlement record,
  1877–1904
Probate minutes, 1853–1929
Probate record, 1872–1888
Probate sale book, 1842–1889
Probate record of settlements,
  1864–1867
Tax assessment record, 1850
Vital records (births, 1881–1895,
  1903–1904, 1920–1937; deaths,
  1881–1892, 1902–1905,
  1920–1930; births and deaths,
  1907–1919)
Will records, 1922–1953

Randolph County

Created from St. Clair and Shelby Counties on December 18, 1832, Randolph County gave land to the creation of Cleburne and Clay Counties (1866). The address of the county seat is P.O. Box 2490, Wedowee, AL 36278. Lands were granted through the Montevallo or Mardisville Land Office until 1905 and then through the Montgomery Land Office until it closed in 1927; see chapter 11 in this volume, "Federal Land Records."

Birth records (1886–1905), death records (1886–1905), census records (1850–1880), Civil War records, and cemetery records have been published for Randolph County; also see Marilyn Davis Barefield, *Historical Records of Randolph County, Alabama* (Greenville, S.C.: Southern Historical Press, 1985), and the new county heritage book. For extensive bibliographies, see the sources cited in chapter 2 in this volume, "Internet, Books, Bibliographies, Periodicals, Newspapers, and Manuscripts," but especially Collier, *Alabama County Data and Resources* (2nd ed.); and Barefield, *Researching in Alabama* (rev. ed.).

For Randolph County research, there is the Randolph County Public Library, 736 College Street, Roanoke, AL 36274. The Northeast Alabama Genealogical Society, P.O. Box 674, Gadsden, AL 35902, publishes *Northeast Alabama Settlers;* and the AlaBenton Genealogical Society, c/o The Alabama Room, Box 308, Anniston, AL 36202, publishes *AlaBenton Genealogical Quarterly.* For current addresses of historical societies, web sites, and public libraries, see the Internet web site of the Alabama Department of Archives and History.

Listed below are the records available on microfilm or as original records at the Alabama Department of Archives and History; the list comes from the archives' inventories. Some gaps in records and scattered issues of newspapers are not indicated. The archives' newspaper microfilm can be borrowed on interlibrary loan through local public libraries. Specific newspapers are listed at the web site of the Alabama Department of Archives and History. Other records are available at the county courthouse. For other vital records, see the next chapter. Many county records, including some not listed below, can be borrowed on interlibrary loan through LDS family history centers.

Cemetery census, 1983
Child labor affidavits, 1908
Confederate pension records, 1930–1951
Deed records, 1897–1905
Inventory records, 1897–1930
List of registered voters, 1907–1908
Marriages, 1930–1951
Newspapers, 1895–1898, 1903–1982
Pension records, 1904–1907
Probate minutes, 1897–1923
Vital records (births, 1886–1942; deaths, 1920–1942)
Wills and bonds, 1897–1945

Russell County

Russell County was created on December 18, 1832, from Montgomery and Pike Counties. It lost area to Lee County on December 5, 1866, and exchanged land with Lee County on September 30, 1932. The address of the county seat is P.O. Box 969, Phenix City, AL 36868. Lands were granted through the Montgomery Land Office (1834–1927); see chapter 11 in this volume, "Federal Land Records."

Marriage records and the federal census (1850 and 1860) have been published for Russell County; also see Russell County Historical Commission, *The History of Russell County, Alabama* (Dallas, Tex.: The Author, 1982). A county heritage book is being prepared for publication. For extensive bibliographies, see the sources cited in chapter 2 in this volume, "Internet, Books, Bibliographies, Periodicals, Newspapers, and Manuscripts," but especially Collier, *Alabama County Data and Resources* (2nd ed.); and Barefield, *Researching in Alabama* (rev. ed.). For current addresses of historical societies, web sites, and public libraries, see the Internet web site of the Alabama Department of Archives and History.

Listed below are the records available on microfilm or as original records at the Alabama Department of Archives and History; the list comes from the archives' inventories. Some gaps in records and scattered issues of newspapers are not indicated. The archives' newspaper microfilm can be borrowed on interlibrary loan through local public libraries. Specific newspapers are listed at the web site of the Alabama Department of Ar-

chives and History. Other records are available at the county courthouse. For other vital records, see the next chapter. Many county records, including some not listed below, can be borrowed on interlibrary loan through LDS family history centers.

Bonds, returns, and sales, 1837–1842

Bonds of administrators and deceased, 1850–1853

Deed and mortgage records index, 1836–1908

Deed records, 1885–1904

Estate case files index

Inventories, appraisements, and sales, 1837–1908

Letters testamentary, 1886–1942

Marriages, 1834–1950

Newspapers, 1856–1994

Orphans and Probate Court docket, 1843–1848

Orphans and Probate Court minutes, 1846–1923

Petitions and reports, 1906–1942

Probate annual and final settlements, 1865–1942

Probate partial and final settlements, 1856–1859

Sheriff jail register, 1892–1895

Tax assessment record, 1861

Vital records (delayed birth certificates, 1943–1962)

Will records, 1838–1942

Sanford County

See Lamar County.

Shelby County

Created on February 7, 1818, from Montgomery County, Shelby County lost territory to the creation of St. Clair County on November 20, 1818; Jefferson County on December 13, 1819; Chambers, Coosa, Randolph, Talladega, and Tallapoosa Counties on December 18, 1832; and Baker or Chilton County on December 30, 1866. It also had numerous border changes with Baker or Chilton, Jefferson, and St. Clair Counties. The address of the county seat is P.O. Box 467, Columbiana, AL 35051. Lands were granted through the Huntsville (closed 1905) and Tuscaloosa (closed 1866) land offices, then through the Montgomery Land Office until it closed in 1927; see chapter 11 in this volume, "Federal Land Records."

Cemetery, marriage, and other records have been published for Shelby County, as well as a county heritage book. For extensive bibliographies, see the sources cited in chapter 2 in this volume, "Internet, Books, Bibliographies, Periodicals, Newspapers, and Manuscripts," but especially Collier, *Alabama County Data and Resources* (2nd ed.); and Barefield, *Researching in Alabama* (rev. ed.). For current addresses of historical societies, web sites, and public libraries, see the Internet web site of the Alabama Department of Archives and History.

Listed below are the records available on microfilm or as original records at the Alabama Department of Archives and History; the list comes from the archives' inventories. Some gaps in records and scattered issues of newspapers are not indicated. The archives' newspaper microfilm can be borrowed on interlibrary loan through local public libraries. Specific newspapers are listed at the web site of the Alabama Department of Archives and History. Other records are available at the county courthouse. For other vital records, see the next chapter. Many county records, including some not listed below, can be borrowed on interlibrary loan through LDS family history centers. The Birmingham Public Library has many Shelby County records on microfilm.

Applications for headstones for Confederate soldiers, c. 1979

Chancery court records, 1839–1884

Chancery court minutes, 1896–1916

Deed records index, 1819–1905

Deed records, 1835–1901

Final record, 1869–1934

Marriages, 1824–1930

Military discharge record, 1920–1946

Naturalization record, c. 1891–c. 1901

Newspapers, 1868–1879, 1883–1893, 1923–1996

Orphans Court records, 1818–1859

Probate record, 1863–1930

Record of patients at alms house, c. 1899–c. 1913

School censuses, 1916, 1918, 1920, 1924

Tax assessment record, 1850

Tract book, c. 1819–c. 1900

Vital records (births and deaths, 1902–1915; births, 1920–1929; deaths, 1920–1929)

Registration of voters, 1908, 1910, 1912, 1914, 1919, 1922, 1924

Will records, 1896–1930

St. Clair County

Created from Shelby County on November 20, 1818, St. Clair County lost area to Benton or Calhoun (1832, 1836), Cherokee (1836), DeKalb

(1836), Etowah (1868), Jackson (1834), Jefferson (1819, 1823), Randolph (1832), and Talladega Counties (1832). It exchanged territory with Shelby County on February 7, 1899, and with Jefferson County in September 1915. The address of the county seat is 129 Fifth Avenue, Ashville, AL 35953. Lands were granted through the Huntsville (closed 1905) and Tuscaloosa (closed 1866) land offices, then through the Montgomery Land Office until it closed in 1927; see chapter 11 in this volume, "Federal Land Records."

Cemetery, marriage, census (1870), Confederate service, newspaper abstracts, and miscellaneous records for St. Clair County have been published; also see W. H. Cather, *History of St. Clair County* (Ashville, Ala.: Southern Aegis, 1897); Mattie Lou Teague Crow, *History of St. Clair County* (Huntsville: Strode, 1973); and the new county heritage book. For extensive bibliographies, see the sources cited in chapter 2 in this volume, "Internet, Books, Bibliographies, Periodicals, Newspapers, and Manuscripts," but especially Collier, *Alabama County Data and Resources* (2nd ed.); and Barefield, *Researching in Alabama* (rev. ed.).

For current addresses of historical societies, web sites, and public libraries, see the Internet web site of the Alabama Department of Archives and History. The St. Clair Historical Society, Ashville Museum and Archives, Box 1570, Ashville, AL 35953, publishes *Cherish: The Quarterly Journal of the St. Clair County Historical Society*. The Northeast Alabama Genealogical Society, P.O. Box 674, Gadsden, AL 35902, publishes *Northeast Alabama Settlers*.

Listed below are the records available on microfilm or as original records at the Alabama Department of Archives and History; the list comes from the archives' inventories. Some gaps in records and scattered issues of newspapers are not indicated. The archives' newspaper microfilm can be borrowed on interlibrary loan through local public libraries. Specific newspapers are listed at the web site of the Alabama Department of Archives and History. Other records are available at the county courthouse. For other vital records, see the next chapter. Many county records, including some not listed below, can be borrowed on interlibrary loan through LDS family history centers.

Administrators' record, 1871–c. 1952
Census record, 1880

Confederate pension record, 1899–1912
Deed record, 1886–1903
Executors record, 1871–1924
Final settlement record, 1871–c. 1930
Guardians' record, 1871–1943
Military discharge records, 1919–1944
Newspapers, 1885–1993
Partial settlement record, 1874–1942
Probate Court minutes, 1856–1927
Probate Court record, 1850–1858
Record of estates, 1885–1908
Vital records (births, 1893–1906; deaths, 1881–1895)
Will records, 1906–1938

Sumter County

Sumter County was created as an original county on December 18, 1832. It lost land to the creation of Choctaw County on March 1, 1870. The address of the county seat is P.O. Box 70, Livingston, AL 35470. Lands were granted through the Huntsville (to 1821), St. Stephens (to 1833), Demopolis (1833–1866), Tuscaloosa (1822–1866), and Montgomery (1866–1927) land offices; see chapter 11 in this volume, "Federal Land Records."

Poll and/or voting lists (1833–1861) and estate records (including wills) have been published for Sumter County. Also for this county, see Ralph M. Lyon, *A Bibliography of Writings about Sumter County* (n.p., n.d.); Virginia O. Foscue, *The Place Names of Sumter County, Alabama* (University: University of Alabama Press, 1964); and Nelle Jenkins, *Pioneer Families of Sumter County, Alabama* (Tuscaloosa: Willo, 1961). A county heritage book is being prepared for publication. For extensive bibliographies, see the sources cited in chapter 2 in this volume, "Internet, Books, Bibliographies, Periodicals, Newspapers, and Manuscripts," but especially Collier, *Alabama County Data and Resources* (2nd ed.); and Barefield, *Researching in Alabama* (rev. ed.). Local libraries include the Sumter County Public Library, Monroe Street, Livingston, AL 35470, and the Julia Tutwiler Library, University of West Alabama, Livingston, AL 35470. For current addresses of historical societies, web sites, and public libraries, see the Internet web site of the Alabama Department of Archives and History.

Listed below are the records available on microfilm or as original records at the Alabama Department of Archives and History; the list comes from the archives' inventories. Some gaps in records and scattered issues of newspapers are not indicated. The archives' newspaper microfilm can be borrowed on interlibrary loan through local public libraries. Specific newspapers are listed at the web site of the Alabama Department of Archives and History. Other records are available at the county courthouse. For other vital records, see the next chapter. Many county records, including some not listed below, can be borrowed on interlibrary loan through LDS family history centers.

Administrators record, 1871–1935

Census, 1880

Census of Confederate veterans, 1907

Confederate pension record, 1920

Confederate volunteers, 1863

Deed records, 1833–1901

Dog tax receipt books, 1891–1916

Estate case files, 1835–1953

Executors' record, 1871–1917

Final settlement record, 1871–1953

Guardians' record, 1871–1932

Inventory record, 1871–1950

Jury lists, 1847, 1859

Lists of registered voters, 1902–1940

Military discharge record, 1917–1954

Newspapers, 1836–1840, 1843–1868, 1871–1996

Oaths of allegiance, 1865

Partial settlement record, 1871

Pension record, 1915–1937

Poll tax record, 1901–1938

Orphans and Probate Court case files, c. 1835–c. 1953

Orphans and Probate Court minutes, 1833–1944

Orphans and Probate Court record, 1833–1937

Sixteenth section lands journal, 1840–1851

Tax assessment record, 1850, 1856, 1858–1861

Tract book, 1833–1834

Vital records (births, 1888–1891, 1909–1916; deaths, 1909–1916; births and deaths, 1917–1919)

Will records, 1827–1938

Talladega County

Created from St. Clair and Shelby Counties on December 18, 1832, Talladega County gained territory from Benton or Calhoun County (1836–1850) but lost ground to the creation of Cleburne and Clay Counties (1866). Talladega County also had various boundary changes with Clay County (1877–

1894). The address of the county seat is P.O. Box 755, Talladega, AL 35161. Lands were granted through the Montevallo or Mardisville Land Office until 1905 and then through the Montgomery Land Office until it closed in 1927; see chapter 11 in this volume, "Federal Land Records."

Cemetery, census (1850–1880), and marriage records have been published for Talladega County. Historical background can be found in E. Grace Jemison, *Historic Tales of Talladega* (Huntsville: Strode, 1984); and "Sketches of Talladega County, Alabama" (Birmingham: Works Projects Administration, 1938). A county heritage book has been published. For extensive bibliographies, see the sources cited in chapter 2 in this volume, "Internet, Books, Bibliographies, Periodicals, Newspapers, and Manuscripts," but especially Collier, *Alabama County Data and Resources* (2nd ed.); and Barefield, *Researching in Alabama* (rev. ed.). For current addresses of historical societies, web sites, and public libraries, see the Internet web site of the Alabama Department of Archives and History.

Some resources specifically for Talladega County include the Talladega Public Library, 202 South Street East, Talladega, AL 35160, which has local newspapers, city directories, and genealogical, biographical, and subject files. The Northeast Alabama Genealogical Society, P.O. Box 674, Gadsden, AL 35902, and publishes *Northeast Alabama Settlers*.

Listed below are the records available on microfilm or as original records at the Alabama Department of Archives and History; the list comes from the archives' inventories. Some gaps in records and scattered issues of newspapers are not indicated. The archives' newspaper microfilm can be borrowed on interlibrary loan through local public libraries. Specific newspapers are listed at the web site of the Alabama Department of Archives and History. Other records are available at the county courthouse. For other vital records, see the next chapter. Many county records, including some not listed below, can be borrowed on interlibrary loan through LDS family history centers.

Absentee voters list, 1926–1929	Chancery court minutes,
Abstract of records of chattel	1854–1876
mortgages, 1894–1897	Circuit court minutes, 1917–1939
Audit report, 1920–1931	Claims docket, 1896–1900
Chancery court dockets,	Confederate pension record,
1839–1899	1900–1939

Deed record index, c. 1833–1909

Deed records, 1833–1902

Deed and mortgage files, 1899–1903

Delinquent taxes docket, 1895

Election officer warrants, 1937–1940

Equity court minutes, 1893–1914

Exemption record, 1872–1914

Fee book, 1871–1884

Final record, 1869–1874

Lists of registered voters, 1902–1927

Marriages, 1833–1936

Military discharge record, 1930–1945

Miscellaneous record, 1820–1966

Newspapers, 1840–1842, 1844–1845, 1847–1850,

1852–1853, 1856–1857, 1859–1892, 1895–1990

Orphans Court minutes, 1843–1850

Poll book, 1890–1899

Poll tax records, c. 1901–1954

Probate Court minutes, 1850–1926

Probate docket, 1857–1887

Report of lands redeemed, 1911

Road book, 1905

Tax assessment records, 1850, 1852, 1853, 1886–1887

Trial docket, 1853–1931

Will records, c. 1833–c. 1853

Wills and inventories, c. 1852–1907

Will book and final record, 1856

Tallapoosa County

Created on December 18, 1832, from Montgomery and Shelby Counties, Tallapoosa County lost land to Macon County on February 2, 1846; Lee County on December 5, 1866; and Elmore County in December 1866. The address of the county seat is 125 N. Broadnax Street, Dadeville, AL 36853. Lands were granted through the Montgomery Land Office (1834–1927); see chapter 11 in this volume, "Federal Land Records."

Marriage records and census records (1850–1860) have been published for this county. Among the several historical works on the Tallapoosa area, see William Presley Ingram, *A History of Tallapoosa County* (Birmingham: The Author, 1985); Tallapoosa County Bicentennial Committee, *Tallapoosa County: A History* (Alexander City, Ala.: The Author, 1976); and Sandra Scott Wilson, *Some Pioneers of Tallapoosa County* (Dadeville, Ala.: Tohopeka Chapter DAR, 1991). A county heritage book is being prepared for publication. For extensive bibliographies, see the sources cited in chapter 2 in this volume, "Internet, Books, Bibliographies, Periodicals, Newspapers, and Manuscripts," but especially Collier, *Alabama County Data and Re-*

sources (2nd ed.); and Barefield, *Researching in Alabama* (rev. ed.). For current addresses of historical societies, web sites, and public libraries, see the Internet web site of the Alabama Department of Archives and History.

Listed below are the records available on microfilm or as original records at the Alabama Department of Archives and History; the list comes from the archives' inventories. Some gaps in records and scattered issues of newspapers are not indicated. The archives' newspaper microfilm can be borrowed on interlibrary loan through local public libraries. Specific newspapers are listed at the web site of the Alabama Department of Archives and History. Other records are available at the county courthouse. For other vital records, see the next chapter. Many county records, including some not listed below, can be borrowed on interlibrary loan through LDS family history centers.

Administrators record, 1871–1898
Apprentice record, 1884–1930
Bond record, 1855–c. 1880
Child labor affidavits, 1908–1916
Declaration of intention,
    1914–1921
Deed records, 1885–1903
Dower record, 1872–c. 1913
Guardians record, 1871–1931
Executors minutes, c. 1924–1936
Executors record, 1871–1926
List of registered voters, c.
    1902–c. 1923
Marriages, 1835–1931
Military discharge records,
    1919–c. 1947
Naturalization records, 1915–1924

Newspapers, 1883–1900,
    1905–1996
Petitions and reports, 1874–1927
Probate accounts, 1848–1874
Probate decrees in final
    settlement, 1874–1926
Probate sale of real estate for
    distribution, 1872–c. 1922
Orphans and Probate Court
    minutes, 1835–c. 1934
Real estate sale record, 1872–c.
    1919
Tax assessment, 1857
Vital records (births, 1881–1907,
    1920–1935; births and deaths,
    1908–1919; deaths, 1881–1938)
Will records, 1835–1930

Tuscaloosa County

Tuscaloosa County was created from Montgomery County on February 6, 1818, and originally included part of eastern Mississippi. It lost ground to Marion (February 13, 1818, December 19, 1820), Cahawba or Bibb (November 20, 1818, December 20, 1820), Greene (December 13, 1819), Perry

(December 13, 1819), Pickens (December 19, 1820), Walker (December 26, 1823), Fayette (December 24, 1824, January 20, 1832), and Hale (January 30, 1867) Counties. The address of the county seat is 714 Greensboro Ave., Tuscaloosa, AL 35401. Lands were granted through the Huntsville (closed 1905) and Tuscaloosa (closed 1866) land offices, then through the Montgomery Land Office until it closed in 1927; see chapter 11 in this volume, "Federal Land Records."

Cemetery, census (1850–1880), Confederate service, genealogical chart, marriage, newspaper abstract (1881–1886), tax (1889, 1894), and amnesty oath (1865) records have been published for Tuscaloosa County, as well as a county heritage book; also see Alton Lambert, *History of Tuscaloosa County*. For extensive bibliographies, see the sources cited in chapter 2 in this volume, "Internet, Books, Bibliographies, Periodicals, Newspapers, and Manuscripts," but especially Collier, *Alabama County Data and Resources* (2nd ed.); and Barefield, *Researching in Alabama* (rev. ed.).

The Tuscaloosa Public Library, 1801 River Road, Tuscaloosa, AL 35401, has a genealogical collection of locally oriented holdings, including newspapers (1958–), Tuscaloosa city directories (1929–, some years missing), maps, and files on people, families, and subjects. For current addresses of historical societies, web sites, and public libraries, see the Internet web site of the Alabama Department of Archives and History.

Listed below are the records available on microfilm or as original records at the Alabama Department of Archives and History; the list comes from the archives' inventories. Some gaps in records and scattered issues of newspapers are not indicated. The archives' newspaper microfilm can be borrowed on interlibrary loan through local public libraries. Specific newspapers are listed at the web site of the Alabama Department of Archives and History. Other records are available at the county courthouse. For other vital records, see the next chapter. Many county records, including some not listed below, can be borrowed on interlibrary loan through LDS family history centers.

Census record, 1880

Chancery court minutes, 1883–1917

Circuit court minutes, in equity, 1917–1928

Confederate pension record, 1928–1931

Confederate veterans record, 1893–c. 1904

Deeds index, c. 1818–c. 1904

Deed records, 1818–1901

Estate case files, c. 1825–1938

Guardians record, 1830–1892

Inventory record, c. 1837–c. 1890

Marriages, 1884–1921, 1930–1933

Military discharge index, 1919–c. 1980s

Military discharge record, 1919–1945

Miscellaneous record, 1820–1966

Newspapers, 1830–1832, 1835–1837, 1840–1855, 1857–1990

Overseers of the poor record, 1818–1833

Petitions and orders for letters of administration, 1911–1928

Poll tax records, 1893, 1901–1965

Poll tax exemption records, 1934–1938

Probate Court conveyances index, 1892–1894

Orphans and Probate Court minutes, 1824–1928

Probate record, 1893–c. 1900

Tax assessment record, 1848

Vital records (births, 1895–1907; births and deaths, 1895–1900, 1905–1922)

Will records, 1898–1928

Walker County

Walker County was created on December 26, 1823, from Jefferson, Marion, and Tuscaloosa Counties. It lost land to Fayette (1824), Hancock or Winston (1850), Blount (1877), and Cullman (1953) Counties. The address of the county seat is P.O. Box 1447, Jasper, AL 35501. Lands were granted through the Huntsville (closed 1905) and Tuscaloosa (closed 1866) land offices, then through the Montgomery Land Office until it closed in 1927; see chapter 11 in this volume, "Federal Land Records."

Cemetery records, a voter list (1867, includes personal data on each voter), and census records (1830–1880) have been published for Walker County; also see John Martin Dombhart, *History of Walker County: Its Towns and Its People* (1937; reprint, as volume five of *Annals of Northwest Alabama*, [Jasper, Ala.: Carl Elliott Books, 1987]). Another source is the new county heritage book. For extensive bibliographies, see the sources cited in chapter 2 in this volume, "Internet, Books, Bibliographies, Periodicals, Newspapers, and Manuscripts," but especially Collier, *Alabama County Data and Resources* (2nd ed.); and Barefield, *Researching in Alabama* (rev. ed.). The Jasper Public Library, 20 East 18th Street, Jasper, AL 35501, has local newspapers (1884–), maps, some Jasper city directories, and files on individuals, subjects, and families. *Alabama Family History and Ge-*

nealogy News is published by North Central Alabama Genealogical Society, Box 13, Cullman, AL 35056–0013; and *Walking Back in Time* is published by the Walker County Genealogical Society, P.O. Box 3408, Jasper, AL 35502–3408.

Listed below are the records available on microfilm or as original records at the Alabama Department of Archives and History; the list comes from the archives' inventories. Some gaps in records and scattered issues of newspapers are not indicated. The archives' newspaper microfilm can be borrowed on interlibrary loan through local public libraries. Specific newspapers are listed at the web site of the Alabama Department of Archives and History. Other records are available at the county courthouse. For other vital records, see the next chapter. Many county records, including some not listed below, can be borrowed on interlibrary loan through LDS family history centers.

> Administrators and executors settlements, 1873–1888
> Confederate pension applications, 1913–1914
> Deed records, 1877–1901
> Divorces, 1891–1935
> Final record, 1877–1929
> Inventories and appraisements, 1881–1897
> Military discharge record, 1919–1944
> Newspapers, 1886–1995
> Poll tax record, 1901–c. 1948
> Probate minutes, 1877–1929

Washington County

Created on June 4, 1800, from Adams and Pickering Counties of the Mississippi Territory, Washington County, originally, on paper, extended across half of today's Mississippi and all of Alabama. It lost land to the creation of Baldwin and Wayne Counties in 1809 and to Clarke County in 1812. With the creation of the Alabama Territory in 1817, it split into Washington County of Mississippi and Washington County of Alabama. The latter lost ground to the creation of Choctaw County in 1847. The address of the county seat is P.O. Box 146, Chatom, AL 36518. Federal lands were granted through the St. Stephens (to 1867), Mobile (1867–1879), and Montgomery (1867–1927) land offices; see chapter 11 in this volume, "Federal Land Records."

Marriage records; tax lists and censuses (1795–1880, 1886–1891); the index to deeds; and other Washington County records have been published; also see Jacqueline Anderson Matte, *The History of Washington County*, 2 vols. (Chatom, Ala.: Washington County Historical Society, 1982, 1989). A county heritage book is being prepared for publication. For extensive bibliographies, see the sources cited in chapter 2 in this volume, "Internet, Books, Bibliographies, Periodicals, Newspapers, and Manuscripts," but especially Collier, *Alabama County Data and Resources* (2nd ed.); and Barefield, *Researching in Alabama* (rev. ed.). The Washington County Public Library, P.O. Box 1057, Chatom, AL 36518, has extensive materials for local history research, including newspapers, maps, photographs, private manuscript collections, and files on families, individuals, and subjects. The address of the Genealogical Society of Washington County is P.O. Box 456, Chatom, AL 36518. For current addresses of historical societies, web sites, and public libraries, see the Internet web site of the Alabama Department of Archives and History.

Listed below are the records available on microfilm or as original records at the Alabama Department of Archives and History; the list comes from the archives' inventories. Some gaps in records and scattered issues of newspapers are not indicated. The archives' newspaper microfilm can be borrowed on interlibrary loan through local public libraries. Specific newspapers are listed at the web site of the Alabama Department of Archives and History. Other records are available at the county courthouse. For other vital records, see the next chapter. Some pre-1817 Washington County records today are in the local records of Washington County, Mississippi. Many county records, including some not listed below, can be borrowed on interlibrary loan through LDS family history centers.

> Bonds, c. 1803–c. 1906
> Chancery court record, 1805–1827
> County court minutes, 1827–c. 1850
> County court records, 1827–1844
> Deed records, 1799–1928
> Inventories and appraisements, 1825–1914

List of records, c. 1805
List of registered voters, c. 1902–c. 1932
Marriages, 1826–1929
Military discharge record, 1919–1955
Newspapers, 1899–1996
Probate records, 1827–1938
Superior court record, 1802–1812
Will records, 1827–1938

Wayne County

Created on December 21, 1809, in the Mississippi Territory, Wayne County lost its territory in today's Alabama with the creation of the Alabama territory in 1817. The early records of the county were lost in a fire in 1892.

Wilcox County

Wilcox County was created from Dallas, Marengo, Monroe, and Montgomery Counties on December 13, 1819, but lost territory to Clarke County on January 15, 1831. The address of the county seat is 100 Broad Street, Camden, AL 36726. Lands were granted through the St. Stephens (to 1819), Demopolis (1833–1866), Cahaba or Greenville (1819–1866), and Montgomery (1866–1927) land offices; see chapter 11 in this volume, "Federal Land Records."

The 1860 federal census and Confederate service records have been published for Wilcox County; also see Marilyn Davis Barefield, *Early Records of Wilcox County, Alabama* (Greenville, S.C.: Southern Historical Press, 1988); and Ouida Starr Woodson, *Within the Bend: Stories of Wilcox County* (n.p.: The Author, 1988). A county heritage book is being prepared for publication. For extensive bibliographies, see the sources cited in chapter 2 in this volume, "Internet, Books, Bibliographies, Periodicals, Newspapers, and Manuscripts," but especially Collier, *Alabama County Data and Resources* (2nd ed.); and Barefield, *Researching in Alabama* (rev. ed.). For current addresses of historical societies, web sites, and public libraries, see the Internet web site of the Alabama Department of Archives and History.

Listed below are the records available on microfilm or as original records at the Alabama Department of Archives and History; the list comes from the archives' inventories. Some gaps in records and scattered issues of newspapers are not indicated. The archives' newspaper microfilm can be borrowed on interlibrary loan through local public libraries. Specific newspapers are listed at the web site of the Alabama Department of Archives and History. Other records are available at the county courthouse. For other vital records, see the next chapter. Many county records, including some not listed below, can be borrowed on interlibrary loan through LDS family history centers.

Abstract of records of chattel
   mortgages, 1938–1940
Chancery court minutes,
   1848–1882
Chattel mortgage records,
   1854–1900
Circuit court case files,
   1890s–1937
County court case files,
   1880–1935
Deed records, 1820–1901
Inventory record, 1861–1864
Jail lists, 1878–1935
Land books, 1888–1917
Lists of registered voters, 1868,
   1902–1918 (incomplete), 1922
Lot book, 1924–1931
Marriages, 1841–1851, 1913–1936
Miscellaneous record, c.
   1879–1930

Newspapers, 1850–1851,
   1868–1883, 1887–1996
Plat books, 1920–1927
Poll tax record, 1886, 1896–1897,
   1901, 1901–1906
Probate dockets and fee books,
   1853–1855
Orphans and Probate Court
   minutes, 1821–1929
Road book, 1923–1928
Road tax record and receipts,
   1909–1924
Sheriffs jail registers, 1878–1935
Tax abstracts, 1907–1947
Tax assessment records,
   1849–1942
Tax sale record, 1870–1887
Vital records (births and deaths,
   1905–1908; deaths, 1908–1915)
Will record, 1898–1934

Winston County

Created as Hancock County on February 12, 1850, from Walker County, its name was changed to Winston County on January 22, 1858, and it gave up territory to the creation of Cullman County on January 25, 1877. The address of the county seat is P.O. Box 147, Double Springs, AL 35553. Land was granted through the Huntsville Land Office until 1905, then through the Montgomery Land Office until it closed in 1927; see chapter 11 in this volume, "Federal Land Records."

Census records (1850–1880), a voter list (1867, giving personal information on each voter), a death register (1888–1910), and marriages (1891–1900) have been published for this county. Several books have been published on Winston County, especially about local support of the Union during the Civil War, as well as a county heritage book. For extensive bibliographies, see the sources cited in chapter 2 in this volume, "Internet, Books, Bibliographies, Periodicals, Newspapers, and Manuscripts," but especially Collier, *Alabama County Data and Resources* (2nd ed.); and Barefield, *Researching in Alabama* (rev. ed.). *Alabama Family History and Genealogy News* is published by North Central Alabama Genealogical Society, Box 13, Cullman, AL 35056–0013. For current addresses of historical societies, web sites, and public libraries, see the Internet web site of the Alabama Department of Archives and History.

Listed below are the records available on microfilm or as original records at the Alabama Department of Archives and History; the list comes from the archives' inventories. Some gaps in records and scattered issues of newspapers are not indicated. The archives' newspaper microfilm can be borrowed on interlibrary loan through local public libraries. Specific newspapers are listed at the web site of the Alabama Department of Archives and History. Other records are available at the county courthouse. For other vital records, see the next chapter. Many county records, including some not listed below, can be borrowed on interlibrary loan through LDS family history centers.

Circuit court case files, 1887–1932
Confederate pension records, 1896
County court records, 1891–1934 (incomplete)
Deed records, 1891–1902
Jury lists, 1889–1910
Lists of registered voters, 1902–1935
Marriages, 1931–1955
Newspapers, 1901–1905, 1918–1924, 1945–1994
Poll tax record, 1903–1918
Probate minutes, 1901–1928
Results of elections, 1935–1952
Tax assessment records, 1891–1926
Vital records (births and deaths, 1888–1918)
Will records, 1891–1925

15. VITAL RECORDS: BIRTHS, DEATHS, DIVORCES, AND MARRIAGES

Government-required civil registration of vital records has a long history in Alabama. Many such early records required by the French and Spanish governments are indexed in Jerome Lepre's *Index to the Records of Old Mobile's Cathedral of the Immaculate Conception* (Pascagoula, Miss.: Jackson County Genealogical Society, 1995). Civil marriage records began in the counties in 1799.

Birth and death vital records began as civil county records in 1881 when the state of Alabama created for each county a health department, charged with keeping information on births and deaths. These records, although often incomplete, frequently survive among the holdings of individual county courts of probate for as late as 1908. In 1909 a state vital records office became the archives of Alabama birth and death records. The state vital records office began a statewide compilation of marriages in 1936 and divorces in 1950.

Individual county health departments of Alabama can request and obtain electronically copies of vital records for the general public for a fee. The Center for Health Statistics, Office of Vital Records, Department of

Health, P.O. Box 5625, Montgomery, AL 36103-5625, can also provide these records by mail. By either means, the cost of a search and copy is currently twelve dollars. Indexes to death, divorce, and marriage records are available from the Center for Health Statistics and can also be borrowed through LDS family history centers.

NOTES ON ACCESS TO MODERN VITAL RECORDS IN ALABAMA, 1909 TO PRESENT

Birth Records

Access to state government birth records in Alabama, 1909 to the present, are restricted to only the individual or to the individual's guardian. LDS family history centers and many major Alabama libraries offer on microfilm an index to Alabama birth certificates, 1917–1919. Proof of year of birth can be learned from such open public records as the federal census (1790–1930). Similarly, identities of parents can sometimes be learned from sources that include social security records and death certificates.

Adoption Records

For information on obtaining access to adoption records in Alabama, contact the Alabama Department of Human Resources, Family and Children's Services Division, 50 N. Ripley Street, Montgomery, AL 36130. Currently, biological birth certificates are open to adoptees, under certain conditions, when the adoptee becomes age nineteen. Several books are available on obtaining information on adoptions, including Jayne Askin and Molly Davis, *Search: A Handbook for Adoptees and Birth Parents* (Phoenix, Ariz.: Oryx Press, 1992). For more information on adoption records and procedures, write for a free pamphlet (and enclose a self-addressed, stamped envelope) from the Genealogy Department, Allen County-Fort Wayne Public Library, P.O. Box 2270, Fort Wayne, IN 46801, or the Alabama Department of Archives and History, P.O. Box 300100, Montgomery, AL 36130-0100.

Death Records

Alabama's Center for Health Certificates has made widely available a microfilm index to the state death certificates, 1908–1959. The index gives

COUNTY CODES
USED IN ALABAMA VITAL RECORDS INDEXES

County	Code	County	Code
Autauga	01	Houston	35
Baldwin	02	Jackson	36
Barbour	03	Jefferson	37
Bibb	04	Lamar	38
Blount	05	Lauderdale	39
Bullock	06	Lawrence	40
Butler	07	Lee	41
Calhoun	08	Limestone	42
Chambers	09	Lowndes	43
Cherokee	10	Macon	44
Chilton	11	Madison	45
Choctaw	12	Marengo	46
Clarke	13	Marion	47
Clay	14	Marshall	48
Cleburne	15	Mobile	49
Coffee	16	Monroe	50
Colbert	17	Montgomery	51
Conecuh	18	Morgan	52
Coosa	19	Perry	53
Covington	20	Pickens	54
Crenshaw	21	Pike	55
Cullman	22	Randolph	56
Dale	23	Russell	57
Dallas	24	St. Clair	58
DeKalb	25	Shelby	59
Elmore	26	Sumter	60
Escambia	27	Talladega	61
Etowah	28	Tallapoosa	62
Fayette	29	Tuscaloosa	63
Franklin	30	Walker	64
Geneva	31	Washington	65
Greene	32	Wilcox	66
Hale	33	Winston	67
Henry	34		

County Codes

Guide to the Soundex System

Used in Alabama Vital Records Indexes

The Soundex filing system, alphabetic for the first letter of surname and numeric thereunder as indicated by divider cards, keeps together names of the same and similar sounds but of variant spellings.

To search for a particular name, you must first work out the code number for the surname of the individual. No number is assigned to the first letter of the surname. If the name is Kuhne, for example, the index card will be in the "K" segment of the index. The code number for Kuhne, worked out according to the system below, is 500.

Soundex Coding Guide

Code	Key Letters and Equivalents
1	b,p,f,v
2	c,s,k,g,j,q,x,z
3	d,t
4	l
5	m,n
6	r

The letters a, e, i, o, u, y, w, and h are *not* coded.
The first letter of the surname is *not* coded.

Every Soundex number must be a 3-digit number. A name yielding no code numbers, as Lee, would thus be L-000; one yielding only one code number would have two zeros added, as Kuhne, coded as K-500; and one yielding two code numbers would have one zero added, as Ebell, coded as E-140. Not more than three digits are used, so Ebelson would be coded as E-142, *not* E-1425.

When two key letters or equivalents appear together, or one key letter immediately follows or precedes an equivalent, the two are coded as one letter, by a single number, as follows: *Kelly,* coded as K-400; *Buerck,* coded as B-620, *Lloyd,* coded as L-300; and *Schaefer,* coded as S-160.

If several surnames have the same code, the cards for them are arranged alphabetically by given name. There are divider cards showing most code numbers, but not all. For instance, one divider may be numbered 350 and the next one 400. Between the two divider cards there may be names coded 353,

350, 360, 365, and 355, but instead of being in numerical order they are interfiled alphabetically by given name.

Such prefixes to surnames as "van," "Von," "Di," "de," "le," "Di," "D'," "dela," or "du" are sometimes disregarded in alphabetizing and in coding.

The following names are examples of Soundex coding and are given only as illustrations.

Name	Letters Coded	Code No.
Allricht	l.r.c.	A-462
Eberhard	b.r.r	E-166
Engebrethson	n.g.b	E-521
Heimbach	m.b.c	H-512
Hanselmann	n.s.l	H-524
Henzelmann	n.z.l	H-524
Hildebrand	l.d.b	H-431
Kavanagh	v.n.g	K-152
Lind, Van	n.d	L-530
Lukaschowsky	k.s.s	L-222
McDonnell	c.d.n	M-235
McGee	c	M-200
O'Brien	b.r.n	O-165
Opnian	p.n.n	O-155
Oppenheimer	p.n.m	O-155
Riedemanas	d.m.n	R-355
Zita	t	Z-300
Zitzmeinn	t.z.m	Z-325

Native Americans, Orientals, and Religious Nuns

Researchers using the Soundex system to locate religious nuns or persons with American Indian or oriental names should be aware of the way such names were coded. Variations in coding differed from the normal coding system.

Phonetically spelled oriental and Indian names were sometimes coded as if one continuous name, or, if a distinguishable surname was given, the names were coded in the normal manner. For example, the American Indian name Shinka-Wa-Sa may have been coded as "Shinka" (S-520) or "Sa" (S-000). Researchers should investigate the various possibilities of coding such names.

Religious nun names were coded as if "Sister" were the surname, and they appear in the Soundex indexes under the code "S-236." Within the code S-236, the names may not be in alphabetical order.

Guide to the Soundex System

the name of the deceased (with the surname sometimes in soundex code), code for county of death, date of death, and state certificate number (volume and number). Given names do not always appear in strict alphabetical order in this index and much of the index uses soundex codes for surnames. Microfilm of the death certificates for 1908 to 1972 are available for loan through LDS family history centers.

The index can also be accessed at the Internet web site Ancestry.com. Using the index on the Internet solves such problems as not knowing the year of death, having deaths recorded in the wrong annual index, and the fact that the index often uses soundex codes for surnames. However, the electronic version of this index sometimes omits names found in the microfilm copy. Ancestry.com also includes many death indexes from other states, creating something of a way of searching the nation as a whole for a death record. Records of deaths can also be found in a number of sources including newspapers, federal census records (1849–1880), social security records, estate records in courts of probate, etc.

Divorce Records

Divorce in what became the state of Alabama started with the Mississippi Territory and required approval by the local courts and the legislature. Court records on any individual divorce, 1798 to present, should be requested from the clerk of the court in the county where the decree was issued. Alabama also required legislative approval of court-sanctioned divorces until 1864. Divorces approved in legislative acts have been published; see Donald F. Watson, *Divorces Copied from Printed Acts of Alabama, 1818–1864* (Montgomery: Alabama Department of Archives and History, 1971). The Center for Health Statistics has made widely available a microfilm index to Alabama divorces for 1950 to 1959. The index gives name of husband, first name of wife, code for county of divorce, date of divorce, and state certificate (volume and page). The Center has also made available microfilm of divorce records, 1938–1992. The Alabama Department of Archives and History has county divorce reports, 1818–1829 and an index to divorces, 1908–1927. All of the above records and indexes can be borrowed on microfilm through LDS Family History Centers.

Marriage Records

An act of 1799 in the Mississippi Territory required registration of marriage licenses and bonds in each county Orphans Court (renamed the Probate Court in 1850). Each marriage license required a marriage bond, wherein someone, often the bride's father, offered property worth two hundred dollars as security for the legality of the marriage. Starting in 1888, bonds were only required if the groom was under age twenty-one and/or the bride was under age eighteen. Permission from parents could substitute for a bond. Beginning in late 1904, bonds no longer became necessary. (Some counties, even in the early years when recording marriage licenses, declined to also record the accompanying bonds.) In 1909 and 1910 individual county courts of probate in Alabama were required to begin recording personal information on each new bride and groom, although from 1909 and for some years afterwards that data was not always requested or recorded. (Even when this information appears on the marriage record, often compilers of county marriage records omit the information from their publications, as they also often omit the information found on the bonds.)

Alabama's Center for Health Certificates has made widely available microfilm of a statewide index to marriage records for 1936 to 1959. The index gives name of bride or groom, code of county where the license was issued, date of marriage, and state certificate number (volume and page). Surnames use census soundex code. Marriage records for 1936 to 1992 have been microfilmed and can be borrowed through LDS family history centers. Otherwise, the researcher should contact the individual county court of probate for searches and copies of marriage records.

Many books of early marriages from certain counties have been published by various individuals. Often these books contain only the information from the marriage licenses and not from the accompanying marriage bonds. Some incomplete statewide compilations of information from these and other sources have also been made available in print and electronically on CD-ROM computer disks. The information on these lists duplicates much of what has been published by county by various individuals. The Birmingham Public Library, in addition to having the best collection of Alabama marriage records published by county, also has typescripts of "Alabama County Marriage Records," compiled by the Daughters of the American Revolution. These volumes include selected years for Baldwin, Blount, Chambers, Clarke, Colbert, Coosa, Dallas, Escambia, Jefferson, Macon, Mobile, Monroe, Montgomery, St. Clair, Talladega, and Washington Counties. For a published volume of miscellaneous Alabama marriage records, see Jordan R. Dodd and Norman L. Moyes, eds., *Alabama Marriages, Early to 1825* (Bountiful, Utah: Precision Indexing, 1990).

16. MILITARY
RECORDS

No specific guide to Alabama military records exists, although the Alabama Department of Archives and History has lists of its basic military holdings, 1776–1975, in the Military Records section of its web site. Several national guides and sources help in researching Alabama soldiers and their campaigns, including

Deputy, Marilyn, et al. *Register of Federal United States Military Records: A Guide to Manuscript Sources Available at the Genealogical Library in Salt Lake City and the National Archives in Washington, DC.* Bowie, Md.: Heritage Books, 1986.

Horowitz, Lois. *A Bibliography of Military Name Lists from Pre-1675 to 1900.* Metuchen, N.J.: Scarecrow Press, 1990.

Karsten, Peter. *The Military in America.* New York: Free Press, 1986.

Neagles, James C. *U.S. Military Records: A Guide to Federal and State Sources, Colonial America to the Present.* Salt Lake: Ancestry, 1994.

Shtrader, Charles R., ed. *Reference Guide to United States Military History.* 5 vols. New York: Facts on File, 1991.

The National Archives microfilm M686 Index to General Correspondence of the [Federal] Record and Pension Office, 1889–1920, includes letters relating to Americans from all wars to 1920. This index includes personal name, geographic location, and military unit. A copy of this microfilm is in the Family and Regional History Program, Wallace State College, Hanceville, Alabama. The National Archives and Records Administration, 700 Pennsylvania Ave. NW, Washington, DC 20408-0001, has the letters referred to in the index.

Works for naval research also exist. Some guides to this material include Lee D. Bacon, "Early Navy Personnel Records at the National Archives, 1776–1860," *Prologue: The Quarterly of the National Archives and Records Administration* 27 (1995): 76–80; and Lee D. Bacon, "Civil War and Later Naval Personnel Records at the National Archives, 1861–1924," 27 (1995): 178–82.

The National Archives has many sources relating to federal military posts, including those in Alabama: National Archives microcopy M617 Returns from U.S. Military Posts, 1800–1900; M661 Historical Information Relating to Military Posts . . . 1700–1900; M903 Descriptive Commentaries from the Medical Histories of Posts; and T817 Lists of the Adjutant General's Office of Carded Records of Military Organizations: Revolutionary War through Philippine Insurrection. Another source is Frances Paul Prucha's *A Guide to Military Posts of the United States, 1789–1895* (Madison: State Historical Society of Wisconsin, 1964).

RECORDS OF SERVICE, 1775–1861

The Alabama Department of Archives and History has microfilm of incomplete card catalogs of service records of Alabama veterans, arranged by war and then alphabetically by soldier, for the American Revolution through World War I. This microfilm is widely available, including through LDS family history centers. For prior to 1865, this film consists of the following:

American Revolution
Territorial Militia and Civil Service (1818)
War of 1812 (1812–1815)
Indian Wars, 1813–1814
State Militiamen, 1820–1865
Texas Revolt from Mexico (1835–1836)
Indian War of 1836
Mexican War, 1845–1848

The Alabama Department of Archives and History also has, inventoried under "Archives and History, Department of," the Alabamians at War Subject Files, 1721–1968. Another source for records of Alabama veterans in early American wars is Pauline Jones Gandrud's *Alabama Soldiers: Revolution, War of 1812, and Indian Wars*, 21 vols. to date (Hot Springs, Ark.: Arkansas Ancestors, 1975–). These volumes consist of data compiled from the notebooks of Ms. Gandrud. Information for the veterans of the American Revolution who moved to Alabama has also been published in Thomas M. Owen, *Revolutionary Soldiers in Alabama* (Montgomery: The Author, 1910); and Virgil White, *Genealogical Abstracts of Revolutionary War Pension Claims* (Waynesboro, Tenn.: National Historical Publications, 1990).

Other sources also document Alabama's participation in the Indian campaigns. For federal volunteers in these conflicts, see Virgil D. White, *Index to Volunteer Soldiers in Indian Wars and Disturbances, 1815–1858* (Waynesboro, Tenn.: National Historical Publishing Company, 1994); Benjamin Achee, *Index to Compiled Service Records, Alabama Units—Creek War, 1836–1837* (Shreveport, La.: The Author, 1971); and Robert C. Horn, *Index to Compiled Service Records for Alabama Soldiers in the Florida Indian War, 1836–1838* (Auburn: Genealogical Society of East Alabama, n.d). Federal pension records from these campaigns are listed in Virgil D. White's *Index to Indian Wars Pension Files, 1891–1926* (1987) and *Index to Old Wars Pension Files* (1987). The service and pension records can be ordered from Military Records, National Archives, 700 Pennsylvania Ave. NW, Washington, DC 20408-0001. Not included in any of the above are claims filed by white civilians for losses in Creek Indian attacks. A list of these claims for 1836 and 1837 is in "Alabama Indian Depredation Claims," a series that begins in *AlaBenton Genealogical Quarterly* with volume 10 (1993): 57–61. The actual files of these claims, if they still exist, have not been located at the National Archives. For historical background on the Indian depredations claims, see Larry C. Skogen, *Indian Depredation Claims, 1796–1920* (Norman: University of Oklahoma Press, 1996).

Alabama troops also served in conflicts with Mexico. Information on Alabamians in the Texas revolt from Mexico (1835–1836) has been published in Clifford Hopewell, *Remember Goliad: Their Silent Tents* (Austin, Tex.: Eakin Press, 1998); Daughters of the Republic of Texas, *Muster Rolls of the Texas Revolution* (Austin, Tex.: The Author, 1986); Gifford White, *They Also Served—Texas Service Records from Headright Certificates* (Nacogdoches, Tex.: Ericson Books, 1994); and Bill Groneman, *Alamo Defenders: A Genealogy* (Austin, Tex.: Eakin Press, 1990). For records of Texas bounty land to these men and their heirs, write to Texas State Land Office, General Land Office, 1700 N. Congress Avenue, Austin, TX 78701, and use Thomas Lloyd Miller, *Bounty and Donation Land Grants of Texas, 1835–1888* (Austin, Tex.: University of Texas Press, 1967). For other sources on the revolt from Mexico, see Jean Carefoot, *Guide to Genealogical Resources in the Texas State Archives* (Austin: Texas State Library, 1984). Texas Land Title Abstracts are indexed on the Ancestry.com web site on the Internet.

Several different sources document service in the Mexican War, 1846–1848. These works include Steven R. Butler, *Alabama Volunteers in the Mexican War, 1846–1848: A History and Annotated Roster* (Richardson, Tex.: Descendants of Mexican War Veterans, 1996); George Stewart Peterson, *Known Military Dead during the Mexican War* (n.p., 1957); Barbara Schull Wolfe, *Index to Mexican War Pension Applications* (Indianapolis, Ind.: Heritage House, 1985); and Virgil D. White, *Index to Mexican War Pension Files* (Waynesboro, Tenn.: National Historical Publishing Company, 1989). Another source is National Archives microfilm M616 Index to Compiled Service Records of Volunteer Soldiers Who Served during the Mexican War. The Alabama Department of Archives and History has, under "Archives and History, Department of," an index to Mexican War rosters, 1846–1847. For personal information on men who enlisted in the regular U.S. Army for the Mexican War, see reel 23 of National Archives microcopy M233 Register of Enlistments in the U.S. Army, 1798–1914, a copy of which is in the Family and Regional History Program of Wallace State College in Hanceville, Alabama. This reel has records in volumes 46 and 47.

OTHER SPECIAL FEDERAL SOURCES FOR EARLY MILITARY SERVICE

Service records of officers of the federal army and navy have been published. These works include Francis Bernard Heitman, *Historical Register and Directory of the United States Army, from Its Organization . . . to*

March 2, 1903 (Washington, D.C.: Government Printing Office, 1903); and Edward W. Callahan, *List of Officers of the Navy of the United States and of the Marine Corps, from 1775 to 1900* (New York: L. R. Hamersley, 1901).

Alabama sent thousands of volunteer soldiers to a number of federally sponsored military campaigns categorized as the Indian Wars (1784–1811), the War of 1812 (1812–1815), the Indian Wars (1815–1855), and the Mexican War (1846–1848). Military Records, National Archives, 700 Pennsylvania Ave. NW, Washington, DC 20408-0001, has the service records of these men. Until 1855, these veterans, their widows, and their heirs could claim federal bounty lands for this service. Veterans and their widows could claim pensions for the War of 1812 in 1867 and for other early conflicts much later. Searches and copies of these records can be obtained by writing to the National Archives at the above address.

Extensive personal information on veterans, widows, and heirs of veterans can be found in the above mentioned bounty land files. The federal government ceased granting lands for military service in 1855. An index to the bounty land warrants of the War of 1812 is National Archives microcopy M848 War of 1812 Military Bounty Land Warrants, 1815–1858, a copy of which is at the Birmingham Public Library. War of 1812 bounty land claims are filed at the National Archives, among the pension files, when the veteran and/or survivor had both. The other 300,000 to 450,000 bounty land claims, without regard to pensions, are filed alphabetically by name of the veteran at the National Archives in the "unindexed bounty land warrant applications." Requests for a search for a bounty land file for pre-1855 wars sometimes benefit from adding the words "search unindexed files."

Pension files also frequently contain extensive information on veterans or their widows. Several finding aids help in identifying federal pensions. Virgil D. White has published nationwide indexes to all federal pensions for American wars from the American Revolution to 1860, all of which are cited above. Other resources include Craig R. Scott, *The "Lost" Pensions: Settled Accounts of the Act of 6 April 1838* (Lovettsville, Va.: Willow Bend Books, 1996); and Alycon Trubey Pierce, *Selected Final Pension Payment Vouchers, 1818–1864, Alabama* (Lovettsville, Va.: Willow Bend Books, 1997), both of which cover the American Revolution through the Mexican War, 1846–1848. For the same pensions, there also exists National Archives microcopy T718 Ledgers of Payments, 1818–1872, to U.S. Pensioners, a copy of which is at the Family and Regional History Program, Wallace State College, Hanceville, Alabama. An 1883 list of federal pensioners for the War of 1812 (and the Civil War) was published as *U.S. Senate Executive Document 84, pt. 1, 47th Congress, 2nd Session, Serial no. 2078* (Washington, D.C.: Government Printing Office, 1883) and has been reprinted in various forms, including on computer CD-ROM. The Alabamians have been published in *War of 1812 Pensioners and Others on the Pension Rolls as of January 1, 1883* (Cullman, Ala.: Gregath, 1982).

CIVIL WAR RECORDS, 1861–1865, GENERAL

For a basic introduction to Civil War records and research, see Brian A. Brown, *In the Footsteps of the Blue and Gray: A Civil War Research Handbook* (Shawnee Mission, Kans.: Two Trails Genealogy Shop, 1996), which even includes a list of some of the many Civil War Internet web sites. Another approach is taken in Sherry Harris, *Civil War Records: "A Useful Tool,"* 2 vols. (Granada Hills, Calif.: The Author, 1990–1993). Most Civil War regimental histories published before 1920 are available on microfiche, such as Robert E. Lester's *Civil War Unit Histories,* 5 vols. (Bethesda, Md.: University Publications of America, 1992). A set of this microfiche is in the Family and Regional History Program, Wallace State College, Hanceville, Alabama.

More and more information appears on the Internet for help in Civil War research. These web sites often include rosters, unit histories, queries for information, and much more. Among the best of these web sites is the American Civil War home page.

The greatest single repository for Civil War records for Alabama or anywhere else is Military Records, National Archives, 700 Pennsylvania Ave. NW, Washington, DC 20408-0001. The National Archives and Records Administration's best general guide is *Guide to Genealogical Research at the National Archives* (Washington, D.C.: National Archives, 1986). Researchers should also consult *Military Service Records: A Select Catalog of National Archives Microfilm Publications* (Washington, D.C.: National Archives, 1985); and Michael Musick, "Honorable Reports: Battles, Campaigns, and

Skirmishes—Civil War Records and Research," *Prologue: The Quarterly of the National Archives and Records Administration* 27 (1995): 259–77. For statistics on the infantry regiments of both armies, see William F. Fox, *Regimental Losses of the Civil War, 1861–1865* (Albany, N.Y.: Albany Publishing, 1889).

With the creation of the Record and Pension Office in the War Department in 1889, an effort began in the federal government to consolidate information on military service in a usable form. This need had become critical as more and more old soldiers and their heirs needed evidence from these records for purposes of applying for military service pensions. The organizing of individual service data for Union soldiers, the men for whom most often requests for information came, received top priority. Consequently, the records of the federal veterans of the Civil War were not as centralized as those later put together for the data of other veterans. For example, the Confederate service records, done last, were placed in a very accessible order by a clerical staff that by then had acquired considerable experience in organizing information. Consequently, although genealogically valuable records for federal service in the Civil War more likely survive in today's National Archives—more valuable than the fragmentary surviving records gathered at the end of the war for the Confederates— often the information on the Union soldiers and sailors proves harder to access. For background on these efforts, see Mabel E. Deutrich, *Struggle for Supremacy: The Career of General Fred C. Ainsworth* (Washington, D.C.: Public Affairs Press, 1962). More information on the compiled service records will be given below.

The Tutwiler Library of Southern History and Literature (Southern History), Birmingham Public Library, has one of the most extensive collections of southern Civil War printed works available anywhere. Many of these works and books for other states, printed before 1920, are on microfiche in the Family and Regional History Program, Wallace State College, Hanceville, Alabama. For books, manuscripts, articles, regimental histories, etc. relating to the Civil War, see

Cole, Garold L. *Civil War Eyewitnesses: An Annotated Bibliography of Books and Articles, 1955–1986.* Columbia: University of South Carolina Press, 1980.

Coulter, E. Merton. *Travels in the Confederate States: A Bibliography*. Baton Rouge: Louisiana State University Press, 1994. This work provides extensive reviews of a number of firsthand accounts of the Civil War.

Dornbusch, Charles Emil. *Military Bibliography of the Civil War*. 4 vols. New York: New York Public Library, 1961–1987.

Meredith, Lee W. *Guide to Civil War Periodicals*. 2 vols. Twenty-nine Palms, Calif.: Historical Indexes, 1991, 1997.

Murdock, Eugene Converse. *The Civil War in the North*. New York: Garland, 1987. Not indexed by unit; the table of contents is better access to this valuable book than its crude indexes.

Nevins, Allen, James I. Robertson, and Bell I. Wiley. *Civil War Books: A Critical Bibliography*. Baton Rouge: Louisiana State University Press 1967. Not indexed by unit, this work is the best source for evaluation of printed works on the Civil War.

Sellers, John R. *Civil War Manuscripts: A Guide to Collections in the Library of Congress*. Washington, D.C.: Library of Congress, 1986.

Smith, Albert E. *Civil War Diaries and Personal Narratives, 1960–1994: A Select Bibliography of Books in the General Collections of the Library of Congress*. Washington, D.C.: Library of Congress, 1997.

War Department. Office of the Chief of Staff. *Bibliography of State Participation in the Civil War, 1861–1866*. Washington, D.C.: Government Printing Office, 1913.

Wright, John H. *Compendium of the Confederacy: An Annotated Bibliography*. Wilmington, N.C.: Broadfoot, 1989. The best bibliography of publications on the Confederacy.

The most extensive compilations of Civil War material ever compiled are the 128 books (sixty-nine "volumes" in four series, plus the general index; volumes 54 and 55, a special index to series I, were never published) known as *The War of the Rebellion: A Compilation of the Official Records* (1881–1901), also called the *ORs*, and a thirty-volume companion: *The Official Records of the Union and Confederate Navies in the War of the Rebellion*. These volumes are a series of grammatically cleaned-up official letters and reports for the Civil War. Even obscure incidents of the Civil War are covered in these volumes. Many persons are named in these volumes, for the widest variety of reasons. For background on this work, see Alan C. Aimone and Barbara A. Aimone, *A User's Guide to the Official Records of the War of the Rebellion* (Shippensburg, Md.: White Mane, 1993).

Three companies now offer these volumes on CD-ROM computer disk, an inexpensive and very precise means of searching these volumes, by any word, name, or unit, that is far superior to the incomplete original indexes. (However, the original indexes are invaluable for identifying persons referred to only by surnames in the records). Also of help in sorting out which volumes to read are the National Archives' five-volume *Military Operations of the Civil War* (Washington, D.C.: National Archives, 1986); and Ronald A. Mosocco's *The Chronological Tracking of the American Civil War in the Official Records of the War of the Rebellion* (Williamsburg, Va.: James River Publications, 1993). Volume 1 of *Military Operations* has been microfilmed by the National Archives, with additional material, as microcopy M1036; and volumes 2 through 5 have been microfilmed as M1815. Broadfoot Publishing Company has publishing an indexed supplement, consisting of over one hundred volumes, for the *ORs*.

The above supplement includes the event cards. These records appear at the beginning of the National Archives microfilm of each Civil War unit's compiled service records and give something of the unit's history and organization. These cards have also been microfilmed separately as "Compiled Records Showing Military Service," National Archives microfilm M861 for the Confederates and M594 for the Union.

To learn about events on any day during the Civil War, there currently exist three works. These chronologies are Robert E. Denny, *The Civil War Years: A Day-by-Day Chronicle of the Life of a Nation* (New York: Sterling Publishing, 1992); Chris Bishop and Ian Drury, *1,400 Days: The Civil War Day by Day* (New York: Gallery Books, 1990); and Navy History Division, *Civil War Naval Chronology, 1861–1865* (Washington, D.C.: Navy Department, 1971).

Aside from the thousands of biographies of Civil War personages, there are also some encyclopedic sources that provide information on soldiers, sailors, and civilians of the period. These works include Stewart Sifakis, *Who Was Who in the Civil War*, 2 vols. (New York: Facts on File, 1988); John T. Hubbell and James W. Geary, eds., *Biographical Dictionary of the*

Union (Westport, Conn.: Greenwood Press, 1995); and James Spencer, *Civil War Generals: Categorical Listings and a Biographical Directory* (New York: Greenwood Press, 1986). Some special source materials for research in the wounded of both armies is the Broadfoot Company's well-indexed (including by unit) reprint of *Medical and Surgical History of the Civil War*.

As most of the fighting of the American Civil War took place outside of Alabama, few maps of the state were created as a result of that conflict. Some Civil War maps of Alabama, chiefly around Mobile Bay, do appear in George B. Davis et al., *The Official Military Atlas of the Civil War* (Washington, D.C.: Government Printing Office, 1891–1895), which is available as a reprint. A geographical index to this book is found in Noel S. O'Reilly et al., *Civil War Maps: A Graphic Index to the Atlas to Accompany the Official Records of the Union and Confederate Armies* (Chicago: Newberry Library, 1987). For other maps, see *A Guide to Civil War Maps in the National Archives* (Washington, D.C.: National Archives, 1986); and Richard W. Stephenson, *Civil War Maps: An Annotated List of Maps and Atlases in the Library of Congress* (Washington. D.C.: Library of Congress, 1989).

Several massive compilations of Civil War source material have been compiled by the Broadfoot Company of Wilmington, Delaware, with special indexes that include place names in Alabama and elsewhere. These include Broadfoot's CD-ROM disk of *The War of the Rebellion*; and the well-indexed reprint editions of such works as *Confederate Military History; Confederate Veteran; Southern Bivouac; Southern Historical Papers; Medical and Surgical History of the Civil War; The Union Army: A History of the Military Affairs in the Loyal States;* and *Order of the Loyal Legion of the United States.*

CIVIL WAR RECORDS, 1861–1865, CONFEDERATE SERVICE

For Confederate research, guides include James C. Neagles, *Confederate Research Sources* (Salt Lake: Ancestry, 1986); and J. H. Segars, *In Search of Confederate Ancestors: The Guide* (Murfreesboro, Tenn.: Southern Heritage Press, 1993). For background information on the C.S.A. (Confederate States of America), see Richard N. Current, ed., *Encyclopedia of the Confederacy,* 4 vols. (New York: Simon & Schuster, 1993).

Military Records, National Archives, 700 Pennsylvania Ave. NW, Washington, DC 20408-0001, has the largest collection of Confederate records. These materials and others are described in detail in Henry Putney Beers, *The Confederacy* (originally pub. 1968; Washington, D.C.: National Archives, 1986); Elizabeth Bethel and Craig R. Scott, *Preliminary Inventory of the War Department Collection of Confederate Records (Record Group 109)* (Athens, Ga.: Iberian Press, 1994); and *Preliminary Inventory No. 169: Treasury Department Collection of Confederate Records* (Washington, D.C.: National Archives, 1967). From the Beers book, the Alabama unit records on page 304 and most of the Confederate hospital records on pages 181 and 176 (including the Stout Collection) have been obtained on microfilm for the Family and Regional History Program, Wallace State College, Hanceville, Alabama. The Alabama Department of Archives and History has the records for the Alabama hospitals in Richmond, Virginia, 1861–1865.

The National Archives' compiled service records can contain almost any information but usually only give information on each soldier's date and place of enlistment, circumstances of absences, and final discharge. These files were compiled from original records that survived the war in federal custody. Records for many of the soldiers and even for some entire units were lost and therefore not used in the compiled service records. The National Archives Southeast Region, Wallace State College, the LDS family history centers, and many other libraries have National Archives microfilm of the Confederate compiled service records for all of the southern states. Janet B. Hewett has published, through the Broadfoot Company, *The Roster of Confederate Soldiers, 1861–1865*, 16 vols. (Wilmington, N.C., 1995–1996), a printed version of National Archives microcopy M253 Consolidated Index to Compiled Service Records of Confederates.

The compiled service records are divided between troops raised by the Confederate government and units created by individual states. When someone appears in the indexes to these records but the microfilm of his unit cannot be found, sometimes his service record will be located under "miscellaneous" in the last reels of the microfilm for the state from which his unit served. The service records for some states, notably Florida, Louisiana, and North Carolina, have been or are being published, although not by the National Archives. Service records of Confederate units raised by the state of Alabama appear in National Archives microfilm M311, and the records for service in non-state Confederate service are found in M258 (military units) and M331 (staff). In some units, as much as 60 percent of the Confederate servicemen do not have compiled service records at the National Archives.

The Confederacy-wide indexes to service records, previously described, do not include all records from the National Archives. Among these other materials are the thousands of alphabetical files in National Archives microcopy M347 Unfiled Papers and Slips Belonging to Confederate Compiled Service Records and the records of the navy and marines in National Archives microfilm M260 (the marines are found in reel 7). All of these microfilms are available at the Family and Regional History Program, Wallace State College, Hanceville, Alabama. Other records of Confederate marines are found in the books on the Confederate marines by Ralph W. Donnelly. Some orders not found in individual service records are listed in Edgar Ray Luhn Jr., *Luhn's Edition CSA AIGO Special Orders Series* and *Luhn's Edition CSA AIGO General Orders*.

For information on a Confederate held as a prisoner of war start with the information found in his service record, then search National Archives microcopy M598 Selected Records of the War Department Relating to Confederate Prisoners of War (records are arranged by prison camp, although there are some general indexes on reels 1 to 6). For research suggestions, see Muriel Phillips Joslyn, "Was Your [Confederate] Civil War Ancestor a Prisoner of War?" *Ancestry Newsletter* 11, no. 4 (1993): 1–5. For Confederates who died in federal custody, see National Archives microcopy M918 Confederate P.O.W.'s: Soldiers and Sailors Who Died in Federal Prisons and Military Hospitals in the North, available through LDS family history centers.

Some other National Archives microfilms relating to southerners include M409 Index to Letters Received by the Confederate Secretary of War, 1861–1865; M410 Index to Letters Received by the Confederate Adjutant, Inspector General, and the Confederate Quartermaster General; and M686 Index to General Correspondence of the [Federal] Record and Pension Office, 1889–1920. For more information on some of these lesser-known sources, see "Reading the Lost Letters of the Confederate Government,"

Heritage Quest, no. 73 (January–February 1998): 91–92; and DeAnne Blanton, "Confederate Medical Personnel," *Prologue: The Quarterly of the National Archives and Records Administration* 26 (1994): 80–84. The National Archives microcopy M345 Union Provost's Marshal's File of Papers Relating to Individual Civilians indexes by every name thousands of miscellaneous records of all sorts on southern soldiers and civilians found in M345 and also in M416 Union Provost Marshal's File of Papers Relating to Two or More Civilians. A microfilm copy of M345 and M416 is available at the Family and Regional History Program, Wallace State College, Hanceville, Alabama.

The Alabama Department of Archives and History has many Civil War holdings relating to Confederate Alabamians. Among the records arranged by military unit are photocopies of the original muster rolls in the National Archives. Other miscellaneous material arranged by unit includes the "Fowler" copies, rosters of Alabama Confederate units made during the Civil War and containing information and soldiers not found in the records of the National Archives. Some of the Fowler copies for Alabama units in the Army of Tennessee were apparently lost during the war. Almost all, if not all, of the names found in the Fowler copies appear in the card catalog described below. These regimental files also contain some Civil War documents, biographical material, unit histories, and related materials. The Alabama Department of Archives and History also has, cataloged under "Archives and History, Department of," the Civil War and Reconstruction files. This material includes such headings as "Biography," "Flags," "Cemeteries," "Deserters and Traitors," "Personal Narratives," and "Veterans." In the records of the adjutant general, the researcher can find registers of officers, 1860–1864; registers of state volunteers, 1860–1865; and Army of Alabama records, 1861–1865. The state auditor's records include impressment vouchers, 1863–1864.

The Alabama Archives also has a card catalog of information on Alabama Confederate soldiers. Widely available on microfilm, this catalog indexes some original Civil War records, Alabama's state pensions to resident Confederates, state censuses of Confederate veterans in 1907 and 1921, and the state census of widows of veterans of 1927. These cards even include, for some veterans, lists of Civil War battles in which they served. Names of hundreds of soldiers for whom no other record of service survives appear in this card catalog. The Alabama Department of Archives and History is placing these cards on its Internet web site. The Alabama Archives also has separate card catalogs on microfilm of Confederate soldiers (including resident Confederate pensioners after the war) and a card catalog on microfilm of militiamen, 1820–1865. Also found in the archives are two reels of "Miscellaneous Confederate Pension Records" that include alphabetical lists of parents, widows, administrators, and other persons related to deceased Confederate soldiers (information taken from compiled service records now in the National Archives); lists of slaves used by the Confederate army; and Mountain Creek Soldiers Home headstones. This microfilm is also available through LDS family history centers and in the Family and Regional History Program at Wallace State College, Hanceville.

Civil War cemetery records that include Alabamians who never returned home have been published for some states. For Confederate soldiers who died and were buried in Virginia cemeteries, see Thomas M. Spratt, *Men in Gray Interments: Virginia Cemetery Series*, 8 vols. to date (Lovettsville, Va.: Willow Bend Books, 1996). For Alabama soldiers buried in Georgia, see Georgia Division, United Daughters of the Confederacy, *Roster of Confederate Graves*, 8 vols. (Atlanta: The Author, 1996). Mississippi burials are listed in Betty Couch Wilshire, *Mississippi Confederate Grave Registrations*, 2 vols. (Bowie, Md.: Heritage Books, 1989). For the dead in the Confederate cemetery in Chattanooga, see *Roster of Our Dead Buried in the Confederate Cemetery* (Chattanooga, Tenn.: N. B. Forrest Camp, UCV, 1894). The Sherman Pompey Collection of information on burials of Civil War soldiers, arranged by state, is available on microfilm through LDS family history centers and at the Family and Regional History Program at Wallace State College, Hanceville, Alabama.

For biographies of major Confederate figures see the following:

Allardice, Bruce C. *More Generals in Gray*. Baton Rouge: Louisiana State University Press, 1995.

An Official Guide of the Confederate Government from 1861 to 1865 at Richmond. Richmond, Va.: n.d.

Crick, Robert K. *Lee's Colonels: A Biographical Register of the Field Officers of the Army of Northern Virginia*. Dayton, Ohio: Morningside Press, 1992.

Davis, William C. *The Confederate General.* Harrisburg, Pa.: National Historical Society, 1991.

Moebs, Thomas Truxton. *Confederate States Navy Research Guide.* Williamsburg, Va.: Moebs Publishing, 1991.

Wakelyn, Jon L. *Biographical Dictionary of the Confederacy.* Westport, Conn.: Greenwood Press, 1977.

Warner, Ezra J. *Generals in Gray.* Baton Rouge: Louisiana State University Press, 1959.

Welsh, Jack D. *Medical Histories of Confederate Generals.* Kent, Ohio: Kent State University Press, 1996.

Some special lists of Confederates, including many Alabamians, are found in Muriel Joslyn, *Immortal Captives: The Story of 600 Confederate Officers and the United States Prisoner of War Policy* (Sharpsburg, Pa.: White Mane, 1995); Charles F. Pitts, *Chaplains in Gray* (Nashville, Tenn.: Boardman Press, 1957); R. A. Brock, *Paroles of the Army of Northern Virginia* (New York: Antiquarian Press, 1962), incomplete, also known as the "Appomattox Roster"; and Greg S. Clemmer, *Valor in Gray: The Recipients of the Confederate Medal of Honor* (Staunton, Va.: Heathside Publishing, 1996).

Photographs of Confederate soldiers from all states are included in William A. Albaugh III, *Confederate Faces* (Salona Beach, Calif.: The Author, 1970); William A. Albaugh III, *More Confederate Faces: Photographs of Confederates* (Washington, D.C.: ABS Printers, 1972); William A. Turner, *Even More Confederate Faces* (Orange, Va.: Moss Publications, 1983); and D. A. Serrano, *Still More Confederate Faces* (Bayside, N.Y.: Metropolitan Company, 1992). The U.S. Army History Institute, Carlisle Barracks, PA 17013-5008, copies Civil War soldiers' photographs loaned to them. They also accept donations of information on all American veterans.

Several sources exist for background on a Confederate unit. Alabama units appear exclusively in Willis Brewer, *Brief Historical Sketches of Military Organizations Raised in Alabama during the Civil War* (Montgomery: Alabama Department of Archives and History, 1966), reprinted from Brewer, *Alabama: Her History, Resources, War Record, and Public Men,* 589–705. For the whole Confederacy, there is Joseph H. Crute, *Units of the Con-*

federate States Army (Midlothian, Va.: Derwent Books, 1987); and Stewart Sifakis, *Compendium of the Confederate Armies,* 10 vols. (New York: Facts on File, 1992). Many unit histories that include rosters of Alabama Civil War companies, regiments, etc. have been and are being published. Some Civil War rosters are included in Alabama's genealogical periodicals. Unit histories also appear in the many serial sets of books reprinted and indexed (including by unit) by the Broadfoot Company, including *Confederate Military History* (with more than 400 biographies and family histories of Alabama Confederate veterans), *Confederate Veteran, Southern Historical Society Papers,* and *Southern Bivouac.*

Many Confederates left the horrors of federal prison camps by becoming "Galvanized Yankees," former Confederates in the federal army. An index to these records is on reels 23 to 26 of National Archives microcopy M1290 Index to Compiled Service Records of Volunteer Union Soldiers Not Enlisted by State. The service records of the former Confederates in the First through Sixth U.S. Volunteers are in National Archives microcopy M1017. For historical background on these men, see Dee Brown, *The Galvanized Yankees* (Lincoln: University of Nebraska Press, 1963). All of this microfilm is in the collection of the Family and Regional History Program, Wallace State College, Hanceville, Alabama.

CONFEDERATE SERVICE PENSION RECORDS

Each of the former Confederate states and the states of Kentucky, Missouri, and Oklahoma eventually offered some form of pensions to their respective *resident* Confederate veterans and widows; see Desmond Walls Allen, *Where to Write for Confederate Pension Records* (Bryant, Ark.: The Author, 1991). Indexes have been published for the pension files of Arkansas, Florida, Georgia, Kentucky, Mississippi, Missouri, Oklahoma, Tennessee, and Texas. Supplements to the Georgia pension index are found in Ted O. Brooke and Linda Woodward Geiger, *Index to Georgia's Confederate Pension Supplements* (Cumming, Ga.: The Authors, 1999); and F. W. Weatherbee, *Georgia Veterans and Their Widows Who Applied for Government Pensions in Alabama* (Carrollton, Miss.: Pioneer Publishing, 2000). Virginia resident Confederate pensions can be accessed through the Library of Virginia web site. The records created by these states frequently contain a great deal of personal information on Alabamians.

The Confederate pension microfilm for most states is available through LDS family history centers. Some related works that mention Alabamians include Bobbie J. McLane and Capitola Glazner, *Arkansas 1911 Census of Confederate Veterans*, 3 vols. plus index (Hot Springs: Hot Springs National Park, 1977); and Gustavus W. Dyer and John T. Moore, *The Tennessee Civil War Veterans Questionnaires*, 5 vols. (Greenville, S.C.: Southern Historical Press, 1985).

Alabama first gave money to disabled Confederate veterans for artificial limbs in 1867 and 1876. A general pension act for indigent resident Confederate veterans and widows of veterans was first passed in 1891. Pensions were also given to Alabama veterans/widows of veterans living in states that did not give Confederate pensions. The Jefferson Manly Falkner Soldiers' [Confederate veterans] Home opened at Mountain Creek in Chilton County as a private institution in 1902. The state took it over the next year and operated it until it closed in 1939. In its last years, the home's residents were widows. Records of this institution are in the Alabama Department of Archives and History. For background information on the home, see R. B. Rosenburg, *Living Monuments: Confederate Soldiers' Homes in the New South* (Chapel Hill: University of North Carolina Press, 1995).

Alabama's pensions to resident Confederate veterans and widows of veterans, and to veterans and widows of veterans of Alabama service residing in states not giving Confederate pensions, represent the best of the records generated by a state Confederate pension program. The original records are at the Alabama Department of Archives and History. Microfilm of these records is widely available. Alabama's basic Confederate pension files are in alphabetical order and are cross referenced by the names of the widows. A typical file includes the veteran's unit and dates of service, as well as residence at the time that he or his widow applied for a pension. Additional information may include details of birth, marriage, property, and health of the applicant. In 1920, widow pensioners had to complete a detailed personal questionnaire, now found in their files, that included such information as the names of their respective fathers.

The Alabama Department of Archives and History has microfilmed its censuses of Confederate veterans for 1907 and 1921 and of widows for 1927. Copies of the microfilm are widely available, including through LDS family history centers. The 1907 census has also been published and has a state-wide index: *Master Index to 1907 Census of Alabama Confederate Soldiers* (Cullman, Ala.: Gregath Company, n.d.) In that census, each veteran had to provide his place of birth (usually county and state), military service, and date of birth. In the 1921 census, each veteran also had to provide the names of his respective children, their places of residence, and occupations. The 1927 census of Confederate widow pensioners asked each woman for specific information on her marriage.

The Alabama Department of Archives and History has other related records among the department's state holdings:

> Archives and History, Department of
>> 1907 Census Questionnaires (arranged by unit for Alabama units, alphabetically for other states)
>> Confederate Veterans and Widows (by county)
>
> Auditor, State
>> Confederate Pension Journals, c. 1885–1938
>
> Pension Commission
>> Pension Letters and Reports, 1921–1957
>
> Pensions and Securities
>> Annual Pension Lists, 1937–1974
>
> Veterans Affairs
>> Confederate Widows Files, c. 1952–1974

Other pension records at the Alabama Department of Archives and History include correspondence with the pension office, including information on Civil War service by veterans and widows unable to prove service, although this material has no index. The Alabama Archives also has records of pension payments, 1899–1915, 1920–1925, 1927–1928, and 1930, a way of estimating when a pensioner died by when he or she no longer received pension payments. It also has files on rejected pension applications, 1919–1938; records of Alabama's Confederate soldiers' home; and applications for artificial limbs, 1865–1900.

CIVIL WAR RECORDS, 1861–1865, FEDERAL SERVICE

Records of Alabamians, black and white, in the United States service during the Civil War can be difficult to locate. An Alabamian who reached the Union lines might have worked as a scout, a forager, a spy, a soldier in any Union unit that happened to be present (particularly Tennessee units but even units from Illinois and New York), a contractor north of the Ohio River, or as a sailor in the navy.

Unlike the Confederate records, the records for Union service frequently are not centralized, lack comprehensive indexes, and are not on microfilm. No guides like the Neagles and Segars books on the Confederate sources exist for the Union soldiers. For detailed descriptions of the records for information on Union soldiers at the National Archives, see *Inventory No. 1: Records of the Headquarters of the Army; Inventory No. 17 Records of the Adjutant General's Office; Inventory No. 187: General Records of the Department of the Treasury;* and *Inventory No. 17: Inventory of the Records of the Accounting Offices of the Department of the Treasury.*

Federal compiled service records for soldiers, black and white, at the National Archives frequently give such valuable genealogical information as county of birth and age. These records can be searched and copies can be ordered from Military Records, National Archives, 700 Pennsylvania Ave. NW, Washington, DC 20408-0001. Filed at the end of the last reel of the Union service records microfilm for a particular unit can be found miscellaneous additional records, arranged alphabetically by soldier. Some of these papers refer to men not found in the unit's compiled service records. The National Archives is currently completing the microfilming of all of the federal Civil War service records. This microfilm should be available through LDS family history centers when completed.

The Broadfoot Publishing Company has made available on computer CD-ROM disk *Roster of Union Soldiers, 1861–1865,* a nationwide index by state. Broadfoot has also published the same index in book form. Service records of the biracial First Alabama Cavalry Regiment (USA) have been published in Glenda McWhirter Todd, *First Alabama Cavalry USA Homage* to *Patriotism* (Bowie, Md.: Heritage Books, 1999); and William Stanley Hoole, *Alabama Tories: The First Alabama Cavalry, U.S.A., 1862–1865* (Tuscaloosa: Confederate Publishing Company, 1960), with the individual service records abstracted from National Archives microfilm M276. Other works on this First Alabama Cavalry are being prepared for publication; also see "What Has Become of All the Old Boys? The 1st Alabama Cavalry, USA," *Alabama Family History and Genealogy News* 21, no. 1 (2000): 22–23. For other records of white federal soldiers enlisted from Alabama, see "Some Forgotten Alabama Union Soldiers," *Alabama Family History and Genealogy News* 17, no. 2 (1996): 12–19; Ernest Klein, "Union Soldiers in Our Midst," *Alabama Family History and Genealogy News* 17, no. 4 (1996): 5–9; Donald Bradford Dodd, "Unionism in Confederate Alabama" (Ph.D. diss., University of Georgia, 1969); Henry G. Sellers Jr., *Some Union Soldiers from a Place Called Crowdabout* (Gulf Breeze, Fla.: The Author, n.d.); and Johnny Potter, *First Tennessee and Alabama Independent Vidette Cavalry* (Chattanooga: Mountain Press, 1995). Copies of the medical records of the Alabama federal soldiers and Mexican War veterans in the National Archives have been microfilmed for the Family and Regional History Program, Wallace State College, Hanceville, Alabama.

An estimated ten thousand African Americans from Alabama served in the federal military during the Civil War. Specific Alabama units included the First Alabama Siege Artillery (6th–7th U.S. Colored Heavy Artillery); First Alabama Regiment Infantry (55th U.S. Colored Troops); Second Alabama Regiment Infantry (110th U. S. Colored Troops); Third Alabama Regiment Infantry (111th U.S. Colored Troops); and the Fourth Alabama Regiment Infantry (106th U.S. Colored Troops). An index to the compiled service records at the National Archives of the African American soldiers is Janet B. Hewett, ed., *The Roster of Union Soldiers, 1861–1865: U.S. Colored Troops in the Civil War,* 2 vols. (Wilmington, N.C.: Broadfoot, 1997).

Aside from the extensive information found in the soldiers' muster-in rolls and compiled service records, the National Archives also has extensive information on the African American soldiers in the records of the Bureau for Colored Troops, Record Group 94, records of the Adjutant General. For other information on their records, see "A Soldier's Story: The Records of Hubbard Pryor, Forty-Fourth United States Colored Troops," *Prologue: The Quarterly of the National Archives and Records Administration* 31 (1999): 266–72; Jeannette Braxton Secret, *Guide to Tracing Your African American Civil War Ancestor* (Bowie, Md.: Heritage Books, 1997); and Budge Weidman, "Preserving the Legacy of the United States Colored Troops," *Prologue: The Quarterly of the National Archives and Records Administration* 29 (1997): 91–94.

Lists of federal Civil War officers have been published. These works include U.S. Adjutant General's Office, *Official Army Register of the Volunteer Force of the United States Army for the Years 1861, '62, '63, '64, '65* (Washington, D.C.: Government Printing Office, 1867), the modern reprint includes a comprehensive index; Guy V. Henry, *Military Record of Civilian Appointments in the United States Army* (New York: Carleton, 1870); and William H. Powell and Edward Shippen, *Officers of the Army and Navy (Regular) Who Served in the Civil War* (Philadelphia, Pa.: L. R. Hamersley & Co., 1892).

One sometimes successful way of locating a service record for a soldier in the federal service, no matter what his regiment, is to have a search made for a pension record. A list of federal pension records for the Civil War is National Archives microcopy T288 General Index to Pension Files, 1861–1934, available in the Family and Regional History Program, Wallace State College, Hanceville, Alabama, and also, when it can be read, at the Ancestry.com web site on the Internet.

Records of spies, guides, and scouts are not often found in service records. Hired by individual officers, these men and women usually have no compiled service records because they did their work outside of the regular military. Fragmentary records exist for the service of some of these people, however, in entry 95 of Record Group 110, Records of the Povost Marshal and entry 874, pt. iv, Record Group 393, Records of Continental Commands (for the Army of the Cumberland). In Record Group 110, Records of the Provost Marshal, can be also found some reports and pay receipts for intelligence agents. Names of some of these operatives from Entry 36 of Record Group 110 appear in "Union Spies, Guides, Scouts, Railroad Operatives and Other Personnel, 1862–1865," *Georgia Genealogical Magazine* 33 (1993): 165–75. The spies listed in Entry 31 of Record Group 110 have a special index at the National Archives prepared by DeAnne Blanton. The spies and guides paid by individual quartermasters have an index in Record Group 92, Records of the Quartermaster General, entries 232.

Records of people held prisoner by the Confederate States of America are fragmentary, consisting in some camps of only the lists of dead. For records of specific camps, see Henry Putney Beers, *The Confederacy* (Washington, D.C.: National Archives and Records Administration, 1986). NARA's holdings include the hospital at the Confederate prison camp at Cahaba, Alabama. In entry 10 of Record Group 249, Records of the Commissary General of Prisoners, National Archives, can be found letters written by and about missing, captured, or released Union soldiers of the Civil War. The indexes, arranged by year and then alphabetically, are in entry 9. The Alabama Department of Archives and History has a card catalog on microfilm of records of Civil War soldiers, in Alabama, other than Alabama residents. This catalog includes federal prisoners in the hospital records for Selma, Alabama. Books about Cahaba/Cahawba, Alabama's most famous Confederate prison, include Jesse Hawes, *Cahaba: A Story of Captive Boys in Blue* (New York: Burr, 1888); William O. Bryant, *Cahaba Prison and the Sultana Disaster* (Tuscaloosa: University of Alabama Press, 1990); and John Lundquist, *Cahaba Federal Prison, Cahaba, Alabama: A Partial Roster of Interned Union Prisoners, 1862–1865* (Minneapolis, Minn.: The Author, 1997). John Lundquist is preparing an expanded version of his work. For historical background information on records of civilians held as prisoners by the Confederacy, see Mark E. Neely Jr., *Southern Rights: Political Prisoners and the Myth of Confederate Constitutionalism* (Charlottesville: University of Virginia Press, 1999).

For information on other federal Civil War records, see Kenneth W. Munden and Henry Putney Beers, *The Union: A Guide to Federal Archives Relating to the Civil War* (Washington, D.C.: National Archives and Records Administration, 1986). Several National Archives microfilm publications lead to letters and information on federal service in the Civil War. These sources include M502 Registers of Letters Received by the Secretary of the Treasury Relating to Claims, 1864–1887; M1290 Index to Compiled Service Records of Volunteer Union Soldiers Not Enlisted by State; M495 Indexes to Letters Received by the Secretary of War, 1861–1870; M1064 Letters Received by the Commission Branch of the Adjutant General's Office, 1863–1870; Registers of the records and proceedings of the U.S. Army General Courts-Martial, 1809–1890; and M725 Indexes to Letters Received by the Office of the [Federal] Adjutant General, Main Series. The National Archives has a number of other scattered records that relate to federal Civil War service, including correspondence received by the paymaster; the quartermaster claims; and the often poorly indexed records of the Volunteer Service Division, Enlisted Branch, Colored Soldiers Bureau, etc. of Record Group 94, Records of the Adjutant General.

Federal soldiers buried in national cemeteries are included in the federal government's series *The Roll of Honor*, expanded, reprinted, and indexed by the Genealogical Publishing Company, which has also made these volumes available on CD-ROM computer disk. Mimi Jo Butler's *Cobb County, Georgia, Cemeteries*, vol. 3, *Marietta National Cemetery* (Marietta, Ga.: Cobb County Genealogical Society, 1994), includes names of thousands of federal soldiers who died during the Atlanta campaign. A list of the first headstones provided to any federal veteran, wherever buried, is National Archives microcopy M1845 Card Records of Headstones Provided for Deceased Union Civil War Veterans, 1879–1903. Another related National Archives microfilm is M2014 Burial Registers for Military Posts, 1768–1921. The Sherman Pompey Collection of information on burials of Civil War soldiers, arranged by state, is available on microfilm through LDS family history centers and at the Family and Regional History Program at Wallace State College, Hanceville, Alabama.

Beyond the personal information and individual service data found in the records of the National Archives, additional information on the experiences of the soldiers can be learned from the thousands of books and articles on the individual units, campaigns, leaders, etc. Information on official federal units has been compiled in the following:

Bahn, Gilbert S. *Infestation of Yankees: Reference Guide to Union Troops in Confederate Territory*. Baltimore: Clearfield, 1998. This work indexes Frederick Phisterer, *Statistical Record of the Armies of the United States* (Washington, D.C.: Government Printing Office, 1883).

Dyer, Frederick H. *Compendium of the War of the Rebellion*. Des Moines: Dyer Publishing, 1908.

Fox, William F. *Regimental Losses of the Civil War, 1861–1865*. Albany, N.Y.: Albany Publishing, 1889.

The Union Army: A History of the Military Affairs in the Loyal States. 8 vols. 1908; reprint, Wilmington, N.C.: Broadfoot Publishing, 1997. This work does not include Alabama or the African American units, although it does cover the Tennessee regiments (volume 4) in which some Alabamians served. The navy is covered in volume 7. For blockade runners, see Rebecca Livingston, "Civil War Cat-and-Mouse Game: Researching Blockade-Runners at the National Archives," *Prologue: The Quarterly of the National Archives and Records Administration* 31 (1999): 179–89.

Welcher, Frank J. *The Union Army, 1861–1865: Organization and Operations*. 2 vols. Bloomington: Indiana University Press, 1989.

FEDERAL SERVICE CIVIL WAR PENSIONS

General federal service disability pensions began in 1890, although severely disabled war-injured veterans, widows and orphans of federal soldiers killed in the war, and impoverished parents of federal soldiers killed in the war began receiving pensions earlier. For pensions based on federal service, including those for black soldiers, see National Archives microcopy T288 General Index to Pension Files, 1861–1934 (also accessible through the Internet web site Ancestry.com); T289 Organization Index to Pension Files (Alabama is on reels 25 and 26 and, along with Arkansas, Arizona, Florida, Georgia, and Idaho, is available at the Family and Regional History Program, Wallace State College, Hanceville, Alabama); M1785 Index to Pension Application Files of Remarried Widows Based on Service in the Civil War and Later Wars; and M686 Index to General Correspondence of the [Federal] Record and Pension Office, 1889–1920. An 1883 list of federal pensioners for the Civil War and the War of 1812 was published as *U.S. Senate Executive Document 84, Pt. 1, 47th Congress, 2nd Session, Serial No. 2078* (Washington, D.C.: Government Printing Office, 1883) and has been reprinted in various forms, including on computer CD-ROM. The Alabamians have been published in *War of 1812 Pensioners and Others on the Pension Rolls as of January 1, 1883* (Cullman, Ala.: Gregath, 1982).

Federal Civil War pension files must be requested from Military

Records, National Archives, 700 Pennsylvania Ave. NW, Washington, DC 20408-0001. When ordering a pension file, insist on having copies made of all of the contents of the file. Another veterans' source is National Archives microcopy M1749 Historical Registers of National Homes for Disabled Volunteer Soldiers, 1866–1938.

The Grand Army of the Republic was a veterans' organization of men who served in the federal military during the Civil War and who never took up arms against the United States. Most of the annual proceedings of the Alabama Division of the GAR, including obituaries of members and other biographical information, are in the holdings of the Library of Congress. For more information, see "Alabama Department of the Grand Army of the Republic (G.A.R.) Union Veterans," *Alabama Family History and Genealogical News* 19, no. 1 (1998): 6–11; and Albert E. Smith Jr., *The Grand Army of the Republic: A Guide to Resources in the General Collections of the Library of Congress* (Washington, D.C.: Library of Congress, 1996).

CIVIL WAR RECORDS, 1861–1865, CIVILIANS

Civilian involvement with the state of Alabama and the Confederacy finds documentation in obscure sources. Records of these companies and individuals are sometimes found in National Archives microcopy M346 Confederate Papers Relating to Citizens or Business Firms, available from LDS family history centers as reels 1664682 through 1665838 and on microfilm at the Family and Regional History Program, Wallace State College, Hanceville, Alabama.

The Family and Regional History Program also has on microfilm "Receipts and Dispersements, July 14, 1861–December 10, 1864," hundreds of receipts of payment made to recruiting agents, suppliers, and paymasters for the Alabama troops. The same microfilm also includes an 1864 record of receipts of persons paid for distributing salt to indigent families of Confederate soldiers. The Alabama Department of Archives and History has affidavits for salt from families of Autauga, Butler, Choctaw, Clarke, Conecuh, Coosa, Monroe, Montgomery, and Tallapoosa Counties. Sherry Harris has published other records of salt allotments to Alabama families as *1862 Alabama Salt List* (Granada Hills, Calif.: Harris Press, 1993). What records that survive of Confederate sequestration and confiscation of property for Alabama are found among the Confederate court records in the National Archives Southeast Region (currently at, but soon to move from, 1557 St. Joseph Avenue, East Point, GA 30344).

Military Records, National Archives, 700 Pennsylvania Ave. NW, Washington, DC 20408-0001, has quartermaster records of Confederate civilian workers, free and slave, in entries 56, 57, and 60 of Record Group 109, War Department Collection of Confederate Records. The index, entry 58, can be searched by mail. These records include slaves. For historical background on African American services to the Confederacy, see Charles Kelly Barrow et al., *Forgotten Confederates: An Anthology about Black Southerners* (Southern Heritage, 1995).

Thousands of Alabamians traveled north of the Ohio River voluntarily to escape the war. They left no official records of their migration, although many of them lived in the already established communities of southerners in the southern counties of Illinois and Indiana, especially around Jeffersonville, Indiana. Some remained in the North as late as the 1870 census. Federal soldiers sent other civilians north as "political prisoners." Records of some of them are found in the records of the Louisville, Kentucky, prison camp, on reel 95 of National Archives microcopy M598 Selected Records of the War Department Relating to Confederate Prisoners of War. Records of many civilians, from this microfilm, held by the federal government as political prisoners have been published in *Alabama Family History and Genealogy News* 21, no. 2 (2000): 18–19. Information on the reasons for arrest of some of these individuals can be found in the previously mentioned papers of the Union Provost Marshal in National Archives microfilms M345 and M416. Some civilians, as well as soldiers, were court-martialed by the United States government during the Civil War. The records of their trials are at the National Archives. Their names appear in National Archives microcopy M1105 Registers of the Proceedings of the U.S. Army General Courts Martial, 1805–1890.

MILITARY RECORDS, POST-CIVIL WAR TO THE PRESENT

The best guide for seeking information on modern military service is Richard S. Johnson's *How to Locate Anyone Who Is or Has Been in the*

Military (San Antonio: MIE Publishing, 1993). Veterans organizations of many military units have web sites on the Internet. Christina K. Schaefer's *Great War: A Guide to the Service Records of All the World's Fighting Men and Volunteers* (Baltimore: Genealogical Publishing Company, 1998) is a guide to research libraries and organizations for research on military personnel of Alabama and the United States, for all wars.

Federal records of military service from 1917 to the present must be requested by the veteran or his heirs from National Personnel Records Center, 9700 Page Boulevard, St. Louis, MO 63132. The NPRC has a web site on the Internet. Records for earlier service should be sought from the National Archives and Records Administration, 700 Pennsylvania Ave. NW, Washington, DC 20408-0001.

Some other sources are available in courthouses and libraries, although usually death certificates were not filed in Alabama for military or private citizens who died in foreign lands, even during wars. Individual Alabama county probate courts have local registers of military service records, for World War I to the present, that provide some personal information. Contemporary local newspapers published casualty lists, news on soldiers/sailors, letters from local service men, and obituaries of war dead. The Alabama Department of Archives and History has microfilm of many county copies of service records for World War I and later, as well as Alabama's largest collection of Alabama newspapers; see chapter 14 in this volume, "City, County, and Community Sources." For the dead of the Spanish-American War and the beginning of the Philippines Insurrection, see Clarence Stewart Peterson, *Known Dead during the Spanish-American War and the Philippines Insurrection, 1898–1901* (Baltimore: The Author, 1958).

The National Archives, 700 Pennsylvania Ave. NW, Washington, DC 20408-0001, has some records of modern military service. The first Spanish-American War pensions are included in National Archives microcopy T289 Organization Index to Pension Files of Veterans Who Served between 1861 and 1900. Alabama is on reel 1. This microfilm is available at the Family and Regional History Program, Wallace State College, Hanceville, Alabama, for Alabama, Arkansas, Arizona, Florida, Georgia, and Idaho. National Archives microcopy T288 General Index to Pension Files, 1861–

1934, includes some pensions for the Spanish-American War, World War I, etc.; this microfilm is available at the Birmingham Public Library and the Family and Regional History Program. For sources for research in the Philippine Insurrection (1899–1913), see Trevor K. Plante, "Researching Service in the U.S. Army during the Philippine Insurrection," *Prologue: Quarterly of the National Archives* 32 (2000): 124–29. Researchers seeking soldiers of the First World War should consult Michael Knapp, "World War I Service Records," *Prologue: The Quarterly of the National Archives and Records Administration* 22 (1990): 300–3; and Mitchell Yockelson, "They Answered the Call: Military Service in the United States Army during World War I, 1917–1919," *Prologue: The Quarterly of the National Archives and Records Administration* 30 (1998): 228–35. Also for World War I, see

Amerine, William H. *Alabama's Own in France.* New York: Eaton & Gettinger, 1919.

Bureau of Naval Personnel. *Officers and Enlisted Men of the United States Navy Who Lost Their Lives during the World War.* Washington, D.C.: Government Printing Office, 1920.

Haulsee, W. M., et al. *Soldiers of the Great War.* 3 vols. Washington, D.C.: Soldiers Record Publishing Association, 1920. This book of photographs of World War I does not include many of the Alabamians. For a more complete list, see Thomas M. Owen, *History of Alabama and Dictionary of Alabama Biography,* 4 vols. (Chicago: S. J. Clarke, 1921), 1: 458–74.

Pilgrimage for the Mothers and Widows of Soldiers, Sailors, and Marines . . . in the Cemeteries of Europe. Washington, D.C.: Government Printing Office, 1930. This work publishes names and addresses of widows and mothers of soldiers buried in Europe. For additional information, see Constance Potter, "World War I Gold Star Mothers Pilgrimages," *Prologue: The Quarterly of the National Archives and Records Administration* 31 (1999): 140–45, 210–15; Michael G. Knapp and Constance Potter, "Here Rests in Honored Glory: World War I Graves Registration," *Prologue: The Quarterly of the National Archives and Records Administration* 23 (1991): 190–93; and Joan S. Clemens, "The Gold Star Book: Personal Memories of Alabamians Who Died in the Great War," *Alabama Heritage* (summer 1995): 34–35.

Roundtree, Maude. *The Cross of Military Service*. Jackson, Tenn.: World
War Insignia Commission, 1927. This work includes service records of
World War I veterans with their Confederate ancestors.

Federal World War I draft records for the whole United States are in the
National Archives Southeast Region, arranged by draft board. Currently,
these records are being transcribed for the whole United States. What has
been done so far is available on the Internet at web sites such as Ancestry.
com. These records have been also microfilmed by the Genealogical Society
of Utah and are made available through the LDS family history centers.
The Family and Regional History Program at Wallace State College,
Hanceville, Alabama, has a set of these for Alabama and some adjoining
states. For information on using these records, see Desmond Walls Allen,
"World War I Draft Registration Records," *Heritage Quest*, no. 71 (September–October 1991): 26–28; and John J. Newman, *Uncle We Are Ready! Reg-
istering American Men, 1917–1919* (Salt Lake City, Utah: Heritage Quest,
2001).

The Alabama Department of Archives and History has extensive military holdings that include microfilmed service records for Alabama soldiers
for the militia, 1873–1898; the Spanish-American War, 1898; and World War
I (1917–1918). This microfilm is widely available in major Alabama genealogical libraries. The Alabama Archives also has, inventoried under "Archives and History, Department of," the Alabamians at War Files,
1721–1968, including World War I draft lists and lists of World War I and
II and Korean War dead. Under "Adjutant General," the Alabama Archives
has rosters and card catalog indexes to service records, 1872–1919. For descriptions of Alabama's Spanish-American War units, see Thomas M.
Owen, *History of Alabama and Dictionary of Alabama Biography*, 4 vols.
(Chicago: S. J. Clarke, 1921), 2: 1262–64. The Alabama Department of Archives and History also has, under restricted access, some service records
(DD214s) of some Alabama soldiers, 1930–1975.

Sources for later conflicts include lists of the killed in action from the
Korean War and the Vietnam War on a CD-ROM computer disk at all
LDS family history centers. For other sources, see Robert M. Browning Jr.,
U.S. Merchant Vessel War Casualties of World War II (Annapolis: Naval In-

stitute Press, 1996), this book lists ships not sailors; Theodore J. Hull, "Electronic Records of Korean and Vietnam Conflict Casualties," *Prologue: The Quarterly of the National Archives* 32 (2000): 54–59; and Ann Bennett Mix, *Touchstones: A Guide to Records, Rights, and Resources for Families of American World War II Casualties* (Bountiful, Utah: American Genealogical Lending Library, 1996). For the World War II dead of the U.S. Marines, Navy, and Coast Guard, see *State Summary of War Casualties* [Alabama] (Washington, D.C.: U.S. Navy, 1946), a copy of which is at the Alabama Department of Archives and History. Lists of United States dead from World War II can also be accessed through the web site of the National Archives and Records Administration.

Other records deal with POWs from Alabama. For Alabama prisoners of war in World War II, the Korean War, and the Vietnam War, see Robert E. Davis, *Ex-POWs of Alabama* (Montgomery: Montgomery Chapter AX-POW, 1984). For records of German and Italian prisoners of war who died in the United States, see Kenneth S. Record, *World War I and World War II Axis Burials in the United States* (Jacksonville, Fla.: The Author, 1997).

17. SPECIAL RECONSTRUCTION-ERA RESOURCES

The end of the Civil War left Alabama in turmoil. Blacks tried to keep new rights while whites tried to regain old ones. Thousands of Alabamians were missing and many others were crippled, indigent, or homeless. Most of the individual capital was gone while much of the state's infant railroads and factories were in ruins. However, Reconstruction also generated a number of genealogically and historically valuable records of Alabama.

Alabama and all states of the former Confederacy, with the exception of Tennessee (which reentered the Union by ratifying the Fourteenth Amendment to the U.S. Constitution), had to hold special elections to restore the state to the Union. In preparation for the elections, a 1866 state census was taken. The Alabama Department of Archives and History has made this census widely available on microfilm. It shows, for each family, the number of killed, wounded, and missing during the war. This census has no index. For other information on federal census records of the period, see chapter 12 in this volume, "Census Records."

For Alabama, almost all of the registrations of black and white males qualified to vote to restore the state to the Union survive in some form, by state senate district and county, at the Alabama Department of Archives and History. Sometimes information that survives in the oath books does not exist in the voter registration books. The Alabama Department of Archives and History has the originals of all of these records and has made microfilm of the registration books widely available. Naturalization information was recorded for almost all foreign-born voters, but few counties aside from Mobile and Tuscaloosa had foreign-born men in 1867. Dale County's returns provide the names of employers in some instances. The registers for Henry, Lee, Perry, and Russell Counties at least sometimes give place of birth. The records for Walker and Winston Counties are spectacular, giving county and date of birth for almost everyone taking the oath to register. Carolyn McGough Rowe has published the records for Marion, Mobile, Walker, and Winston Counties. Having an ancestor who voted in the 1867 election became a requirement for voting under Alabama's state constitution of 1901. For background on these records for the whole South, see "The South's 1867 Returns of Qualified Voters and Their Value in Genealogical Research," *Heritage Quest*, no. 54 (1994): 62–63.

Many white southerners found themselves disqualified from full citizenship for being officers above the rank of colonel, government employees, commerce raiders, persons with property valued over twenty thousand dollars, former United States congressmen, graduates of a United States military academy, governors, former officers of the United States, or prison officials/guards. They were required to petition the governor of their state and the president of the United States to have their full citizenship restored. From 1867 to 1898, when universal amnesty was passed, only an act of Congress could restore citizenship. A detailed explanation of this situation and the categories of persons excluded from voting appear in "The Civil War: Amnesty and Pardons," in *Ancestry VIII* (Augusta: Augusta Genealogical Society, 1984), 13–16. Separate but complete lists of the presidential and congressional pardons for the whole country are published in Carolyn M. Rowe's *Index to Individual Pardon Applications from the South, 1865–1898* (Pensacola: The Author, 1996). The petitions for pardons and amnesty through 1867, often containing personal information, are reproduced on National Archives microcopy M1003, available at the National Archives Southeast Region and at the Family and Regional History Program, Wallace State College, Hanceville, Alabama. Pardon files for 1868 to

1898 must be sought from Entry 500 40A-H21, Record Group 233, Center for Legislative Studies, National Archives and Records Administration, Washington, DC 20408-0001.

Many southerners (black and white) also petitioned the federal government for compensation for property destroyed or seized by the federal army and navy. Although these claims often contain genealogical data, the loyalty and credibility of the claimants was often suspect. The only comprehensive index to the claimants is Entry 366, Record Group 56, General Records of the Treasury, National Archives and Records Administration, Washington, DC 20408-0001. This index includes citations to records in National Archives microcopy M502 Registers of Letters Received by the Secretary of the Treasury Relating to Claims, 1864–1887. For more information on Civil War claims, see Kenneth W. Munden and Henry Putney Beers, *The Union: A Guide to Federal Archives Relating to the Civil War* (Washington, D.C.: National Archives, 1986). For information on records of claims against federal confiscation of property, see "Without Right of Conquest: The Civil War Occupation and Restoration of the Findlay Foundry of Macon, Georgia," *Prologue: The Quarterly of the National Archives and Records Administration* 29 (1997): 301–15.

The most famous of the above southern property claims were those brought before the Commissioners of Claims (also known as the Southern Claims Commission) between 1871 and 1880. These often genealogically rich files were for property lost to Union military forces by black and white southerners who claimed, at least after the war, loyalty to the Union during the war. The claims frequently contain information from neighbors. More than 80 percent of these claims were rejected from lack of evidence or from proof of attempted deceit.

The various alphabetical lists of these claims contain errors and misleading identifications. In some instances for approved claims, for example, the wrong counties appeared on early lists, with those mistakes reprinted and repeated on later lists. In some instances, the property taken or destroyed was in a different county and even state than that where the person filing the claim finally made a claim. The most extensive list of the claims before the Commissioners of Claims is found in Gary B. Mills's *Southern Loyalists in the Civil War: The Southern Claims Commission* (Baltimore: Genealogical Publishing Company, 1994). For background on these claims, see Sarah Lawson, "Records of the Southern Claims Commission," *Prologue: The Journal of the National Archives and Records Administration* 12 (1980): 207–18.

Obtaining a copy of a claim can be complicated. The approved claims are in Record Group 217, Records of the Accounting Office of the Department of the Treasury, National Archives and Records Administration, Washington, DC 20408-0001. The approved claims for Alabama are available as National Archives microcopy M2062 Southern Claims Commission Approved Claims, 1871–1880: Alabama. Most of the claims that were disapproved by the Southern Claims Commission are included in National Archives microcopy M1407 Barred and Disallowed Case Files of the Southern Claims Commission, 1871–1880. The reports on decisions of the disallowed claims are on microfilm in the Family and Regional History Program, Wallace State College, Hanceville, Alabama; see U.S. Commissioners of Claims, *Summary Reports of Claims* (1871–1881). These are the "reports" referred to in the indexes to the disallowed claims.

When a claim is missing from any of the above, it can usually be found in the Court of Claims congressional (not regular) case files in Record Group 123 of the National Archives and Records Administration, Washington, DC 20408-0001. To obtain the citation to such a file, see the previously mentioned comprehensive index to the claimants in National Archives' Entry 366, Record Group 56, General Records of the Treasury, or write to Index Section, U.S. Court of Claims, 717 Madison Place NW, Washington, DC 20005. The National Archives has microfilmed an index to most of these records as microcopy M2007 United States Court of Federal Claims Docket Cards for Congressional Case Files, 1884–1937.

Federal tax records are on microfilm at the National Archives Southeast Region, near Atlanta, Georgia, for Alabama and the rest of the South for 1865 and 1866 and, as original records, for 1867 to 1873. The records are arranged by state and then by district. Such items as gold watches, professions, pianos, buggies, alcohol manufacture, and tobacco were taxed. Often Americans chose to ignore these poorly enforced and inconsistently collected taxes. For a detailed description of these records and their background, see Cynthia G. Fox, "Income Tax Records of the Civil War Years,"

Prologue: The Journal of the National Archives and Records Administration 18 (1986): 250–59. The Alabama returns on microfilm are National Archives microcopy M754 Internal Revenue Assessment Lists for Alabama, 1865–1866. This microfilm is widely available at large libraries.

The Civilian Records Branch, National Archives and Records Administration, Washington, DC 20408-0001, also has the 1865–1866 federal real-estate property evaluations made for Barbour, Calhoun, Chambers, De-Kalb, Henry, Randolph, Russell, and St. Clair Counties. These records have been microfilmed for the Family and Regional History Program of Wallace State College, Hanceville, Alabama, along with a list that appears to be of federal Civil War veterans living in those counties.

Records of the branches of the Freedman's Savings and Trust Company in Huntsville and Mobile at least partially survive, although records for the Montgomery branch are lost. Within the depositor registers, thousands of individual investors, most but not all of whom were African American and former slaves, left detailed personal information useful in identifying their accounts. Sometimes this extensive family information goes back decades into slavery. These records were copied as part of National Archives microcopy M816 Registers of Signatures of Depositions in Branches of the Freedman's Savings and Trust Company, 1865–1874. Huntsville accounts, 1–1698, appear on reel one, and Mobile accounts, 777–1567, 1572–2326, and 4287–9173, appear on reel two. The account identification information for the Huntsville branch, accounts 1–791, has been published in Fred Charles Rathburn's *Names from Huntsville, Alabama,* 2 vols. (Littleton, Colo.: The Author, 1986). The index to deposit ledgers for the Huntsville branch serves as a crude index to the registers of signatures of depositions and appears on reel one of National Archives microcopy M817 Indexes to Deposit Ledgers in Branches of the Freedman's Savings and Trust Company, 1865–1874. The deposit ledgers do not survive, although the registers of signatures, containing the personal information, are on reel one of the previously mentioned M816.

A nationwide every-name index to the microfilm of the Freedmen's Bank records has been prepared by the Genealogical Society of Utah on CD-ROM computer disk. For how to use the microfilmed records, see "Documentation for Afro-American Families: Records of Freedman's Savings and Trust Company," *National Genealogical Society Quarterly* 76 (1988): 139–46. Information on records of this bank that have not been microfilmed is found in Reginald Washington, "The Freedman's Savings and Trust Company: African American Genealogical Research," *Prologue: The Quarterly of the National Archives and Records Administration* 29 (1997): 170–81. Descriptions of all of the records that survive from the federally created Freedman's Bank are found in Debra L. Newman, *Black History: A Guide to Civilian Records in the National Archives* (Washington, D.C.: National Archives Trust, 1984), 189–92; and *Black Studies: A Select Catalog of National Archives Microfilm Publications* (Washington, D.C.: National Archives Trust, 1984).

The National Archives and Records Administration, Washington, DC 20408-0001, has extensive records of the activities of the Bureau of Refugees, Freedmen, and Abandoned Lands in Alabama and elsewhere, as well as a center for research in these documents. Freedman's Bureau records contain records of recently freed former slaves and of various relationships between blacks and whites immediately after the Civil War, and some records of confiscation of Confederate property. However, this material is poorly organized and barely indexed, when indexed at all. One index from a relative few of these documents is Jacqueline A. Lawson's *An Index of African Americans Identified in Selected Records of the Freedman's Bureau* (Bowie, Md.: Heritage Books, 1995). Some records of this agency have been abstracted on the Freedmen's Bureau's Internet web site.

Several published works help in understanding Freedman's Bureau sources. For an overview of what survives for the Freedman's Bureau, see Elaine C. Everly, "Freedmen's Bureau Records: An Overview," *Prologue: The Quarterly of the National Archives and Records Administration* 29 (1997): 95–99; and the description of Record Group 105 in *Guide to Federal Records in the National Archives of the United States* (Washington, D.C.: National Archives Trust, 1996). Ideas on using these documents can be found in *Guide to Genealogical Research in the National Archives* (Washington, D.C.: National Archives and Records Administration, 1983), 177, 180. Examples of what can be found in such records appear in Barry A. Couch and Larry Madares, "Reconstructing Black Families: Perspectives from the Texas Freedmen's Bureau Records," *Prologue: The Quarterly of the National*

Archives and Records Administration 18 (1986): 109–22. Microfilms of Freedman's Bureau records, including those for the nation as a whole, have detailed descriptions in *Black Studies: A Select Guide to National Archives Microfilm Publications* (Washington, D.C.: National Archives Trust, 1984).

Some Freedman's Bureau records specifically for Alabama include microcopy M809 Records of the Assistant Commissioner for the State of Alabama and M810 Records of the Superintendent of Education for the State of Alabama. Local office records, in Alabama and elsewhere, have not been microfilmed, although they survive in the National Archives and Records Administration. The Alabama Department of Archives and History has in its state government documents the Freedman's Hospital Records, 1868–1875.

Index

South Alabama, University of, 20
South Carolina, 5, 49, 99. *See also* southern
   research
South Flomaton, 107
Southern Historical Collection, 22
Southern History Collection. *See* Bir-
   mingham Public Library
southern research, 22, 46–47, 49
southern unionist claims, 252–53
southwest Alabama, 32
Spain, 4, 31, 43, 71–72
Spanish-American War, 246–48
Sparta, 85
spies (Civil War), 240–41
Springville, 27
St. Clair County, 89, 200–2, 254
St. Stephens, 4, 6, 72, 82, 84
stars ("fell on Alabama"), 3
state officials, 31
State Oil and Gas Board, 14
steamboats, 5, 13
steel, 5
Stevenson, 27
subject files, 43
Sumter County, 103, 202–3
Supreme Court (federal), 101
Sylacauga, 27, 114

Talladega, 27, 114, 204
Talladega County, 203–5
Tallapoosa County, 205–6
Tallassee, 27
Tallassee (East), 27
taxes: federal, 253–54; state, 44
teachers, 44, 50
Tennessee, 5, 22, 99, 235–36. *See also* southern
   research
Tennessee River Valley, 3, 5, 60
Tennessee Valley Authority, 100
Terrell County, Ga., 19
territorial records, 72–73
Texas, 222–23
thesis, 14, 17–18
Thomaston, 27

Thomasville, 27
Thorsby, 6
tobacco, 100
Tombigbee River, 32, 60
topographical maps, 25, 28–29
topography, 3, 6, 16
Toulouse (Fort), 4, 70
town maps, 25–28
towns. *See* cities
township maps, 28, 81–83
townships, 80
tract books, 86
traders (Indians), 47, 62
trails, 13
transportation, 5
*Tributaries: Journal of the Alabama Folklife
   Association*, 17
Troy, 27, 195
Tuscaloosa, 5, 27, 82, 85, 103, 107, 115, 207
Tuscaloosa County, 47, 206–8, 251
Tuscumbia, 27, 108, 144
Tuskegee, 27, 115, 180
Tutwiler Collection. *See* Birmingham Public
   Library

Union Springs, 27, 129
Uniontown, 27, 109
United States Geological Survey (USGS), 25
United States government, 4
university lands, 79
USGS, 25

Valley, The (West Point Pepperell mill
   towns), 115
Vernon, 172
Vidette Cavalry, 239
Vietnam War, 248–49
Virginia, 235
Virginia Gazette, 48
vital records, 9, 214–19. *See also* deaths; mar-
   riages
voter lists (1867–1868), 75–76, 250–51

Walker County, 47, 75, 208–9, 251
Wallace State College (Hanceville), 36, 38, 47,